TONI MORRISON AND THE IDEA OF AFRICA

Toni Morrison's fiction has been read as a contribution to and critique of Western civilization and Christianity. La Vinia Delois Jennings reveals the fundamental role that African traditional religious symbols play in her work. Based on extensive research into West African religions and philosophy, Jennings uncovers and interprets the African themes, images and cultural resonances in Morrison's fiction. She shows how symbols brought to the Americas by enslaved West Africans are used by Morrison in her landscapes, interior spaces, and on the bodies of her characters. Jennings's analysis of these symbols demonstrates that a West African collective worldview informs both Morrison's work, and contemporary African-American life and culture. This important contribution to Morrison studies will be of great interest to scholars of African-American literature.

LA VINIA DELOIS JENNINGS is Associate Professor of Twentieth-Century American Literature at the University of Tennessee, Knoxville.

TONI MORRISON AND THE IDEA OF AFRICA

LA VINIA DELOIS JENNINGS

CAMBRIDGE
UNIVERSITY PRESS

CAMBRIDGE UNIVERSITY PRESS
Cambridge, New York, Melbourne, Madrid, Cape Town, Singapore, São Paulo, Delhi

Cambridge University Press
The Edinburgh Building, Cambridge CB2 8RU, UK

Published in the United States of America by Cambridge University Press, New York

www.cambridge.org
Information on this title: www.cambridge.org/9780521885041

First published 2008

Printed in the United Kingdom at the University Press, Cambridge

A catalogue record for this publication is available from the British Library

ISBN 978-0-521-88504-1 hardback

To my Solomon,
Sydnor Johnston Jennings
December 25, 1865–June 23, 1940

Contents

Acknowledgments

A number of people consistently brought positive energy to the writing of this book, and I would be remiss not to remember them below.

I thank my sister La Ronica Maria Jennings for reading the draft of this book when it was only an "idea" of twenty pages and giving me thoughtful feedback. I also wish to thank Yahya Jongintaba (Jon Michael Spencer) for the supportive comments he made at a symposium in Richmond where I was invited to present what at that time was just the beginning of a very gratifying academic investigation.

I am grateful that I know Trudier Harris, a divine example of collegial support. In addition to reading this manuscript and making helpful suggestions, she has assisted me throughout my scholastic development. While I was a doctoral student at the University of North Carolina at Chapel Hill, I made my first intensive study of Toni Morrison's novels in a seminar that she conducted. She directed my dissertation on sexual violence in the novels of Richard Wright, James Baldwin, and Toni Morrison, and read the manuscript for my first book, a critical introduction to the works of dramatist and novelist Alice Childress. Trudier, I honor you.

For repeated words of encouragement from academic colleagues, I thank Helena Woodard, Isabel Gallego Rodriguez, Kathleen Coyne Kelly, Peter Höyng, David Ikard, Arthur Smith, John Evelev, Oliver Nathaniel Greene, Jr., Janet Atwill, Laura Howes, Charlie Biggs, Charles Maland, Jenn Fishman, Christoph Irmscher, R. Baxter Miller, and Jürgen Grandt.

I also thank Carol Nickle, Larry Doby Horton, Anthony Florian, Ken Lewellen, Gary Bayless, and Jack Randy Farmer, supporters outside of the academy, whose personal and professional care freed me to write.

At Cambridge University Press in the United Kingdom, I thank you, Ray Ryan, for seeing ME when we first spoke. I send a very warm thank you to the preliminary reader whose thorough report was invaluable in refining my manuscript. And I thank Maartje Scheltens, Rosina Di Marzo, and Libby Willis for making the technical transformation of the manuscript into a book painless.

For illustration permissions, I thank the Ashmolean Museum, Oxford, and Bruce R. McPherson at McPherson & Company. For indexing, I thank Dawn Adkins at adkinsindexing.com.

Parts of this book have been presented in various forms in a number of contexts, including Salvador da Bahia, Brazil (Caribbean Studies Association Conference), Port-au-Prince, Haiti (International Conference on Caribbean Literature), Accra, Ghana (African Literature Association Convention), Miami and Birmingham (College Language Association Convention), Cincinnati (Biennial Conference of the Toni Morrison Society), Lugano, Switzerland (Lugano Caribbean Conference), Honolulu (Hawaii International Conference on Arts and Humanities), Knoxville (International and Interdisciplinary Conference), and San Francisco (Modern Language Association Convention). I extend my gratitude to Tobie Pierre Ahlonsou and his University of Abomey-Calavi in Benin classmates who sought me out after my presentation in Accra and to scholars at other academic venues who raised questions that helped refine the contents of this book.

Lastly, I am deeply indebted to Chloe Wofford Morrison, an artistic visionary and a literary genius, and to all the ancestors who looked on as I wrote.

LA VINIA DELOIS JENNINGS
RICHMOND, VIRGINIA; PORT-AU-PRINCE, HAITI;
AND ELMINA CASTLE, GHANA, 2007

Illustrations

Introduction: finding the elusive but identifiable Blackness within the culture out of which Toni Morrison writes

> I don't like to find my books condemned as bad or praised as good, when that condemnation or that praise is based on criteria from other paradigms. I would much prefer that they were dismissed or embraced on the success of their accomplishment within the culture out of which I write.
> I don't regard Black literature as simply books written *by* Black people, or simply as literature written *about* Black people, or simply as literature that uses a certain mode of language in which you sort of drop *g*'s. There is something very special and very identifiable about it and it is my struggle to *find* that elusive but identifiable style.
> Toni Morrison, "Rootedness: The Ancestor as Foundation"[1]

I

An amalgamated West and Central African traditional culture in the African diaspora of the Americas, the culture out of which Toni Morrison writes, sets the decisive criteria for the identifiable qualities of Blackness that her novels of African-American life stylistically exemplify. In addition to possessing an oral, participatory nature and a choral narrator,[2] her narratives draw upon the Middle Passage survival of traditional cosmologies from these regions that New World-enslaved Africans creolized into a collective worldview that Western hegemony and time later subverted in the United States. Because Africa has more than a thousand cultural groups whose traditions and beliefs are tribal and not universal, African philosopher Kwame Anthony Appiah, comparative literature specialist Valentin Y. Mudimbe, and African historiographers have rightly argued against the notion of a monolithic "African worldview." But as literary scholar Gay Wilentz points out, a collective concept is not impractical "in relation to African American history because of the intermingling of cultures from west and central Africa during the slave trade. From the different interactions and retentions of traditions during and after slavery, there evolved a worldview alternative."[3] The combined remnants of that worldview alternative taken from many African civilizations survive, in defamiliarized forms, beneath European-American New World culture. As a collective worldview, it operates largely below the threshold of modern African-American consciousness, influencing the perceptions and actions of its real life human repositories and the imaginary ones that inhabit Morrison's fiction.

A Classics scholar, Toni Morrison is well versed in the ease with which Africa's contributions to other civilizations have been overwritten into nonexistence. It took little time, she asserts, for the Greeks' record of African influence to be explained away as "Egyptomania," in order "to eliminate Egypt as the cradle of civilization *and* its model and replace it with Greece."[4] A similar explaining away occurred with respect to African religious retentions' intersection with and influence on Christianity, New World thought, and American culture. An aesthetic goal of Morrison's fiction is to dust off the survivals of West and Central African traditional civilizations that Christianity obscures in the Western hemisphere. It is a challenging recuperation because the Middle Passage and American slavery from the seventeenth to nineteenth centuries fostered countless cultural suppressions and erasures for inestimable Africans and African Americans. Reflecting reality in its situation of West and Central African traditional religious beliefs as buried but not dead in the African-American personal and collective (un)conscious,[5] Morrison's fiction exposes an African palimpsest upon which European-American culture superimposes itself. Lying latent under that superimposition, and at times commingled with interpolations from indigenous peoples' beliefs, are decipherable, identifiably Black, traditional, cosmological inscriptions thought lost to the North American experience. To evoke their presence Morrison turns to the most discernible African symbol in the Americas, the cross within a circle, which survived the Middle Passage and the transatlantic slave trade. She uses it as the substructure for her literary landscapes and interior spaces, and as a geometric figure performed by or inscribed on the bodies of her characters.

The symbol of the cross within a circle that took root in the Caribbean and culturally migrated to various spaces in the Americas was Kongo's[6] geometric Yowa or cosmogram. The cross within a circle, or "tree" within a circle, from Kongo became the signage under which the creolizing of West and Central African traditional religions occurred in Haiti's Voudoun. Kongo's Yowa united with Dahomey's Vodun (the Fon word for god) to produce the symbol and name under which the Caribbean manifestation of many African peoples' beliefs were preserved in the Western hemisphere. An ancestral cosmogram, the Yowa signifies reincarnation, renaissance, and mediation of spiritual power. Also referred to as "the four moments of the sun," the Kongo Yowa emblematizes in contradistinction to Western thought the "backward" or "counterclockwise" spatialization of time as governed by nature, from east to west or right to left. The east-west rise and descent of the sun and its counterclockwise movement reinforce the flow of time from generation to generation, each spiraling backward into an infinite past. The right, east, or "sunrise" compass point of the horizontal axis of the cross indicates birth and the beginning of life; the left, west or "sunset" point indicates decline and approaching death. The "midday" or summit of the sun on the vertical axis indicates the strongest moment of life, while the southern or "midnight" moment of the sun indicates one's descent into the afterworld. The radius of the cross within the circle invokes the crossroads: the intersection of the physical and metaphysical planes. Their point of contact, where flesh and spirit meet, is the moment when the loa – the gods, spirits, or saints of the Voudoun pantheon – temporarily manifest themselves in serviteurs, devotees of a specific loa. Materially formed by a tree encircled at its base, the vertical axis of the cross in Voudoun is the spiritual avenue by which the immortal loa travel to the mortal realm. The philosophies behind Kongo's Yowa, Dahomey's Vodun, and other West African traditional cosmological beliefs, like those of the Yoruba people in the area now known as Nigeria, found expression in not only Voudoun in the Caribbean but also Voodoo in the United States and Candomblé in Brazil.

Literary scholars have read Toni Morrison's characters and their behaviors mainly through the interpretive lens of Western civilization and Christianity. Critically analyzing them, however, through the socio-religious directives of the cross within the circle and the philosophies of Voudoun, Candomblé, and their two African-based pantheons of gods – respectively the loa and orixás that hark back to West Africa's Vodun – has been uninitiated heretofore. Yet the philosophies, practices, rituals, and divinities of Voudoun, Candomblé, and African traditional religions in general operate as the optimal Black standard in interpreting the deweys' inseparability in *Sula* (1973) as the Voudoun Marassa-Trois invoked as Marassa-Dossu-Dossa (Dew-sō-Dew-sä) or Eva Peace's burning of her son Plum as the maternal prerogative of Ayizan, the preeminent loa of the psychic womb, in the baptism by fire of bruler-zin.[7] The assonant naming of the "blind" horsemen in *Tar Baby* (1981) suggests the "divine" horsemen or loa who "mount" serviteurs in Voudoun possession rituals. And Beloved's extreme and sporadic emotionalism gravitates between dual manifestations of the loa Erzulie. On the one hand, Beloved is the infant Erzulie Ge-Rouge, the tragic goddess of love who laments the shortness of life and the limitations of love. On the other hand, she is the seductive Mistress Erzulie Freida, whose jealous love cannot tolerate rivals and whose symbol is the pierced, red heart of the valentine. These and other spirit personalities, such as the loa Ogoun and Legba of Voudoun and the orixás Yemanjá and Oxóssi of Candomblé, manifest themselves in principal characters throughout Morrison's literary canon.

In order to "Blacken" her fiction, Morrison's writerly vision offers more than the presence of a particular African cosmological or religious artifact; it focuses "on the philosophical-psychological linkages" between Africans and African Americans. Her texts display surviving Africanisms in social roles, behaviors, rituals, and cosmologies embedded in what Wade W. Nobles calls African Americans' "experiential communality," the sharing of particular experiences by a particular group of people through time and space.[8] African survivals have been noted to persist in regional and geographical locations where their carriers are racially segregated or physically isolated from the dominant, host culture; where there is a Black majority; and where African orientations do "not openly conflict with the cultural-behavioral elements of the 'host' society."[9] Racial segregation during the ante-bellum period in the American rural South and in post-bellum northern ghettos, island isolationism like that of Haiti in the Caribbean and Sapelo Island off the Georgia coast, and black majority populations in Louisiana, South Carolina, and Brazil where aspects of Vodun did not openly conflict with Christianity fostered the retention of West and Central African traditional religion derivatives in the Americas.

The above determinants of survivals are directly compatible with the geographical and religious formulations of the Bottom in *Sula*, the Michigan Southside and Shalimar, Virginia in *Song of Solomon* (1977), Dominique in *Tar Baby*, the African-American community on the periphery of Cincinnati in *Beloved* (1987), and Ruby in *Paradise* (1998). These fictive communities are insulated from the dominant Anglo-European culture, and like many African traditional tribes, their members share, at the conscious and unconscious levels, a common conception of unity, balance, reconciliation of opposites, time, death, immortality, accidents, and communal collectivism. Specific, traceable, West and Central African, ethnographic artifacts – the dancing of the Chiwara antelope from Malian cultures, the duping by the trickster spider in Ashanti Anancy fables, and Kongo's sacralizing of a venerable person's or martyr's postmortem remains in a kimbi sack – reinforce an African ethos. Rich, guiding African traditional cosmologies are at the core of Morrison's fiction.

Having knowledge of the particulars of those cosmologies is not essential to the appreciation of her novels, but interpreting her literary art without them diminishes the aesthetic, cultural, historical, and political force of the artist and her artform.

Morrison's novels contain identifiable West and Central African traditional religious subscriptions by which her novels may most effectively be read. Those subscriptions are not implemented as metaphors but as real and discernible presences in African-American life and culture. Critics of her works may parallel these subscriptions with the "mythic" substructuring that James Joyce, for example, employs in *Ulysses* (1922). The association, however, falls short because the "mythic" with respect to West African traditional beliefs and practices transcends the mythological and enters the present moment. The roles, practices, and pantheon of Vodun and its diaspora derivatives not only appear in folktales and legends but survive in the ritual, ceremony, and daily experience of the twentieth and twenty-first centuries. Traditional priests and priestesses still officiate at religious ceremonies performed in a circle and the loa or spirits still incarnate themselves in the bodies of serviteurs. And African-descended peoples in the diaspora of the West continue to syncretize, juxtapose, disidentify, and misidentify the retentions of traditional Africa in modern life. The fictional characters that perform traditional rituals and roles knowingly and unknowingly in Morrison's American and Caribbean settings occupy the secondary and tertiary stops on an east-west trajectory that originated in West and West Central Africa. Starting in the Harlem Renaissance, African-American writers sought, through the drum and other African "relics," to recover an authentic ancestral past that would forge a definable link to Blackness. Morrison's selection of the cross within a circle and the influence of Vodun in the Western hemisphere forges that link and reveals a more complex vision of Black Atlantic cultures. She depicts a compelling overlay of diasporic retentions that moves toward a formulation of diasporic modernism, an alternate form of modernism that strives to disrupt not conventional modernism but dominant perceptions of experience and reality and to reconnect broken bonds between the psychological and the cultural.[10]

II

The following chapters of *Toni Morrison and the Idea of Africa* aim to expose the African palimpsest lying latent in Morrison's fiction and in African-American culture and life. Chapter 2, "Dahomey's Vodun and

Kongo's Yowa: the survival of West and Central African traditional cosmologies in African America," extends the discussion of the cross and circle
cosmogram and the creolization of traditional beliefs and practices under
its signage by the Bakongo and the Fon, Yoruba, and other West African
peoples who contributed to Haiti's Voudoun. Chapters 3, 4, and 5 and
their Kikongo titles – "bandoki" (witches), "kanda" (juniors, living elders,
and ancestors), and "banganga" (specialists) – honor Kongo's profound
impact on African-American social and religious life and on Morrison's
fictional world. The titles convey a methodological approach that inves-
tigates the most historically resilient West and Central African traditional
socio-religious roles that appear as major cultural features of Morrison's
literary aesthetic. African scholar John S. Mbiti asserts that "Because traditional religions permeate all the departments of life, there is no formal
distinction between the sacred and the secular, between the religious and
the non-religious, between the spiritual and the material areas of life." A
study of traditional beliefs and practices "is, therefore, ultimately a study of
the peoples themselves in all the complexities of both traditional and
modern life."[11] In short, traditional beliefs and practices operate through
social roles, subject positions, or personages within the community who
perform in various and decidedly conventional ways in keeping with
religious behavioral expectation and necessity. Thus these chapters interpret the principal centuries-old socio-religious roles and worldviews found
in traditional villages from Senegambia to Kongo-Angola, as Morrison
fictively mediates them in New World cultures. Her treatments of religious
beliefs and practices, the cultural elements that are most resistant to
temporal and spatial changes, correlate with "examinations of preslavery
Africa" and affirm, as Nobles's research posits, that "many [West African]
tribes shared one overriding philosophical system" that they expressed
through religion.[12] Her depictions of African traditional witches, living-
dead ancestors, living elders, medicine (wo)men, and priest(esse)s mirror
identifiable qualities of Blackness, ancient African ways of being and
knowing, that presently linger consciously and unconsciously in African
America.

Chapter 3, "Bandoki: witches, ambivalent power, and the fusion of good
and evil," examines the nonreligious role of the witch and the witch
imaging imposed on female characters in *Sula* (1973), *Beloved* (1987), and
Paradise (1998) as the residual of an African traditional orientation and
(un)consciousness. In a real sense, African Americans are conditioned to
living with and surviving evil since "[w]e may in fact," as Morrison
maintains, "live right next door to it, not only in the form of something

metaphysical, but also in terms of people."[13] In terms of people, evil of the criminal variety often makes the African-American community its haven. Outlaws of both African and European descents who have committed censurable moral evil, crimes that injure others, commonly live in Black neighborhoods as anonymous, undocumented social exiles in order to evade capture and (re)incarceration. Conflating the metaphysical with the human, many African Americans in the twentieth century were familiar with accounts or had direct knowledge of individuals rumored or known to work roots (practice sympathetic magic) or to cast the evil eye – that is, cause misfortune psychically with a glance. Morrison asserts that Black people do not as a default reaction annihilate evil. It functions as a "fourth dimension in their lives." They neutralize it by nondestructive means. They survive it.[14]

The African traditional mind concerns itself with the causes and effects of evil, not its origin, since the concept of the Devil does not exist. Traditional religions recognize misfortunes that are the product of moral evil, acts committed by one person against another that damage relationships. Almost always considered to be female, African witches, the principal agents of moral evil, unconsciously and involuntarily visit dis-ease, death, and material misfortune on familial and communal members in close spatial proximity to them. Witches, who remained within their tribes despite the threat that their presence posed to kings, living elders, and communal stability, were among the first that Europeans enslaved when their value as trade goods rose. Sylvia R. Frey and Betty Wood maintain that

A "considerable part" of the African women sold into slavery in the Americas was reported to have been convicted of witchcraft ... Persons who were suspected of being witches were seized and confined until a slave vessel arrived, whereupon they were transported to the Americas as slaves, by that means continuing and preserving many traditional beliefs and practices in Afro-Atlantic cultures.[15]

If the number of African women accused of witchcraft increased exponentially during the transatlantic slave trade because of material greed, then a surge in witchcraft lore also traveled to the New World even when legitimately divined witches did not.

The African-American communities of the Bottom in Medallion, Ohio; of Cincinnati, Ohio, surrounding the Bluestone Road former way station; and of Ruby, Oklahoma, respectively, deem Sula Peace, Beloved, and Consolata Sosa witches in their midst. As individuals whose practices set them in opposition to institutionalized religion, they are immoral, anti-social destroyers of relationships and revered traditions who use valid and good power for invalid and evil ends. Because the quintessential African traditional witch's craft, in addition to being involuntary, is psychic – she neither mixes potions nor casts spells – Sula, Beloved, and Consolata may in fact be witches without their own cognizance. Self-awareness is immaterial.

In their respective settings the sign of Kongo's four moments of the sun circle and cross appears subliminally inscribed on the natural landscape in order to forward symbolically that a Christian ethos is not the only belief system actively defining the social behavior of select characters or their neighbors' interpretation of them. Morrison elaborates on this traditional influence by assigning the characteristics of the spirits or gods of the Vodun pantheon to some of her central characters as those divinities have been preserved and mediated in the African diaspora of the Western hemisphere. In the twentieth-century United States, African Americans under the domination of Christianity and basing their conception of witchcraft on a Eurocentric model erroneously blurred the practices of Voodoo with witchcraft and regarded both with fear and as a collective of absolute, demonic evil. Nevertheless, as Morrison's fiction posits, traditional witchcraft practitioners, or bandoki – a Kikongo word I have chosen to designate female witches throughout the West and Central African regions – are regarded as principal agents of moral evil but not absolute evil personified.

The four elemental emanations of the face of Sula set up a paradigm of quaternal balance that reconciles conflicting impulses and alludes to the notion of a fourth face, or oppositional dimension, of God. That fourth face, within the frame of an African traditional monistic theodicy, explains malevolence related to Him and other religious powers. A monistic theodicy does not define good and evil as an absolute, exclusive binary but reconciles the two as an ambivalent, inclusive unity. Morrison bases the Bottom's recognition of a fourth or evil dimension of God on the stabilizing balance of the four fundamental constituents of the universe. The passive and feminine elements, earth and water, temper the active and masculine elements, air and fire. The quaternary integration of opposing yet balancing elements and their inclemental influences – cold, rain, heat, and wind – formed the nucleus of ancient and medieval cosmologies. The ambivalent and inclusive quaternity preceded the univalent and exclusive Trinity of Judeo-Christian belief that ushered in the Manichean dualism of absolute good and absolute evil, God and Devil. African traditional cosmologies fuse good and evil in the higher religious powers – God, the gods, and the ancestors – who dispense both blessings and curses, while the agency of witches, also capable of harming and protecting, largely account for humanly precipitated evil.

Morrison completes the character portraits of Beloved and Consolata Sosa as African traditional witches by opening their representations to the possible interpretation that they practice kindoki kia dia, soul or psyche-eating witchcraft, the incorporeal, spiritual, and symbolical eating of a victim's flesh that physically presents itself as a wasting dis-ease. Although Consolata would be considered a sacred priestess in an Africanist community aware of its traditional roots, Christian hegemony and the erosion of memory over time foreclose the possibility of her community interpreting her role as a sacred one, transmuting it to a morally evil one. Embodying the potential for good and evil, these female characters, however, temper oppositional forces in their African-American communities.

Focusing on Morrison's characters whose socio-religious roles compose the familial matrix, Chapter 4, "Kanda: living elders, the ancestral presence, and the ancestor as foundation," discusses *Song of Solomon*, *Tar Baby*, and *Beloved* as an ancestral trilogy with *Tar Baby*'s Caribbean setting, bridging representations of African Americans' present and past, marking the liminal site, the crossroads, of imminent New World ancestral attrition and retention. All African traditional societies believe in an afterworld where the ancestors – living-dead – reside when their earthly lives expire. Benevolent familial advisors if the living properly honor them, ancestors serve active religious roles in which they instruct their surviving lineage whose remembering of them and active calling of their names indefinitely extend their personal immortality in the afterworld. The living-dead ancestor and living relative reciprocally insure the continued life of one another, respectively, in the metaphysical and physical worlds. The death of the ancestor, permanent disremembrance and severance from involvement with earthly kin has yet to occur in the infinite past, where time spatializes backward into an inverted future. The ancestor ultimately becomes collectively immortalized, anonymously subsumed into the graveyard of time.

Sequentially, the plots and settings of *Song of Solomon*, *Tar Baby*, and *Beloved* substructure regressive temporal and spatial images and patterns that map the historical conveyance of ancestorship to the New World and its subliminal survival in the American space. They treat what has been genealogically forfeited and culturally retained in African-American life with respect to the slippage of the ancestor into the interstices of spatial dispossession, temporal discontinuity, and familial disremembrance. Each of these novels addresses, given the confluence of past and present from a traditional perspective, the African-American socio-psychological disconnect brought about by the Middle Passage and an American slavery that prohibited New World Africans from knowing the names of their living-dead kin and from continuing their responsibility of reciprocity to them in the circle of life. Because the ancestors regress in time from the present, to the recent past, to the remote past, understanding the Africanist concept of time is key to interpreting the religious philosophy controlling the simultaneity of past and present in these texts. Although she is not an ancestor, Beloved is the only Morrison character to date with a traceable life in the timeless afterworld. Her ontological profile establishes a paradigm for the concurrence of past and present and the counterclockwise regression of the living-dead through time that Kongo's cosmogram maps.

Abetting critical uncertainty concerning which character functions as the ancestor in each of her novels, Morrison conflates the office of the living-dead ancestor with the living elder, converging and diverging their ontological boundaries to create a hybrid, an "ancestral presence" that mediates the two socio-religious roles at the apex of eldership. The ancestor and the living elder act as a unity. Last with and closest to the ancestor, the ancestral presence disseminates information to the junior lineage and, at moments, exudes supernatural traits not unlike a spiritual being or the ancestor that s/he mediates. The living elder, acting as the ancestral presence, gives earthly "presence" to the absent living-dead ancestor. In *Song of Solomon* Pilate, the ancestral presence, and Macon Dead the first, the ancestor, are prime examples of the conjoining of the former with the latter that fuses their offices and the physical and spiritual planes of the living and living-dead. The representations of Ma'am, Nan, Sixo, Baby Suggs, and Mary Thérèse Foucault, the blind horsemen, and the swamp women provide subjective variations on the expression of the ancestral presence.

Chapter 5 discusses the final social category, "Banganga: the specialists – medicine (wo)men and priest(esse)s," and elevates the general interpretation of "conjurers" in Morrison's fiction to the specific socio-religious roles that the sacred African traditional specialists enact. Stronger in West African traditions than in other parts of the continent, the tradition of the priest receives substantive treatment in Morrison's Western diasporic representations. Morrison imbues her priests and priestesses, the medicinal and psychical healers of their respective communities, with characterizations based on the official priestly roles of the Haitian houngan (Fon for "priest"), the Haitian mambo (the French transcription of the Carib term "great priest/snake"), and the Brazilian mãe de santo (Portuguese for "mother of the saint").

In keeping with their roles of priesthood, and chief among them, is the responsibility of serving as medium between the living and the spirits-each of Morrison's priest(esse)s in some capacity projects the personality or exhibits the characteristics of a maît-tête (the master loa in Voudoun or its equivalent, the head spirit, in Candomblé). The representation of Soaphead Church premières Morrison's treatment of the priest who is the intermediary of a remote God indifferent to earthly affairs, but Shadrack in *Sula* debuts her construction of the African traditional priest subscribed with a loa persona. Shadrack's figuring as a World War I soldier and founder of National Suicide Day, a day intended to cure ritualistically the trauma of uncertain death, follows the Voudoun houngan's methodology of psychosomatic treatment. Unobtrusively written on Shadrack on the battlefield and in his hometown of Medallion are nature and warrior qualities associated with the many manifestations of the loa Ogoun, who is the divinity of war and guardian of the Voudoun hounfor (parish) because of his love of ritual and initiation. Similarly, Pilate Dead's and Consolata Sosa's priesthoods bear the confirmatory markings of master gods or spirits governing their personalities and offices. The tree and root descriptions of Pilate Dead's body in *Song of Solomon* allude to the crossroads loa Legba, who is the guardian of the gateway tree that conducts the intersection of the physical and metaphysical worlds in Voudoun. Modeled on traits that also allude to the influence of Dahomean Vodun, Consolata Sosa, the mãe de santo of a women-centered, Brazilian terreiro or house of Candomblé formulated as the Convent in *Paradise*, has the personage of the Candomblé water priestess Yemanjá, the guardian of women, childbirth, fertility, and witchcraft. In oral charges issued to religious serviteurs and devotees in their communities, Baby Suggs in *Beloved* and Consolata Sosa in *Paradise* reify the central organizing principle of their Vodun-derived religions. Both reaffirm the inseparability of the flesh and the spirit. Finally, Morrison's inclusion in *Song of Solomon* of Circe, an extension of the healer figure M'Dear in *The Bluest Eye* (1970) and the only priest(ess) figure with a classical name, requires an interrogation of the Greek appropriation of the African god. The African divinity's detachment from Africa and Greek appropriation stands in relief to the interpolation of various religious beliefs and practices of the indigenous peoples of the Americas, the Carib Arawakan Indians and Amerindians, into Voudoun and Candomblé.

The concluding chapter, "Identifiable Blackness: Toni Morrison's literary canon at the Western crossroads," raises possibilities for the future direction of Morrison scholarship in light of the West and Central

African traditional survivals that this study uncovers in her novels. Although Henry Louis Gates, Jr. made no mention of Morrison's incorporation of Vodun figures in the five novels she had written when his *Signifying Monkey* appeared in 1988 identifying Esu-Elegbara as a key topos in African-American vernacular theory, her canon similarly draws upon Esu-Elegbara, other West African divinities, Kongo's Yowa, and traditional beliefs in general to qualify her work as irrevocably Black. Morrison accounts for the presence of West and Central African traditional religious survivals in her early novels as vestiges of memories brought forward from her childhood and later insights that Africans helped her identify. While incorporation of these African traditional elements becomes more self-conscious in her work, her initial Africanist recollections and insights intersect with African fiction as recent as Ben Okri's *The Famished Road* (1991) and expand the literary interpretation of twentieth-century African-American fiction as early as Charles W. Chesnutt's *The Conjure Woman* (1899).

Although the philosophical, historical, ethnographical, cultural, and anthropological research of numerous scholars contributes to the African traditional interpretations of Morrison's fiction in this study, the work of a select half a dozen in particular has proved invaluable to understanding her narratives from an African traditionalist viewpoint. Robert Farris Thompson and Joseph Cornet's *The Four Moments of the Sun: Kongo Art in Two Worlds* (1981) and Thompson's *The Flash of the Spirit: Afro-American Art and Philosophy* (1984) masterfully explain, through early African visual art, Kongo and other African survivals that are readily discernible in African America. Thompson, however, credits K. Kia Bunseki Fu-Kiau as his tutor and "one of the richest traditionalist minds in Central Africa."[16] The contents of Fu-Kiau's privately published *The African Book Without Name* (1980) and numerous interviews that the Congolese scholar "who was the first writer who made explicit the implicit paradigms of Kongo thought and ritual"[17] provide Thompson's and Cornet's scholarship with a store house of knowledge used in this study. Scholars from disparate parts of the globe corroborate Fu-Kiau's assertion that the cross was a central part of Bakongo thought before European arrival.[18] A Kenyan scholar's work, John S. Mbiti's *African Religions and Philosophy* (1970) makes intelligible a variety of abstractions – evil, morality, time, and ancestral "death" – as traditional cultural groups interpret them throughout the African continent. Sterling Stuckey's *Slave Culture: Nationalist Theory and the Foundation of Black America* (1987) situates the passage of Kongo's symbol and ritual through the Black Atlantic as the ring shout, a shuffling, counterclockwise, sacred dance that people of the African diaspora perform in a circle to remember their ancestors and to worship God. Along with Zora Neale Hurston's pioneering anthropological study of Voudoun in Haiti, *Tell My Horse* (1938), Voudoun initiate Maya Deren's articulation of the amalgamated religion in *Divine Horsemen: Voodoo Gods of Haiti* (1953) and her documentary featuring footage of loa mounting serviteurs in *Divine Horsemen: The Living Gods of Haiti* (1985) give sensitive outsider and insider perspectives. Deren synthesizes a number of seminal Caribbean studies to produce her carefully nuanced explications of the intelligence at work in Voudoun. Without Deren's insightful exegesis of Voudoun beliefs, this study would be greatly impoverished.

To date, few literary scholars have identified substantively specific African cosmological extractions in Morrison's canon and speculated on what her assertions concerning their presences suggest about the evolution and present state of African-American sacred and secular survivals and culture. Vashti Crutcher Lewis's "African Tradition in Toni Morrison's *Sula*" (1987) posits that Morrison writes from "an African aesthetic" and that the "Africanness of the major character's name ... places a demand on the critic to search for a blueprint for the novel based on an African worldview."[19] Lewis maintains that the relationship between Shadrack and Sula is "metaphorically, a marriage of a traditional West African water spirit/ priest to a water priestess, both oracles of a river god."[20] Next, Holly Fils-Aimé's "The Living Dead Learn to Fly: Themes of Spiritual Death, Initiation and Empowerment in *A Praisesong for the Widow* and *Song of Solomon*" (1995) centers on Milkman Dead, whose name evinces that he is the dead among the living, as a zombie who undergoes a "Vodun" initiation that Pilate, the "poto-mitan [poteau-mitan] of Legba" guides.[21] A comparative literature specialist, Fils-Aimé taught from 1986 to 1988 at Collège International in Haiti where she expanded her knowledge of Voudoun. In the same year that Fils-Aimé's article appeared, Barbara Christian, a native of the Caribbean, echoed Lewis's call for critical African interpretations of Morrison's novels in "Fixing Methodologies: *Beloved*" (1995). Christian cites the title character's resemblance to Erzulie, the Haitian loa of love. Finally, Gay Wilentz's "An African-Based Reading of *Sula*" (1997) affirms an approach "that explores the alternative reality of the novel, allusions to African traditions and cultural milieus, and a cosmology that displaces binding oppositions such as reality/fantasy, science/magic, and good/evil."[22]

Therese E. Higgins, in *Religiosity, Cosmology, and Folklore: The African Influence in the Novels of Toni Morrison* (2001), mounts an inaugural extended examination of specific African markers in Morrison's canon.

Methodologically, she looks at nine groups of Africans selected from all compass points of the continent: "The Lele of Zaire, the Abaluyia of Kenya, the Lovedu of Zimbabwe, the Dogon of the Sudan, the Mende of Sierra Leone, the Shilluk of the Upper Nile, the Tutsis and the Hutus of Rwanda, the Fon of Benin, and the Ashanti, a specific group of Akan people of Ghana."[23] Unlike Higgins's discussion, which draws from African cultures at large and neither identifies Kongo's Yowa nor treats the influence of Dahomey's Vodun in Morrison's texts, the assertions presented in this study reflect the methodology of moving backward in time and space to ascertain the specific cultures that contributed predominantly to the identifiable Blackness – African survivals – at work in modern African-American life and Morrison's fiction. The regressive history of those contributions moves from present African America, to the creolizing of African traditional beliefs in Voudoun in the Caribbean during the transatlantic slave trade, to the West and West Central African regions and cultures that participated in that creolizing and in the centralizing of Kongo's cross and circle cosmogram.

This study is equally invested in reclaiming from the brink of American disremembrance specific cosmological survivals and identifying Morrison's artful use of them as interpretive and aesthetic strategies. It contains extended articulations of traditional beliefs that are not commonly known outside of specialists' circles. The Western academy's ancillary and generalized discussions in the twenty-first century of things African continue to hamper specific literary critical analysis of the continent's cultures that cradled civilization. As critical explicators, we owe it to ourselves and to others to (re)claim the particulars, to dust off the critical palimpsest as well.

The intention of this study is not to exoticize or essentialize Blackness or promote the misleading belief that Morrison exclusively uses the stylistic, aesthetic approaches it discusses. Some of the cosmologies that she treats may overlap with other cultures, and their usage may be found in the works of other writers. Enlisting Morrison's position as my own, "I am not suggesting that some of these approaches have not been used before and elsewhere"; my primary objective is to identify their uses in her work and to posit some reasons why she may have selected them.[24] This study discusses solely Morrison's work, yet she is not alone in producing imaginative African-American fiction steeped in traditions traceable to the Caribbean and traditional Africa. For many readers, Paule Marshall's *Praisesong for the Widow* (1983) and Gloria Naylor's *Mama Day* (1988) immediately come to mind. Moreover, a few literary critics have revisited earlier twentieth-century

American works of fiction with new critical gazes that reveal examples of African traditional cosmologies vis à vis the Caribbean. More than half a dozen articles discussing Erzulie, Esu, and sacred tree symbolisms in Hurston's *Their Eyes Were Watching God* (1937), a likely source for Voodooisms, have been published in the past ten years.[25] With more astute identifications of literary survivals, with deeper, more exacting scholarly interrogations of those identifications, identifiable West and Central African traditional survivals in American life will emerge from the depths of spatial dispossession, temporal discontinuity, familial disremembrance, and Western disrespect. That scholarship will not only restore for readers the African subject to rightful remembrance and interpretation but also validate the Black subject's humanity and the totality of his or her reality in American and global post-enslavement, post-colonial literatures and life.

Dahomey's Vodun and Kongo's Yowa: the survival of West and Central African traditional cosmologies in African America

> From the movement of the sun, Kongo people derive the circle and its counterclockwise direction in a variety of ways. "Coded as a cross, a quartered circle or diamond, a seashell's spiral, or a special cross with solar emblems at each ending – the sign of the four moments of the sun is the Kongo emblem of spiritual continuity and renaissance."
>
> Sterling Stuckey, *Slave Culture*[1]

Toni Morrison's literary work documents, as historical scholarship bears out, that West and Central African traditional socio-religious roles, beliefs, and practices are neither nonexistent nor extinct in African-American life. Despite the documentation of African transatlantic religious retentions in the pioneering anthropological studies of Melville J. Herskovits in the second quarter of the twentieth century and later historiographies by Benjamin Mays, John W. Blassingame, Albert J. Raboteau, Mechal Sobel, Joseph E. Holloway, and others, the dominant impression persists that African-American religious histories began with the African introduction to Christianity in the New World.[2] It is commonly held that virtually no substantial traditional beliefs from West Africa and West Central Africa, the geographical regions from which the majority of Africans brought to the Americas originated, survived beyond African enslavement in the early American South.[3] Historians Sylvia R. Frey and Betty Wood note that "as recently as 1990 Jon Butler confidently asserted that West and West Central African religious systems were shattered beyond repair as a result of the Middle Passage, a process that he describes as a '*holocaust.*'"[4] Refuting the supposition that West and Central Africans totally abandoned their own beliefs and practices and immediately adopted new ones once they arrived in North America, scholarship citing the survival of African traditional religions emphasizes a reconciliatory syncretism with Christianity. The theory of syncretism, however, is slowly giving way to the assertion that early African arrivals juxtaposed, rather than conflated, their traditional beliefs with Christianity. African proselytes adopted and adapted New World beliefs and rituals to accommodate their Old World traditional beliefs and practices. The Christian cross and Catholic saints, for example, took on crossover meanings, while baptism stood for tribal purification rites.

Before New World introduction, traditional religious beliefs thrived alongside encroaching Christianity and Islam in Africa. Arriving on Africa's west coast around the mid fifteenth century, pre-Reformation Portuguese were the first to introduce Christianity to West Africans and West Central Africans in the form of Catholicism. By the seventeenth century's commencement of the organized European slave trade, a small percentage of West Africans professed Christianity and a larger percentage claimed Islam, but the great majority remained faithful to traditional religions.[5] In the ancient kingdoms of Ghana, Mali, and Songhay, centers of Muslim influence, "elements of Islam were often mixed with or adapted to forms of traditional African belief." But not until "shortly before and contemporary with nineteenth-century colonization" were European and American Christian missionaries successful on a large scale in penetrating Africa's interior.[6]

During and after the colonial and revolutionary periods when Africans and their European and American enslavers moved in both directions between Africa and the North American South, first by way of the British and French colonized Caribbean islands and later directly to the southern mainland, traditional beliefs and rituals traveled with them. Most of the human cargo and consequentially the traditional beliefs brought via the Caribbean or directly to the American South were largely from Africa's coastal and interior societies extending from Senegambia in the sub-Saharan west to Kongo-Angola in the west central and southwest.[7] Slave traffickers who routed their trade through the Caribbean segregated members of the same tribe from each other, blending them with disparate other groups to curb the potential for solidarity leading to insurrection. Consequently, newly formed alliances with people from distant and dissimilar cultural regions of Africa's western seaboard and hinterland and Indians newly encountered in the Caribbean spawned syncretized transcultural beliefs and practices that enslaved Africans forwarded in the New World. Slave-market dispersal of West and West Central Africans throughout the American South resulted in a similar hybridity of African religious cultures.

Composed of numerous and varied cult groups, the majority of West and Central Africans believed in a Supreme Being and a pantheon of lesser divinities which facilitated the smooth creolization of African traditional beliefs.[8] Frey and Wood state that "Among the Slave Coast (Bight

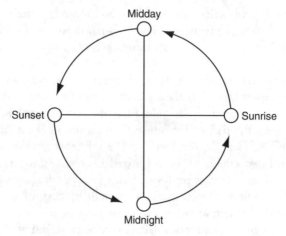

Figure 1. The Kongo Yowa: The four moments of the sun

of Benin) groups whose traditions are most prominent in African American religion, including the Yoruba of southwestern Nigeria and their neighbors, the Ewe, and especially the Fon of [the pre-colonial kingdom of] Dahomey, God was the ultimate power."[9] They believed, like peoples of the distant Kongo-Angola kingdoms, that the Supreme Being, the creator of the universe and resident of the sky, was remote, too high above humans to be concerned with earthly affairs. Lesser spirits were often more important since the administration of human affairs fell under their purview.[10] Possessing ambivalent natures, including the propensity for good and evil, many divinities were thought to bestow prosperity, fertility, and health on the living when the proper propitiatory sacrifices were made to implore their blessings, and to visit misfortune upon those who offended or angered them.

To align the fictional with the factual, Morrison turned to the Caribbean, the crossroads of New World African traditional religious amalgamation, and principally to the creolization of West and Central African socio-religious roles, beliefs, and practices that coalesced in Haiti in Voudoun,[11] the Caribbean transmutation of Dahomey's Vodun. African peoples who were torn from the Dahomean, Fula, Mandingo, Ashanti, Hausa, Yoruba, and Kongo empires and brought to Haiti reconstituted a single religion[12] that centralized its belief in a single geometric symbol imported from Kongo, a cross within a circle mapping the four moments of the sun (see figure 1). Symbolizing the four stages of life, the Kongo Yowa or cosmogram invokes renaissance and reincarnation by paying homage to the ancestors, the living-dead. In the amalgamation of beliefs, historian Sterling Stuckey asserts, Kongo's Yowa "was so powerful in its elaboration of a religious vision that it contributed disproportionately to the centrality of the circle in slavery."[13]

A ground marking used for purposes of initiation and the mediation of spiritual power between worlds, Kongo's quartered circle became one of the most discernible African survivals in the Western hemisphere. In Haiti the Kongo symbol became the religious sign for Voudoun, a creolized religion whose name bore the contribution of the Fon people from Dahomey, the birthplace of Vodun.

The Yowa, emblematizing the four solar positions, resembles the Greek cross but, predating the arrival of the Portuguese on the continent of Africa in 1471 and in Kongo in 1482, it does not signify the crucifixion of Christ.[14] It invokes the indestructibility and circularity of the human soul. African art historian Robert Farris Thompson has explained the ontological symbolism encoded in the Yowa, asserting that "in Kongo immortality is a privilege of right living. In the vernacular imagination, extraordinary persons – those who are generous, strong, and wise in life on a heroic scale – die twice. They die once 'here,' and once 'there,' beneath the watery barrier, the line Bakongo [the people of Kongo] call Kalunga."[15] The horizontal Kalunga line divides the world or mountain of the living on earth (ntoto) from the world or mountain of the dead or "'white clay' (*mpemba*) . . . God is imagined at the top, the dead at the bottom and water [at the Kalunga diameter] in between."[16]

The four disks at the compass points of the cross stand for the four moments of the sun, while the circumference of the circle represents the certainty of reincarnation; three of the solar disks map the phases of life on earth and the fourth marks the spiritual existence beyond the earthly realm. Each disk, forming a tension against its opposing disk, demonstrates balance and unity. Sunrise, the solar disk at the right or east, is the sign of life beginning, and sunset, at the left or west, signifies the inevitable organic process of death. "The summit of the pattern not only symbolizes noon but also maleness, north, and the peak of a person's strength on earth. Correspondingly, the bottom equals midnight, femaleness, south, the highest point of a person's otherworldly strength." The pattern of the sun's natural journey from right to left or east to west, counterclockwise in direction, figures the journey of life on earth and beyond in the afterworld. The counterclockwise spiral of the solar moments suggests a backward movement that spatializes time as it recedes into the past. A variation of the cosmogram replaces the sun disks with arrows symbolizing the four winds of the universe.[17]

In Haitian Voudoun a sacred tree or erect cross serves as the poteau-mitan or center-post for a human circle of worshippers or serviteurs that physically forms the circumference of the Yowa. The vertical axis of the cross in the circle takes on broader significance as a tree or the tree of the cross, the avenue by which the Voudoun loa (Mystères, gods, or spirits) of ambivalent personalities descend to intersect with the horizontal, mortal realm. At the intersection of the axes, the radius of the circle, the physical and the metaphysical or flesh and spirit worlds meet. It is at this inter-section, the crossroads, that the loa, spirits considered divine horsemen, mount or spirit-possess their serviteurs.

In its most recognized North American, Christian manifestation, wor-shippers physically form the Yowa configuration in the ring shout, a shuffling counterclockwise sacred dance performed to remember familial ancestors and to communicate with the ultimate ancestor, God. In a mid-nineteenth-century-manifestation, the Yowa appeared in the First African Baptist Church of Savannah, Georgia, as bored holes forming thirty-six cross and diamond patterns spread throughout the floor of its fellowship hall. Built between 1859 and 1861 by enslaved Africans who started a congregation in 1773, the First African Baptist Church, one of the earliest-formed Black congregations in North America, has an oral history that connects the cosmogram to the Underground Railroad. The Yowa is believed to have camouflaged ventilation holes for runaway slaves hiding between the church floor and a subflooring four feet beneath it. In one of its most recent appearances, an artistic rendering of the Yowa commemo-rates the site of the lower Manhattan African burial ground containing the remains of thousands of free and enslaved seventeenth- and eighteenth-century Africans discovered in 1991 at the corners of Duane and Elk Streets, adjacent to the Ted Weiss Federal Building at 290 Broadway in New York City. The burial ground is the earliest known African-American cemetery. Rodney León, an African American of Haitian descent, designed the permanent exterior memorial that features a circle with a counterclockwise spiral marking its center. Artist Houston Conwill designed *The New Ring Shout*, a handmade Kongo-inspired cosmogram made of terrazzo and polished brass laid in the rotunda floor at 290 Broadway.

A symbol of reincarnation, unification, balance, reconciliation of oppo-sites, and the backward spatialization of time, the Yowa in Morrison's canon repeatedly appears as a substructural signifier marking landscapes, bodyscapes, and interior spaces. Its subliminal presence underscores an identifiable, operational, African traditional worldview by which the social roles and subject positions of her characters – from the malevolent communal member who damages relationships to the benevolent guiding ancestral presence – can most usefully be interpreted.

Historian Philip Curtin estimates that one-third of African Americans are of Kongo and Angola ancestries, which explains, in part, the dominance of the Yowa in African-American culture along with "the presence of Kongo-influenced signs in Black traditional burials across the southeastern United States and the continuity of some of the main gestures of Kongo statuary in Afro-American gesture and stance."[18] Kongo's dominance also explains Morrison's selection of the cross within a circle to substructure natural landscapes, bodyscapes, and interior spaces in her American-set fiction.[19] In *Sula* (1973) cross and circle imaging appears in the geographic mapping of Medallion and the riverside scene involving Sula Peace and Nel Wright just before the drowning of Chicken Little, whose fowl nickname within the context of a Voudoun sacrifice takes on heightened significance. In *Song of Solomon* (1977) the Shalimar children, chanting a ditty chronicling the protagonist Milkman's disremembered ancestors, physically form the cosmogram in a play rendition. A third appearance unfolds in *Tar Baby* (1981), as Jadine Childs performs a mock-possession dance with a tree centered in a peristyle, a circular grove modeled on the sacred precinct in Voudoun where religious ceremonies take place. Swamp spirits or loa look on from the tops of the encircling trees. Ma'am, Sethe's mother in *Beloved* (1987), literally has the quartered circle branded under her breast, while Baby Suggs, holy, calls worshippers from the trees encircling the Clearing to perform the ring shout. In addition to the geography of Ruby bearing the design of the cosmogram, Consolata Sosa and her coven of four in *Paradise* (1998) ritualistically celebrate within a circle of burning candles in the cellar of the Convent the inseparability of spirit and flesh, the defining doctrine of Vodun. Consolata's retention of the African-based religion comes from her early exposure to Candomblé, Vodun's survival in African-Brazilian culture. Inside the cellar ring the women arrange their bodies in various postures figuring a cross.

In the *Paradise* cellar scene, placement of the ancient pre-Christian cross and circle symbol in what was first an embezzler's mansion and then a convent metaphorically underscores the historical superimposition of European-American cultural inscriptions onto an African palimpsest. The embezzler's construction of the mansion laden with ostensibly classical mermaids and nymphs covertly critiques Western culture's fraudulent appropriation of mythical figures that are African in origin but now believed to be exclusively Greek. Replacing the classical with the Christian, transforming the mansion into the Convent, suggests the formidable success that the Portuguese introduction of Catholicism to West Africa had in assisting Greece's appropriation and subversion. The physical embodiment of the historical meeting of the two religions in the Old World and the juxtaposing of them in the New World, Consolata Sosa, a Brazilian orphan who is transported to the United States under Catholic influence and who had been indoctrinated by African-Brazilian Candomblé before her departure, officiates figuratively as the mae de santo (mother of the saint) at the subterranean cross and circle gathering in the Convent's cellar.

The substructural appearance of the cosmogram in each of these novels supplants European and Western inscription, primacy, and domination. It indicates that identifiable West and Central African traditional cosmologies that entered the New World through Voudoun in the Caribbean, Voodoo in the United States, and Candomblé in Brazil continue to inform, to varying degrees, the thoughts and actions of the Black diaspora of the Americas. These cosmological survivals fold seamlessly into Morrison's narratives just as they are invisibly tucked into the (un)consciousness of the African diaspora of the United States. Their presences are not readily acknowledged by modern African America because of the dominance of Christianity and the success that European-American culture has had in demonizing and subverting African traditional beliefs. Nevertheless, Vodun's and the Yowa's myriad covert influences privilege African traditional cosmologies from the west and central regions as the primary socio-religious criteria for interpreting the communal roles and subjectivities of Morrison's characters and for shaping subliminally many African beliefs and practices in African-American life.

Bandoki: witches, ambivalent power, and the fusion of good and evil

What? shall we receive good at the hand of God, and shall we not
receive evil?   Job 2:10

[F]or in their secret awareness of Him, He was not the God of three
faces they sang about. They knew quite well that He had four, and
that the fourth explained Sula.   Toni Morrison, *Sula*[1]

When my sister and I were nine and five years old respectively, my
mother shared with us at bedtime a spellbinding remembrance about
our Great-Aunt Coot, who was reputed to cause misfortune to settle
scores against those who did her wrong in her north Florida community.
A six-year-old girl, recounted our mother, "crossed" our great-aunt and
shortly thereafter the young girl, given to attacks of asthma or epilepsy,
suffocated while playing in a cotton bin. Despite our fledgling grasp of
cause and effect, it was clear to my sister and me that our great-aunt had
willed the tragedy.

In subtle and not so subtle ways, Great-Aunt Coot resembled Sula, the
title character of Toni Morrison's eponymous second novel; she was
attractive, independent, age-defying, and the continual object of male
desire and social controversy. Just as the African-American Bottom community designates the ruthlessly individual Sula a witch, our great-aunt's
name and the terms "Hoodoo," "Voodoo," and "witchcraft" often occupied the same sentence when members of her small panhandle town
discussed her. And similarly to Sula, whose cause of death in 1940 is
undisclosed, Great-Aunt Coot died prematurely in the early 1940s of a
wasting illness that some attributed to cancer and others to counterconjure,
vengeance-magic, or metaphysical retribution.

To learn more about a real life Voodooist deemed a witch by my
extended family, who staunchly embraces Christianity, I turned to surviving elders who had known Great-Aunt Coot in life. Their remembrances
supplemented my research on West Africa's Vodun and Central Africa's

bandoki, the Kikongo word for witches or traditional practitioners of kindoki – the art of exercising unusual ambivalent powers. I discovered that my great-aunt's given name was Jeanette Belser and that despite faded memories of her, there was one aspect of her oral legend that remains constant: those who knew her believed that she had psychic, invisible power. During her life, few people "messed" with her or sought reprisal for the acts of evil that they believed she willed into being.

***

In a 1975 published interview, Toni Morrison asserts that Black people's concepts of evil differ from those that Christianity, the dominant religion of the West, typically informs. Her aim in *Sula* (1973), she explains, was to foreground those differences:

> I was recently reading a most interesting critic who said – and this might apply to other writers as well – that Black writers seem to be focusing on a very different concept of evil, one that is unlike normal concepts of evil. They are focusing on a peculiar way in which Black people experience evil and deal with evil. Now I was certainly very much interested in the question of evil in *Sula* – in fact, that's what it was all about. . . . It never occurs to those people in the novel to kill Sula. Black people never annihilate evil. They don't run it out of their neighborhoods, chop it up, or burn it up. They don't have witch hangings. They accept it. It's almost like a fourth dimension in their lives. They try to protect themselves from evil, of course, but they don't have that puritannical [*sic*] thing which says if you see a witch, then burn it, or if you see something, then kill it . . . They don't destroy evil. It's as though God has four faces for them – not just the Trinity, but four.[2]

Morrison's literary constructions of contemporary African-American perceptions of and responses to evil provide solid socio-historical moorings on which to secure the Blackness of her narratives. Her representations seamlessly detail identifiable qualities of evil and morality that reflect diasporic retentions of creolized West and Central African traditional cosmologies. Despite Judeo-Christian sublimation, African traditional religious beliefs and practices in defamiliarized forms, especially those central to the empires of Dahomey and Kongo, survived the massive cultural chasm wrought by the Middle Passage and more than two centuries of American slavery. Anticipating readerly acceptance of European-American hegemony, Morrison skillfully subverts images of dominant Christianity to expose underlying African cosmological survivals that fold neatly, almost invisibly, into the collective (un)consciousness and culture of the United States. Her novels address the socio-religious worldview of African civilizations that preceded the reigning Western civilization[3] and that hovers at the threshold of recognition in the forms of religious symbols, beliefs, and social roles in twenty-first-century African-American life.

In order to interpret correctly the differently conceived, pre-Christian ideology of evil freed of a priori Western assumptions that *Sula* is "all about," a familiarity with traditional beliefs from Africa's western regions that creolized in Voudoun in the Caribbean and passed into North America is essential. Understanding West and Central African peoples' uniting of good and evil and the balancing fusion of constituent opposites, in large measure, is key to unlocking moral meaning throughout Morrison's literary canon. Without a guiding African traditional world-view, cultural outsidership or disconnectedness renders morally unintelligible the maternally irreconcilable act of Eva Peace, Sula's grandmother, incinerating her son, Plum. Without understanding the Bottom residents' justification for designating Sula a witch in their midst, then the subsequent figuring of the title character of *Beloved* (1987) as "a room-and-board witch"[4] growing inexplicably fat as her mother, Sethe, becomes emaciated is incomprehensible. And without a guiding traditional perspective, the depiction of Consolata Sosa and the women of the Convent in *Paradise* (1998) as cannibalistic "bodacious black Eves" who act "[m]ore like witches" than bitches[5] remains an enigma to many readers.

In each of these novels, the Kongo Yowa, central to unifying West and Central African traditional beliefs in Voudoun, appears as a substructural indicator that Christianity is not the sole arbiter of the religious beliefs and values shaping the personalities and actions of Sula, Eva, Beloved, and Consolata. Establishing Sula as the first of her canon's characters to epitomize moral evil, the defining trademark of the traditional witch, Morrison underwrites the personalities of select characters throughout her narratives with the personality traits of the loa or orixás (spirits or gods), whose roots evolved from the West African Vodun pantheon. In all of Morrison's novels, Black communities set apart from dominant European-American culture retain *in part* an African organizing cosmological (un)consciousness that undergirds their religious life and culture. "In part" must be emphasized because time, diasporic displacement, and the domination of Christianity have overwritten African Americans' active cultural remembrance and acceptance of African religious beliefs, practices, and roles that continue subliminally in Black communities, complicating and conflating the sacred and the profane. Memory overwrite is most evident in the distinction that can be drawn between Sula and Consolata. The African-American communities of Sula and Consolata designate them both witches or, to underscore the West and Central African distinction of the role from its Western counterpart, bandoki. Because of her ruthless individualism, egocentricism, and destruction of personal relationships, Sula's community deems her morally evil. Consolata, on the other hand, performs African-Brazilian Candomblé rituals that are traceable to sacred Yoruba and Vodun practices. In a West African traditional setting or an African-Brazilian one, she would be venerated as a priestess and not disparaged as a witch.

THE FOURTH THAT EXPLAINS SULA

In "The Fourth Face: The Image of God in Toni Morrison's *The Bluest Eye*," Allen Alexander makes the following assertion concerning the complexity of divinity in Morrison's fiction:

In Morrison's fictional world, God's characteristics are not limited to those represented by the traditional Western notion of the Trinity: Father, Son, and Holy Ghost. Instead, God possesses a fourth face, one that is an explanation for all those things – the existence of evil, the suffering of the innocent and the just – that seems so inexplicable in the face of a religious [Christian] tradition that preaches the omnipotence of a benevolent God.[6]

The recognition of a fourth face or evil dimension of God by Sula's neighbors alludes to African traditional thought rooted in the fusion of opposites: the stabilizing balance of the fusion of the four fundamental constituents of the universe: earth, water, fire, and air and the stabilizing balance of the fusion of good and evil. In fact, the cohesive integration of the four oppositional yet complementary elements and their inclemental influences – cold, rain, heat, and wind – formed the nucleus of ancient and medieval cosmologies. Morrison's subliminal subscriptions of Kongo's Yowa – the four moments of the sun cosmogram – and the four faces of God, with the fourth operating in relief to the opposing three, recognize an inclusive and ambivalent quaternal residual at work under an exclusive and univalent Trinity in African-American thought. Her unconscious, monistic, Africanist grounding of divinity in the Bottom community counters the Manichean dualistic indoctrination of absolute good and absolute evil, the separate and distinct binary of God and Devil on which the ethos of the West and the Christian Trinity turns.

The primarily monistic West African beliefs that comprise Voudoun fuse good and evil within the higher religious powers – God, the gods, and the ancestors – who dispense both blessings and curses, while the agency of witches, which also both protects and harms, largely accounts for human precipitated evil. Reifying Morrison's subgrounding of the unconscious influence of a monistic theodicy in African-American life despite the hegemony of a Christian dualism, historical record supports the survival of fractured and reconciled West and Central African traditional beliefs beyond the transatlantic slave trade's Middle Passage and the plausibility that those accused of witchcraft, or moral evil, were among the first to arrive on the shores of North America, first indirectly by way of the Caribbean and then directly to its New World ports from the African continent. African traditional notions of the witch as the embodiment of moral evil were central to early African-American religious experience and those notions, which shape present-day consciousness, linger in identifiable forms.

The non-Western imaging of Sula as a witch unseats entrenched interpretations, taxonomies, and representations of conventional Western witch depictions and prompts the consideration of a theodicy that diverges from a dualistic one and converges with Morrison's monistic fusion of good and evil. In her representation of a belief system that is traditionally Africanist in cosmological make-up, Morrison references the Christian Trinity as a foil to the African traditional quaternity; scene after scene, the former consistently highlights the latter. Morrison tacitly posits that because early enslaved Africans and African Americans consistently syncretized African and Western beliefs, African Americans presently retain residual traditional ideas and expressions brought forward from the Middle Passage. Her representations also support the view that western African traditional beliefs share a common elemental design with other pre-Christian religions and worldviews.

Morrison's ascription of a fourth dimension or face of God that is coeval and coequal with the "faces" of the Trinity – Father, Son, and Holy Spirit – and that negates absolute goodness by serving as a "reservoir"[7] that can discharge evil consciously and unconsciously supports a monistic theodicy. Her ascription inverts conventional dualistic and semi-dualistic perspectives that the evil agent is the separate and binary opposite of God (i.e., the Devil, Satan, or the Anti-Christ). Dualistic and semi-dualistic theodicies entail a notion of separable and, therefore, absolute evil, while monistic theodicies regard everything including evil as an aspect of God.[8]

African traditional cosmologies that allow for a fusion of discordant good and evil in the divine do not diametrically conflict with the Old Testament. The Bottom's belief in a monistic theodicy that coincides with the ambivalent nature of African divinities is applicable to the Judaic God of Abraham and Isaac. Early biblical texts reveal that evil was at times credited to God's agency, yet there was still a reluctance to see evil as a trait intrinsic to God. In the Old Testament "evil" describes God's temptation of Job to test his faithfulness. It also describes God's retribution upon the nation of Israel for unfaithfulness and breaking the covenant of Moses. The Anchor Bible Dictionary provides a summary of Israel's approach to explaining evil attributed to God.

[But Israel, w]ithin the confines of its own henotheism and later monotheism, grappled with explaining the relationship of evil to its conception of God. It did not develop a metaphysical dualism in which evil could be explained as the work of demonic powers. Neither did it develop the concept of a capricious [monistic] God to whom both good and evil could be ascribed. Rather it developed an ethical monotheism ... It resolved to accept the mystery of evil by conceptualizing a creator God with greater freedom to work in ways and for purposes that transcend human understanding.[9]

With the New Testament's shift, however, God no longer "tempt[s] with evil ... but rather rescues from it" and evil is "ascribed to the EVIL ONE, the Devil."[10]

Morrison points to a "secret awareness" of God within a monistic frame that alerts the Bottom to His fourth face, a fourth dimension of His divine nature that explains Sula, malevolence related to Him. The Bottom's awareness of a fourth and decidedly vengeful facet of God is not a novel concept. "[E]ven in the days of unqualified belief in the Trinity," asserts Carl Jung, who wrote extensively on evil, "there was a quest for a lost fourth, from the time of the Neopythagoreans down to Goethe's *Faust*."[11] The precedent for a fourth as part of a whole bearing a dichotomous nature had a much earlier source.

The quaternary Roman/Greek figure of pre-Christian mythology and alchemy, Mercurius, following the tradition of Hermes, is many-sided, changeable, and dual in gender identity. He consists of "the dry and earthy, the moist and viscous." Two of his elements are passive and feminine, earth and water; and two are active and masculine, air and fire. He is both good and evil, and his symbol is a triangle in a square.[12] The quaternity of Mercurius is compatible with the nature of Mawu-Lisa, the Supreme Being of the Fon of Benin, the former kingdom of Dahomey and the birthplace of Vodun. One side of God, Mawu, is female, associated with the earth, the water governing moon, and the west. The other side or nature, Lisa, describes Mawu's twin brother, son, male consort or husband, who is associated with the sky, the fiery sun and the east.[13] The reconciliation and unification of the natural elements and cardinal points associated with Mercurius and Dahomey's Mawu-Lisa interface with the binding of thesis and antithesis in the quaternal structure of the Yowa of the four moments of the sun of Kongo art and religion. Three of the Yowa's solar disks map the phases of life on earth, with the highest indicating the summit of maleness and strength, while the fourth and the lowest maps the spiritual existence beyond the earth in the watery female realm.

While parallel quaternal divinity designs imply an immediate connection between West African traditional thought and Greek mythology, an argument can also be made for a direct link between West Africa and East Africa – sub-Saharan West Africa and Egypt. "[A]lmost all the names of gods came into Greece from Egypt," wrote Herodotus, who is considered the Father of History (484?–425?BC), and according to the Greek historian, classical religion has its roots in African cosmology. A direct link between West Africa and Egypt, however, may explain why some Nigerians believe that Esu and the Egyptian god Shu are one and the same and why there are similarities between the Yoruba Ifa System of Divination and Egyptian hieroglyphics.[14] An east-west connection may also explain, in part, why an early pre-Christ textual source for a fourth face of God associated with evil that surfaced in East Africa potentially supports Morrison's observation that embedded in African-American (un)consciousness is the perception that God has four faces and not just the three of the Trinity.

The book of 1 Enoch, written around 100BC and included in the pseudepigrapha of the Old Testament, cites a four-faced God-image that parallels Morrison's conception. Carl Jung, in his essay "Answer to Job," summarizes the vision of 1 Enoch 40:7.

Enoch sees the four faces of God. Three of them are engaged in praising, praying, and supplicating, but the fourth is "fending off the Satans and forbidding them to come before the Lord of Spirits to accuse them who dwell on earth." The vision shows us an essential differentiation of the God-image: God now has four faces, or rather four angels of his face, who are four hypostases or emanations, of which one is exclusively occupied in keeping his elder son Satan, now changed into many, away from him, and preventing further experiments after the style of the Job episode.[15]

Of questionable character and authorship but known to almost all the New Testament writers, 1 Enoch fell into discredit from the fourth century onward under the ban of Jerome (AD340?–420) and Augustine (AD354–430). It gradually passed out of circulation and became lost to the knowledge of Western Christendom until 1773 when an Ethiopic version was found in Abyssinia and brought to Europe. A Greek version surfaced in Akhmim at Cairo in 1886.[16] Prophesy from the noncanonical 1 Enoch receives a single biblical reference in Jude 1:14. Composed of a single chapter of twenty-five verses and one of the shortest New Testament books, Jude exhorts its readers to contend for the faith. Morrison's naming and depiction of Jude Greene, Nel Wright's unfaithful husband in *Sula*, suggests Morrison's knowledge of Enoch's apocryphal record via the New Testament.

The Bottom's four divinations of Sula's facial birthmark mime Enoch's vision. With the last performing in opposition to the first three, the four shifting interpretations of "the scary black thing"[17] over Sula's eye turn on elemental interplay. The birthmark metamorphoses from a photosynthesizing, air-producing, air-aromatizing rose to a water-born but earthbound tadpole to an earth-crawling snake and, finally, to ashes, the aftermath of air consuming fire. The fourth interpretation, supplanting the other three, takes on an ominous malevolence since the ashes are evidence of misfortune that Sula allegedly causes. The community comes to suspect that Sula psychically set her mother on fire and that the configuration above her eye quintessentially signifies "Hannah's ashes marking her [as evil] from the very beginning."[18] Sula's fluid physiognomy reveals her elementally dynamic, good and evil shifting natures. Morally, she is a fusion of opposing impulses that form a necessary unity and not a competing duality. Unlike Christianity that calls for evil to be cast out and the flesh subdued in order that spirit may reign, from an Africanist perspective both good and evil are essential to balance, wholeness, and wellness.

Morrison embeds fused oppositional quaternities of a similar order in the narrative details of *Sula* to elaborate a monistic worldview. In the novel more than a score of fours and configurations of three-and-one appear accenting moments of (con)fusion, terror, oppression, contempt, death, hatred, menace, evil, betrayal, racism, and the bizarre. In the confusion of post-traumatic angst, the four fingers of each hand of Shadrack,[19] whose World War I story opens the novel, fuse into the fabric of his shoestrings and the eyeholes of his high-topped shoes, creating panic in the recuperating soldier. Feeling inexorable terror when the stateside hospital releases him, he plunges down four steps to escape the floating menace of paper-thin patients and the medical staff robed in white.

Shadrack's doubtful journey back to wholeness ushers in Helene Wright's journey through an oppressive South and to the dreaded Louisiana home of her youth. Four or five black faces regard her disapprovingly when she flashes a dazzling smile at the Anglo conductor who humiliates her for walking through the "whites only" coach. A further reminder of the United States's separate but unequal treatment of non-whites, the specific time of four o'clock marks her degradation in the

Meridian sun where racist Jim Crow law mandates that she and her daughter Nel relieve themselves in the bushes during train stops. Helene imitates the example of a fat woman with four children, three boys and one girl, and is soon an adept leaf folder. Three surviving generations – Rochelle, Helene, and Nel – gather at the New Orleans Sundown home of Cecile Sabat to pay respect to the dead fourth. Four Virgin Mary icons decorate the Sundown house, three in the front room and one in the bedroom where the dead body of Nel's great-grandmother lay.

Helene's estrangement from her New Orleans French Creole past gives way to the narration of early disappointments and conflicts in Eva Peace's three-story home with four flights of stairs. The high-pitched, big-city laughing woman of her estranged husband, Boyboy, leaning on the smallest of four sickle-pear trees in Eva's front yard triggers a lifetime of hatred in Eva. Mr. Buckland Reed contests Eva's insistence on the school admission of the four-year-old dewey, one of her three adopted sons, arguing "that one there was one year old when he came, and that was three years ago."[20] Notwithstanding their ages, the trio of deweys never grows taller than forty-eight inches: four feet. Her "fourth" son, Plum, becomes a heroin addict.

Uniting the disordered Peace home and the ordered Wright home, Sula and Nel, becoming fast friends, thwart the menace of four Irish boys who harass them after school. Sula slashes off the tip of her fourth finger to diffuse their threat. The next summer, the two girls, on the cusp of young womanhood, pass by the "four blocks" that compose all the "sporting life" in the Bottom on their way to play in a "square of four leaf-locked trees of four cornered shade,"[21] just before the river death of Chicken Little. The young boy's unidentifiable body, missing for three days, reaches the embalmer on the fourth day after his drowning.

In the wake of her mother setting Plum on fire, Hannah Peace, Eva's daughter, evilly wonders about Eva's love for her children on Wednesday, the fourth day of the week. The question is the second of four strange things. The fourth strange thing that happens before Hannah's death is Eva's misplacement of her comb that is usually never out of place. The fourth strange thing could be Hannah's dream of a red bridal gown if Sula's craziness is not counted as the third.

In Part Two of *Sula*, four dead robins, an ill omen, herald the social disorder that Sula's return to Medallion will cause after her ten-year absence. And Nel's discovery of Jude and Sula "down on all fours naked"[22] is one instance of that omen's fulfillment. In time, Nel fears that she will go to the box with four handles or coffin, a metaphor for the grave, without experiencing male intimacy again after Jude's marital infidelity and abandonment. After her last dialogue with Sula, Nel rapidly descends four flights of stairs, leaving the deathly ill Sula to concentrate on the four boards covering the window that Eva crashed through in her vain attempt to save Hannah burning in the yard below.

Other groups of four in the Bottom confront antagonistic forces. The interview of four colored men to work on the Medallion tunnel does not diminish the year's bitter end that forecasts misfortune and death. Ajax and two other African-American men go to rescue a questionably raced jailed fourth, a drunken Tar Baby, but a racist legal system takes all four to court. Tar Baby, who makes people think about death when he sings, becomes the fourth, along with the three deweys, to join Shadrack on the final National Suicide Day, a celebration Shadrack institutes to confront death. Three or four fainthearted marchers are afraid to enter the white part of town but most intrepidly forge ahead.

Twenty-five years after Sula's death and the tunnel disaster, Nel arrives at Sunnydale, the white-run home for the elderly, at a chilly four o'clock. Terrified, she flees from Eva who implicates her in the death of Chicken Little. Running past the colored part of the cemetery, she views the four "Peace" headstones of Plum, Hannah, Sula, and Pearl, a missing fourth during the course of the story. Married young, Pearl moved to Flint, Michigan, where she wrote sad nonsense letters to Eva, and the reader learns nothing more about her until the novel's end. Not one of Eva's three children but her grandchild, Sula, becomes the evil fourth of the Bottom community.

To signify symbolically a subverted organizing cosmic (un)consciousness that substructures African-American life, religion, and culture, Morrison superimposes on the Bottom community and the greater Medallion landscape a practically invisible four moments of the sun cosmogram replete with adaptations of its religious expressions in Voudoun. The setting of *Sula* originates in the inversion of bottom and top in the Ohio town of Medallion, a French word designating a circular medal bearing figures in relief. The Bottom, where Blacks live, is in the hills or top of Medallion, and the top where whites (mpemba or white clay, the land of things all white or dead) live is in the fertile bottom hemisphere of Medallion. The sign of a medallion also calls to mind engravings appearing within its circumference that hint at vevers, mirrored, laced designs that Voudoun adepts draw with flour, cornmeal, sand, coffee, or ashes in honor of the loa inside the circle enclosing the base of a tree or cross. The inversion of Medallion's top and bottom is achieved only from the perspective of God or, for the purpose of this explication, loa looking down.

A river, the metaphorical Kalunga line, flows at the diameter of Medallion. Moreover, at midtext or at the story's diameter with respect to the plot's timeline,[23] Sula as a living-dead, a person who has "passed on" to the afterworld, takes a post-mortem journey that traverses the river.

In the penultimate scene of the chapter entitled "1922," Sula Peace and Nel Wright retire to a peristyle, "a square of four leaf-locked trees of four cornered shade" that directly parallels the tree-ringed worship area of Voudoun where in its center the loa descend to the horizontal mortal realm through the vertical axis, a central tree or poteau-mitan. The two girls lie with the tops of "their foreheads almost touching in the midst of these leaf-locked trees, their bodies at a 180 degree angle," forming the diameter of the circular cosmogram – the horizontal, mortal axis. Within the peristyle Sula traces vevers, "intricate patterns," in a generous bare spot that she clears. The girls form with twigs two circular holes that merge into one, then fill the newly made hollow circle in the peristyle with debris that symbolizes the unification of the material and the spiritual.[24] As she lies on the ground, the coil of Sula's hair around her arm echoes the four moments of the sun's spatialization of time, the backward spiraling of ancestry from generation to generation. Moments later, Sula, inversely, ascends the vertical axis of a nearby double beech tree, escorting Chicken Little, the metaphorical initiate who shortly will soundlessly disappear beneath the watery Kalunga. Sula's inverted movement must be stressed because while the loa descend the vertical axis to the mortal realm, mortals do not ascend it to the spiritual realm. Her movement up the vertical axis indicates that she possesses powers that surpass those of the ordinary person. After descending the double beech tree, Sula picks Chicken Little "up by the hands and [swings] him outward then around and around" before he sails into the river.[25] The nickname the young boy possesses, within the context of Voudoun, becomes especially ironical since chickens, ritualistically killed in special rites, undergo the preparation of ventailler, the "ceremonial gesture of waving them in the air just prior to their sacrifice."[26]

The final scene of the novel is imagistically replete with concentric circles, a road encounter mapping the horizontal, mortal axis, and the implication that Sula's spirit resides, like a loa, in the vertical axis of a tree. Leaving the colored section of the tree-named cemetery Beechnut Park[27] where a few curious Bottom spectators came twenty-five years earlier to witness a witch's, Sula's, interment and sing "Shall We Gather at the River," – a Kalunga reference – Nel, "hurrying along the road with the sunset in her face"[28] and, therefore, west meets Shadrack, the novel's traditional priest figure,[29] heading in the opposite direction, east. As the two pass one another, "each thinking separate thoughts about the [dead of the] past,"[30] they pace the horizontal axis of the mortal realm. Gazing at the tops of trees, Nel whispers to Sula, intimating that her long-deceased best friend, now a living-dead, hovers above as spirits do in the vertical axis of the treetops. Earlier in Beechnut Park, when Nel passes the four headstones marking the graves of the three Peace children and one Peace grandchild who have all predeceased the family's matriarch, the narrative's assertion, "They were not dead people,"[31] invokes the renaissance and reincarnation symbolism of Kongo's Yowa. The assertion amplifies Nel's sudden spiritual awakening that aligns with Bakongo thought that the cemetery is "not a final resting-place . . . but a door (mwelo) between [the] two worlds . . . of the living and of the [living-]dead, circumscribed by the cosmic journey of the sun."[32] The tree-named cemetery ideologically intersects the horizontal earth site with the vertical site of spiritual transference.

The cry that Nel utters, the vocalizing of her epiphany that the missing presence in her life has not been her estranged husband, Jude, but Sula who has passed on, reprises the structural symbolism of the four moments of the sun cosmogram substructuring Medallion's geography. In Voudoun the living and the living-dead insure the continuation of one another in their respective ontological realms. It is the duty of the living to prevent the living-dead from moving from personal immortality to collective immortality and death in the graveyard of time. Nel has failed to connect with Sula to insure her best friend's personal immortality in the afterworld, especially since Sula does not have children to perform that vital service. Calling "Sula" repeatedly (and name calling is important to insure the living-dead's vivification) as elemental objects, mud and a breeze, shift around her, Nel issues "a fine cry – loud and long – but it had no bottom and it had no top, just circles and circles of sorrow."[33] In the four moments cosmogram, counterclockwise spirals of the sun similar to those of a snail shell or seashell represent the spatialization of time[34] and the defiance of mortality. The melding of elemental and cardinal opposites validates the melding of opposites within the human psyche, within nature, and within the mortal and immortal worlds.

The fourth that explains Sula and Morrison's rendering of the African traditional culture that substructures that explanation draw upon the monistic theodicy of Voudoun and its reconciliation and unification of opposites. The fourth face or evil dimension of God or the gods, the four divinations of Sula's birthmark with the fourth reconciling with the opposing three, and the reconciliation and fusion of quaternities throughout the narrative all pull interpretive energy from the worldview encoded in the four moments of the sun cosmogram with which Morrison subtly frames the Medallion setting. The cosmological strategy configuring the town's landscape also wields powerful explicative power over the Bottom's designation of Sula as a witch, the principal agent of moral evil.

THE PRINCIPAL AGENT OF MORAL EVIL – SULA AS AFRICAN NDOKI PARADIGM

Evil is an "essentially contested concept."[35] There is no essentialist definition that fixes it as firm, basic, and unquestionable. John Kekes in *Facing Evil* (1990), conceding imprecision, interprets it as "undeserved harm . . . as it affects human beings" even though a "full account would have to consider animals and perhaps also plants, other organisms, and possibly sentient beings not presently known."[36] David Parkin dismisses it as an abstraction and argues, "Evil *is* not any *thing*: it denotes rather an area of discourse concerning human suffering, human existential predicaments and the attempted resolution of these through other humans and through non-human agencies, including a God or gods."[37] Yet morality has to be considered in concert with evil since evil is a negative aspect of any moral system.

Morality largely figures in the primary sense of "evil" as recorded by the Oxford English Dictionary:

"Evil" as "the antithesis of GOOD in all its principal senses" . . . may be interpreted widely or narrowly: "In the widest sense: that which is the reverse of good; whatever is censurable, mischievous, or undesirable . . . [e.g.] *moral* [and] *physical* evil." In the narrower sense, evil is "what is morally evil; sin, wickedness." Thus, the narrow sense is specifically moral, while the wide sense includes it, as well as all other forms of evil.[38]

Therefore undeserved harm may issue from "moral evil," evil that can be defined as chosen human agency or culpability. For example, if Shadrack, the post-traumatically shocked World War I veteran in *Sula*, lured the townspeople of the Bottom in Pied Piper fashion to the tunnel being built by the white labor force in Medallion *knowing* that the tunnel is on the brink of collapse and *hoping* that they will confront death (which is the reason he institutes National Suicide Day), then his chosen act that leads to their drowning would be directly attributable to moral evil. From a West and Central African traditional perspective, his commission of moral evil may also include the unconscious *willing* of the forepoles bracing the tunnel's wall shield to slip, culminating in those near by losing their lives.[39]

In contrast to Western theology, which is concerned with "the origin of evil, traditional African religions," according to historians Sylvia R. Frey and Betty Wood, "were preoccupied with the causes and effects of evil." The concept of absolute evil, the idea of the Devil, was foreign to most African cultures. Traditional religions recognized misfortunes that were the product of moral evil, "acts ... committed by one human being against another, which damaged relationships."[40] Frey and Wood assert that "The principal agents of moral evil were witches possessed involuntarily [and unconsciously] by the spirit of evil, who by their very nature 'set to destroy relationships' and to visit disease, death and material loss upon the people. In order to neutralize their evil effects, Africans had frequent recourse to [ba]nganga" – ritual experts such as priests, mediums, diviners, herbalists, and rainmakers.[41]

Sula's fourth face confirms her commission of moral evil in light of her damaged relationships with Eva, Nel, and the women of the Bottom community. Her gender especially predisposes her to the Africanist interpretation that she is a witch. Religious cultures as geographically removed from each other as Nigeria's Yoruba and Kongo's Azande share the belief that the practitioner of witchcraft may be male or female. Yet, Thomas E. Lawson points out, in the African religious world at large "the maker of witchcraft is that unknown individual, almost always considered to be a woman, who uses valid and good power for invalid and evil ends."[42] Traditional religions "accorded great recognition to the mystical power of women,"[43] and women's biology cast them as evil since menstruation signified an innate biological power linked with the moon and the tides of the sea. In Ashanti life, for example, villagers feared menstruating women, and in cultures throughout Africa women were the primary specialists in evil, "a threat to public order, an unbearable strain on traditional social organization[, and] a challenge to revered tradition."[44] Sula's first act of evil, Chicken Little's drowning, occurs when she is approaching puberty and the commencement of her menses, signifying the activation of her innate biological power linked with the moon, the tides of the sea, and witchcraft.

Witchcraft in traditional terms is by and large a spiritual activity that involves no magical control or palpable apparatus. The Gã of the Ghana seaboard, like many tribal groups, simply believe it to be the projected will from the mind of the witch. "A witch," as Edward E. Evans-Pritchard observes in his research on the Central African Azande, "performs no rite, utters no spell, and possesses no medicines. An act of witchcraft is a psychic act."[45] The African public identification of bandoki is still problematic because their actions are completely private, secret, and unconscious. Since bandoki are often asleep "when the soul of their witchcraft-substance flit[s] on its errand of destruction," they therefore practice witchcraft unconsciously and involuntarily. In Azande culture as late as the early twentieth century, Evans-Pritchard reported, "[W]itchcraft is so much a daily consideration, is so much taken for granted, and so universal," that any woman might easily suppose that since anyone may be a witch, it is possible that she is one herself.[46] The very presence of the witch resulted in the release of evil and rarely would her psychically projected power assault strangers: family and community members were its most common targets.[47] The obeah woman who appears in literature as the "island conjure woman" is a recognized West African Middle Passage survivor, but she is not a traditional witch. A derivative of the Ashanti word "obaye,"[48] obeah requires magic, ceremonies, incantations, and potions. Peoples of European ancestry in mid-eighteenth-century America and the British Caribbean misapplied the term. Practitioners of obeah are sacred specialists not traditional witches.

If *Sula* is all about the African-American community's conception of evil and the culturally specific ways in which Black people define moral malevolence and deal with its commissioner, then the novel's formulation of its title character as a traditional witch establishes the blueprint for later witch images in Morrison's canon. Morrison's prototype for an African witch in the traditional sense crystallizes when one considers that Sula is not required to make any conscious overture or practice any magical arts to validate herself as one since she may be a witch without knowing it herself. She, like my Great-Aunt Coot whose story prefaces this chapter, is capable of willing misfortune into being whether she is cognizant of it or not. Sula's mere presence in the Bottom; her close, physical proximity when disaster and death occur; and her impulsive psychic leanings, which damage relationships and disrupt social order, position her squarely in the malevolent role. Sula implements a willful egocentrism as powerful witchcraft-substance to stir up misfortune. Her admission to Nel that she had sex with her husband Jude because "there was this space" inside her head and he filled it destroys the two women's longstanding friendship and speaks to the potency of Sula's latent or active psyche that fearlessly and selfishly transgresses social boundaries.[49] And her psychic potency has deadly potential. Her early unleashing of latent power in the form of "dark thoughts" precedes Chicken Little's drowning.[50]

Geoffrey Parrinder, who has published extensively on West African traditional religions and psychology, validates Morrison's observation that unlike European and Puritan American witch-hunting, expulsion, hanging, or burning of the accused did not automatically resolve African witch divinations. The Bottom does not expel Sula or threaten her with annihilation since its African traditional counterpart would not have dealt with her in that manner:

There is no doubt that Africans fear and hate witches, and therefore take stern measures to curb their activities. . . .

Yet while Africans fear witches they do not hunt them out incessantly. Many people are believed to be witches, but as their powers are generally thought to be in abeyance they are not unduly disturbed. Only when there seems to be evidence that the witch is on the prowl, and men sicken, is action taken to restrain the witches' [sic] activities.[51]

Few recorded cases of early "witch-hunts" in Africa survive, though there were instances following several deaths when suspects were divined and executed.[52] Apart from these instances, when misfortune was thought to be the result of witchery, those involved often sought communal or victim reconciliation, even in cases where the misfortune targeted a monarch. Evans-Pritchard's twentieth-century observations note that among the Azande there were cleansing rituals that reconciled the witch with her victim.

The witch persona that Sula exemplifies and that the Bottom community does not eject or destroy is necessary to the West African traditional community that allows evil a natural space in opposition to good at every ontological level. The West African traditional worldview allows for a fusion of good and evil within the gods, the ancestors, and living humans. Esu-Elegbara, the Yoruba god in Nigeria, or Legba, his Fon equivalent in Benin (Dahomey), is perhaps the best known of the ambivalent West African divinities and one of the most complex. Depicted with a large phallus despite his gender duality, icons of him appear throughout these two sub-Saharan regions. Esu's personage survived the Middle Passage in the forms of Echu-Elegua in Cuba, Exú-Elegba in Brazil, Papa Legba in the pantheon of the Voudoun loa of Haiti, and Papa La Bas in the Voodoo spirits of the United States. Christian missionaries who went to West Africa tended to distort Esu's nature, equating him with the concept of the Devil, while in reality he contains within him forces both of good and evil and the ability to mediate between heaven and earth.[53] Sources also credit him with being "the head or father of witchcraft,"[54] and like the fourth emanation in Enoch's vision, he has the power to fend off the destructive actions of demons. Below Esu and the other gods are the ancestors, those who long ago or of more recent memory passed on and now inhabit the realm of the living-dead. Considered religious powers, the ancestors are capable of cursing or blessing their living descendants. Their benevolence largely depends on the proper reverence they receive. Africana Studies scholar Simon Bockie explains that with respect to living humans, "evil tendencies are considered an inescapable part of human nature, not something that can be completely eradicated. Such tendencies can only be integrated into the community and kept under control."[55]

Among the Bamanianga of Central Africa, Christian missionaries have been unsuccessful in displacing belief in kindoki, the art of exercising unusual powers, because the culture does not allow for the "idea of purity as a goal, or of warfare against sin, requiring evil to be cast out."[56] Good and evil must be kept at a balance. One must temper the other:

All human beings, it is understood, are a mixture of good and bad to varying degrees. No one can attain perfection in this life. That is possible only to ancestors in the after-death world. Since everyone has both a good and a bad side, the good is to keep the bad side under control, not to let it become worse than need be. The community in order to prosper must be in harmony with its own evil side, just as the individual must strike a successful balance between strengths and weaknesses.[57]

Buakasa Tulu Kia Mpansu, in his study of Kongo's Bandibu, formally defines kindoki as signifying power and force.[58] "Hence kindoki can be termed a quality which makes a particular human being different from the average or ordinary person." Although taken as evil, it is an ambivalent, ambiguous power capable of harming or protecting . . . [and even "h]armful kindoki is allowed a well-defined place in the community so it can be subjected to the checks and balances that keep the group unified and thriving."[59]

If inferences from modern accusations of kindoki provide clues to the social profiles of West and Central African women charged with invisible powers in preceding centuries or in the literary texts of Morrison, then the usual suspects, those socially positioned like Sula, or later Consolata Sosa in *Paradise*, posed threats to male–female bonds, marriage, and motherhood. Unmarried women like Sula and Consolata, women separated from their husbands, and widows were vulnerable targets to charges of kindoki practice. Young women in the first two categories were unquestionably uncontained sexual threats, while unmarried women of advanced age were potential sexual predators. In the case of widows, members of the community might question the circumstances under which their husbands' deaths occurred; and they, too, might be judged sexually dangerous.

In early West and Central African traditional cultures, motherhood was consistently the most revered female role. Thus childlessness, barrenness, or birthing a stillborn baby subjected traditional women to kindoki charges since failing to produce children marked them as anti-maternal – haters, murders, and devourers of children. Because children were considered among the primary targets for undeserved harm, suspected bandoki could not be entrusted with their care. Moreover, they were saboteurs of conception and pregnancy. Childless bandoki were believed to cause infertility and miscarriage in women and impotence in men. They took unborn children from their mothers' wombs and put them back dead.

Proclaiming men not worth keeping, sexually preying on the husbands of her neighbors and best friend Nel and then discarding them, the unmarried, ruthlessly independent Sula is uninterested in making babies, only in herself. Exacerbating her communal designation, rumors that she sleeps with white men grow out of the Bottom men's preoccupation with her sexual freedom. Indulgently privileging her whims and desire over her reproductive duty scandalizes Sula. She is not the ordinary person. Nevertheless, Sula is not the embodiment of absolute evil; and the Bottom resolves not to run her out of town but to withstand her, counteracting her negative evil with positive goodness. Sula is the fulcrum through which necessary, complementary cosmic balance issues.

It is difficult for the Bottom community to pinpoint when Sula's invisible powers began, since if they were not natally inscribed she may have acquired them post-natally.[60] Nevertheless, the community retroactively confirms her possession of extraordinary powers judging by her aberrant physicality:

Among the weighty evidence piling up was the fact that Sula did not look her age. She was near thirty and, unlike them, had lost no teeth, suffered no bruises, developed no ring of fat at the waist or pocket at the back of her neck. It was rumored that she had no childhood diseases, was never known to have chicken pox, croup or even a runny nose. She had played rough as a child – where were the scars? Except for a funny-shaped finger and that evil birthmark, she was free of any normal signs of vulnerability. Some of the men, who as boys had dated her, remembered that on picnics neither gnats nor mosquitoes would settle on her."[61]

Sula's mercurial birthmark and events leading to her acquisition of the "funny-shaped finger" mark her as a traditional witch. First, in accordance with West African traditional belief, the birthmark over Sula's eye when interpreted as a snake or tadpole is a clue to the operation of witchcraft since witches' familiars, among others, are snakes and frogs.[62] Second, her oddly shaped finger is the result of daring self-mutilation to which she resorts in order to intimidate four Irish boys who terrorize her and Nel on their way home from school. Resolved that she and Nel will take the most direct route home and not the path of avoidance, Sula, armed with Eva's paring knife and a "determined but inaccurate" aim, "slashed off only the tip of her finger."[63] As "[t]he four boys stared open-mouth" at the severed flesh of her symbolic phallus, Sula warns through intimation that she is fully capable of inflicting harm on anyone, even on herself. "If I can do that to myself, what you suppose I'll do to you?," she questions them.[64] The boys' inference from her action of their own mutilation, or more specifically castration, sends them scurrying. Sula's self-mutilation is the first in a series of excessive acts that validates her evil dimension. It also gives credence to Eva as her ndoki predecessor. Although it is never verified, rumor cites premeditated self-mutilation as the cause of Eva's missing leg. The community speculates that in order to collect a monthly disbursement for bodily injury from the railroad's insurance company, Eva staged the extreme act of sacrificing her limb.

The drowning of Chicken Little, a child, at Sula's hand in a site that directly replicates a West African sacred precinct further endorses Sula's culpability as the practitioner of harming kindoki, a judgment that would prevail where a traditional worldview determines evil and morality. Morrison's landscape invocation of the Yowa and Voudoun belief destabilizes Christian hegemony with the aura of Voudoun domination. Vashti Crutcher Lewis, who argues that Sula and Shadrack are both oracles of a river god and, respectively, traditional West African water priestess and priest, posits that when Chicken Little "slips from her [Sula's] grip into the water, he is sacrificed to the river god just as it was not uncommon for children to be sacrificed to river gods in Africa, throughout the Bight of Benin."[65] Before the drowning, overhearing her mother Hannah telling friends that despite her maternal love for her, she "just don't like her" psychologically traumatizes Sula. Hannah's painful disclosure plunges Sula into a profound, psychic reverie of "dark thoughts" that Nel, calling from outside, suspends.[66] The significance of that revelation read through a West African lens culminates in the girls retreating to a Voudoun-styled peristyle where Sula and her sacrifice, Chicken Little, climb the vertical axis of a double beech tree. The tree's height provides them with a panoramic vista across the Kalunga river divide, foreshadowing the young boy's impending sacrifice/death.[67] The cosmographic site and the rite that occurs there become the "religious text" by which to read the remaining series of events in *Sula*.

An ominous aspect of his drowning is that "[t]he water darkened and closed quickly over the place where Chicken Little sank."[68] One fully expects Chicken Little to thrash to the surface for air, but the water remains placid, and there is the eerie sense that he has met with death by unnatural misadventure. Ambiguity shrouds Chicken Little's silent disappearance.

A strong belief in traditional thought asserts that a bewitched drowning victim's body does not resurface during or after drowning and a sacrifice duly accepted does not rise. Sula's climbing of the beech tree beforehand, her ascension of the vertical highway that the loa descend, foreshadows Sula's communal positioning as not the ordinary or average person. She is a mortal who has traveled the spiritual plane.

With Chicken Little now consecrated to a watery grave, Sula's primary concern is her own exposure: to confirm if "somebody saw."[69] Her fear of a spectator raises the suspicion of intentionality, and as literary critic Trudier Harris asserts, "there is an ... intentional aura surrounding the drowning."[70] Because accidents, according to traditional thought, do not occur, had she willfully allowed Chicken Little's hands to slip from hers? Risking uncertain danger to ascertain if Shadrack had witnessed her death-dealing act, Sula runs to his cottage for verification, not to the town for help and the possible rescue of the little boy or at the very least the immediate recovery of his body.

Following closely on the ambiguity of Chicken Little's drowning is Sula's role in Hannah's immolation. Her "interest" in watching Hannah burn addresses Sula's ambivalent intrigue with human misfortune and death and provides a glimpse into her psycho-kinetic potential. Once again, in accordance with West and Central African cosmologies, Sula is thought to act from short distances on family and those familiar to her. In construing what causes Hannah's clothes to ignite, the reader steps into one of Morrison's participatory "holes and spaces" – moments when the listener/reader collaborates imaginatively with the author by contributing subjective experience or drawing upon experiential communality.[71] First, the Western reader who is familiar with American rural outdoor canning rituals of the period envisions Hannah standing by a boiling black cauldron with fire encircling its base, the womb symbol that the pre-Christian world associated with witchcraft.[72] The imagined scene subliminally invokes the Western witch-image. Next, the Western reader assumes that the fire ignites Hannah's clothing accidentally, that she carelessly stands too close to the fire or the breeze, mentioned later, connects the fire with her clothing. But indeterminacy frames the scene since the text does not disclose specific causality. The reader's Western frame imaginatively contributes it. Morrison cleverly diverts the narrative focus onto Eva watching from above, and it is through her that the reader discovers, after the fact, that Hannah is on fire. "Before she trundled her wagon over to the dresser to get her comb, Eva looked out the window and saw Hannah bending to light the yard fire." Eva then trundles to the dresser but a strange thing occurs – she cannot find her comb, which is never out of place. On the verge of irritation in her search, she finds it and trundles "back to the window to catch a breeze" and "it was then she saw Hannah burning. The flames from the yard fire were licking the blue cotton dress, making her dance."[73] The comb's disappearance is significant, for it suggests that spiritual or psychic mischief that exceeds the normal is afoot. Eva routinely collects her fallen hair and burns it, a ritual of the Voodoo practitioner, or the ritual of an individual who respects/fears its power, or, at the very least, a holdover from Voodoo that she enacts despite its severance from a religious base.

After hurling her body through the window, Eva, cut and bleeding from attempting to save Hannah, notices and later comments on her granddaughter not far away "watching," oddly transfixed:

When Eva, who was never one to hide the faults of her children, mentioned what she thought she'd seen to a few friends, they said it was natural. Sula was probably struck dumb, as anybody would be who saw her own mamma burn up. Eva said yes, but inside she disagreed and remained convinced that Sula had watch Hannah burn not because she was paralyzed but because she was interested.[74]

In the Bobangi language of Central Africa, Sula means "to be afraid, to run away, to poke, to alter from proper condition to a worse one, be blighted, fail in spirit, be overcome, be overpowered, paralyzed with fear, quail, be stunned."[75] Morrison, who often inverts names with character traits, may be positing that despite Sula's demonstrations of fear – recall the finger cutting and Chicken Little episodes – being paralyzed with fear is uncharacteristic of her. Watching Hannah burn to death, Sula is not afraid, overpowered, or stunned, as an ordinary individual would be. Her perceived "interest" again qualifies her as not the average or ordinary person. In naming Sula, Morrison's selection is a slight variation of "Suba," the West African Bambara word for "ndoki."[76]

Sula's emotional detachment from her mother and her motive for unconsciously wishing Hannah undeserved harm derive from Sula's knowledge in the summer of 1922, the time of Chicken Little's drowning, that Hannah does not like her. The next summer, Hannah's fatal burning occurs while Sula watches from the porch. Here one must remember that being an ndoki does not require the performance of rituals, the casting of spells, or the mixing of potions. Psychic energy alone can produce ill effects. The cognitive power of the ndoki is not inconsistent with theories of parapsychology. "[I]t is a commonplace of poltergeist stories that the poltergeists tend to centre around particular persons, often adolescents, especially girls."[77] In 1923 Sula "was thirteen, [and] everybody supposed her nature was coming down, but it was hard to put up with her sulking and irritation."[78] Furthermore, "fire-raising" or the spontaneous "ignition of material is an activity of the classical poltergeist."[79]

In addition to having psychic power, if a person suspected of kindoki is in the vicinity when harm takes place, even if only by chance, then that person becomes the main suspect in the commission of moral evil.[80] Hence, Sula's status as a practitioner of kindoki is communally verifiable given her close physical proximity to the occurrences of misfortune. Simon Bockie relates a modern true account of misfortune that arises ostensibly from amoral, nonhuman, physical evil or natural agency, yet a Central African community credits the physical presence of an ndoki with moral culpability, guilt by spatial association, even though human motive and agency cannot be tendered. His kindoki is unpremeditated, and its result is underserved:

In 1958 my distant cousin Nsumbu Aaron was killed by lightning in one of the most ferocious tropical storms in the area that year. Since he was with two elder members of the family, one of them [an] ndoki . . ., there was no doubt in people's mind that he was killed by that man's kindoki, or invisible power to do harm.[81]

Before entering the afterworld, a contrite Sula repents for the thrill she felt while watching the burning Hannah jerk and dance. The memory of her mother's sensational conflagration activates her unconscious psyche in sleep and cues a recurring dream in which her physical closeness to the subject of the dream, a baking powder icon, causes the icon to combust spontaneously:

Then she had that dream again. The Clabber Girl Baking Power lady was smiling and beckoning to her, one hand under her apron. When Sula *came near* she disintegrated into white dust, which Sula was hurriedly trying to stuff into the pockets of her blue-flannel housecoat. The disintegration was awful to see, but worse was the feel of the powder – its starchy slipperiness as she tried to collect it by handfuls. The more she scooped, the more it billowed. At last it covered her, filled her eyes, her nose, her throat, and she woke gagging and overwhelmed with the smell of smoke.[82]

Wishing to conceal her culpability for the disintegration/conflagration, Sula strives to obstruct from view the visible proof of the misfortune attributable to her being near by. Bockie supplies a second true account in which the perceived presence of an ndoki in a village explains undeserved misfortune.

[I]n 1955 my half brother Philemon's three children living in Kinshasa [Zaïre's capital] accompanied their mother on vacation to the village. The eldest child, who was about ten years old, could not sleep. Whenever it was time for bed he began to cry, for he was so frightened by bandoki who were trying to catch him. He grew thin and was rushed back to his father in Kinshasa. Since then he has never dared to return to the village. The second child, who was about five years old, became deaf and dumb. His deafness and dumbness are attributed to kindoki. His parents claim that before going to the village he was talking; after returning to Kinshasa, he could neither talk nor hear. Their father, a charismatic Kongo prophet who has devoted his life to living according to God's expectations, has ever since then denounced kindoki for his children's suffering.[83]

Basing its consensus on contrived, circumstantial, and hard evidence, the Bottom judges Sula to be the principal agent of moral evil when after a ten-year absence from Medallion her return is "accompanied by a plague of robins."[84] The peculiarly unsettling avian arrival en masse arouses her neighbors' uneasiness but does not alter their neutrality in responding to the evil:

In spite of their fear, they reacted to an oppressive oddity, or what they called evil days, with an acceptance that bordered on welcome. Such evil must be avoided, they felt, and precautions must naturally be taken to protect themselves from it. But they let it run its course, fulfill itself, and never invented ways either to alter it, to annihilate it or to prevent its happening again. So also were they with people.

What was taken by outsiders to be slackness, slovenliness or even generosity was in fact a full recognition of legitimacy of forces other than good ones. They did not believe doctors could heal – for them, none ever had done so. They did not believe death was accidental – life might be but death was deliberate. They did not believe Nature was ever askew, only inconvenient. Plague and drought were as "natural" as springtime. If milk could curdle, God knows robins could fall. The purpose of evil was to survive it and they determined (without ever knowing they had made up their minds to do it) to survive floods, white people, tuberculosis, famine and ignorance. They knew anger well but not despair, and they didn't stone sinners for the same reason they didn't commit suicide – it was beneath them.[85]

Surviving evil is the Bottom's preferred approach to dealing appropriately with evil, not annihilating it since

[t]here was no creature so ungodly as to make them destroy it. They could kill easily if provoked to anger, but not by design, which explained why they could not "mob kill" anyone. To do so was not only unnatural, it was undignified. The presence of evil was something to be first recognized, then dealt with, survived, outwitted, triumphed over.[86]

Sula's neighbors think in very African traditional ways. In traditional belief accidents do not happen. All misfortunes have assignable agency. Hannah's fiery death cannot be determined an accident because "[a]ll death is believed to be caused by someone's witchcraft-substance, since only persons possessing this are thought to have the power of bringing death." The Tiv in Nigeria, for instance, assume that someone using witchcraft-substance for personal benefit rather than for the good of the community results in death.[87] Legitimizing forces other than good ones, the towns-people uphold that just as there are temperate forces in nature, every person is made up of a balance of good and evil. Thus no one is so ungodly as to necessitate annihilation.

The Bottom citizenry tactically enlist folk rituals and a permissive attitude to survive and neutralize Sula's threatening presence. "So they laid broomsticks across their doors at night and sprinkled salt on porch steps. But aside from one or two unsuccessful efforts to collect the dust from her footsteps, they did nothing to harm her. As always the black people looked at evil stony-eyed and let it run."[88] In addition to enlisting spiritual protection – arranging broomsticks, sprinkling salt, and collecting footstep dust used in Voudoun to foil the power of a witch – still other neutralizing approaches are possible.[89]

Finally, the people of the Bottom, who "have lived with various forms of evil all their days," wage a campaign of goodness to counterbalance her evil.

Their conviction of Sula's evil changed them in accountable yet mysterious ways. Once the source of their personal misfortune was identified, they had leave to protect and love one another. They began to cherish their husbands and wives, protect their children, repair their homes and in general band together against the devil in their midst. In their world, aberrations were as much a part of nature as grace. It was not for them to expel or annihilate it. They would no more run Sula out of town than they would kill the robins that brought her back.[90]

Once the community diagnoses Sula as moral evil whose mere presence without motive claims victims, it imputes harmful and bizarre occurrences to her. Because she is preternatural, it believes that she is "set to destroy relationships, to undermine the moral integrity of society, and to act contrary to what custom demands."[91] First, a child target, Teapot, the five-year-old neglected son of Betty, breaks his leg while stepping off Sula's porch after she responds to his query concerning bottles that he might collect. A poor diet of Mr. Goodbars and soda pop contribute substantially to his fracture, but Teapot's mother, Betty, blames Sula. The traditional argument for invisible powers being responsible for Teapot's misfortune interrogates why on this specific occasion and not on another has the boy fallen and broken a bone. He was not walking carelessly and his motive for being on Sula's porch was entirely respectable. If he had not been bewitched, he would not have misjudged his step. The conclusive argu-ment for witchcraft as causality is that all falls do not result in broken bones. Why has this fall produced a broken bone if witchcraft were not behind it? Compare the Teapot incident with the following true account that Edward E. Evans-Pritchard, who conducted research among the Azande of Central Africa, supplies:

A boy knocked his foot against a small stump of wood in the centre of a bush path, a frequent happening in Africa, and suffered pain and inconvenience in consequence. Owing to its position on his toe it was impossible to keep the cut free from dirt and it began to fester. He declared that witchcraft had made him knock his foot against the stump. . . . He agreed that witchcraft had nothing to do with the stump of wood being in his path but added that he had kept his eyes open for stumps, as indeed every Zande does most carefully, and that if he had not been bewitched he would have seen the stump. As a conclusive argument for his view he remarked that all cuts do not take days to heal but, on the contrary, close quickly, for that is the nature of cuts. Why, then, had his sore festered and remained open if there were no witchcraft behind it?[92]

Betty's psycho-cultural investment in believing that Sula is responsible in the harming of Teapot corresponds with passive-aggressive beliefs in ndoki bewitchment. "Beliefs in bewitchment are functional in as much as they are used as a channel through which people can deal with hate, hostility, frustration, jealousy, anxiety, guilt, and sexual fantasies which are not culturally overtly expressed." Teapot's mother may suffer from guilt of maternal inadequacy; she is negligent, or her blame of Sula may emanate from the hate or jealousy of her neighbor. She may also resolve impersonally ambivalent feeling surrounding interpersonal relationships by accusing Sula of bewitching her son. Betty, like the entire Bottom community, may perceive Sula as hostile and unpredictable but cultural values still require her to be friendly, generous, cooperative, and patient. Externally displacing the onus of her internal conflict onto Sula frees her conscience and vindicates her reneging on the prescribed communal behavior.[93]

Next, Mr. Finley chokes on a chicken bone and dies immediately after he looks up and sees Sula. The townspeople "must find and give immediate causes of death," and as theologian John S. Mbiti argues concerning African culture, "[b]y far the commonest cause is believed to be magic, sorcery, and witchcraft. This is found in every African society, though with varying degrees of emphasis; and someone is often blamed for using this method to cause the death of another."[94]

The community also accredits abnormal and sudden changes in the human body to witchcraft. Shadrack tips an imaginary hat to Sula, causing her to flee. Dessie, the observer of their exchange, immediately develops a sty on her eye along with the suspicion that the sudden eruption is the product of watching evil since she has never had an inflamed eyelid. Comparable to the conception of witch hags with warts and sagging green skin in Western depictions, skin lesions, boils, and scales that appear suddenly are common corporeal markers of bandoki activity affecting their victims.

In addition to the injury and death that the community credits to Sula, her "wicked" anti-social behavior solidifies her ndoki status. As a true outcast, one who willfully chooses to transgress traditions without respect for the communal values that the ancestors determine, she threatens public order. Challenging two longstanding revered traditions and violating, albeit allegedly, a third, Sula strains then breaches acceptable village mores. Minor social infractions – failing to wear underwear and to compliment her neighbors' cooking – exacerbate the major ones convincing the Bottom that Sula is mocking God.

Sula's committing Eva to Sunnydale, a rest home for the aged and infirmed, goes counter to the Black cultural dictum regarding the individual's moral obligation to provide for aging elders, especially matriarchs who were once the caregivers. And one of the paramount ways to show "good" character in African society is to honor and respect elders.[95] Even more injurious is Sula's choice of placing Eva in a white-run home whose residents are "dirt poor," demented," and have "no people at all."[96] Eva, a person of means and part of a tribe wherein she has consanguineal ties, should be placed under the care of familiar kin and community, not under the supervision of strangers. Her sound mental faculties compound the gravity of the injury turned insult since she is cognizant of the offense. Sula, contacting her grandmother only when she "needed a little change"[97] during her ten-year absence then sassing and discarding her in a home for the infirm upon her return, epitomizes unconscionable irreverence of the elder.

From a traditionalist, gender-neutral position, Sula's sexual acts are deemed morally reprehensible because they breach personal and social relationships. Sula offends both a close friend and the entire village. Mbiti explains marital sexual misconduct from a traditional perspective:

To sleep with someone else's wife is not considered "evil" if these two are not found out by the society which forbids it; and in other societies it is in fact an expression of friendship and hospitality to a guest to spend the night with one's wife or daughter or sister. It is not the act in itself which would be "wrong" as such but the relationships involved in the act; if relationships are not hurt or damaged, and if there is no discovery of breach of custom or regulation, then the act is not "evil" or "wicked" or "bad."[98]

Hannah's sexual dalliances that do not damage relationships illustrate the de facto social contract of some traditional societies. Her selection of the Bottom women's husbands "compliment" them since it validates that they have chosen desirable men, and she has not practiced possessive mating, breached de facto custom and contract, and "taken" their husbands. She does not want to marry their men, nor is she interested in white men. Harris observes that "In any world but the one Morrison has created, Hannah Peace would be considered a slut. However, Morrison does not allow such a moral judgment in the novel . . . [E]ven the whores who resent her 'generosity' and the women who call her 'nasty' are not inclined to believe that she is evil."[99] A world *does* exist outside of the one Morrison fabricates, one in which suspension of moral judgment against Hannah would occur. It is the Africanist world based on traditional social values and conduct that informs Morrison's fictional one.

Caught having sex with her best friend's husband, who then abandons his family, earns Sula the Bottom's moral censure but "it was the men who gave her the final label, who fingerprinted her for all time" as an unredeemable violator of Black interracial sexual mores. Refraining from sexual intercourse with whites is racially mandated for all, but the community police women more rigorously for compliance with the interracial sex code. The men of the Bottom find Sula "guilty of the unforgivable thing – the thing for which there was no understanding, no excuse, no compassion. The route from which there was no way back, the dirt that could not ever be washed away. They said that Sula slept with white men."[100] Given slavocracy and the sexual exploitation and concubinage of Black women, the men of the Bottom insist that only the explanation of rape be offered as the reason for sexual unions between Black women and white men. Consensual sex is unacceptable. The fact that miscegenation occurred in their families or that they have sex with white women does not lessen their disgust or discourage their intolerance. Unmarried, childless, and female, Sula is a sexual threat to the social equilibrium of the Bottom. "[W]alking around all independent-like" and "act[ing] like a man,"[101] Sula, as a masculinized figure who experiments artistically with her life, is dangerous. Moreover, the alleged commission of her earlier offense against Teapot proves that she is anti-maternal. Her community, of course, does not know about her hand in Chicken Little's death. Male sexual antagonism and male subjection of the female play a major psychological role in the Bottom's indictment of Sula as morally evil. The male witch-hunters have a morbid preoccupation with the sexual activities of the accused woman with whom they may have had sexual relations themselves.

Superseding elder irreverence and interracial sexual transgressions, ruthless individualism is the most egregious moral evil that Sula enacts against the Bottom, as African traditional cultures disdain egocentrism. Lacking a social conscience that prohibits damaging communal relations, Sula, an amalgam of Eva's arrogance and Hannah's self-indulgence, flaunts an egocentric moral code that runs counter to African communal collectivism. She does not count on others, discounts the reliability of self, and feels no compulsion to comply with corporate protocol or submit to its pressures. A flagrant case, Sula's social solipsism outstrips the prized American ethos of rugged individualism and self-reliance. Her solitary traits resonate with those of the ndoki that remain alive in the Congo today: the utterly selfish individualist devoid of mercy.[102] There, according to Bockie, "[t]he only true outcasts are those who willfully choose to go outside the traditions, without respect for the communal values that are determined by the ancestors. They are outcasts by their own choice."[103]

Overhearing Hannah's admission of dislike for her instigates Sula's detachment from others and retreat into self. Her mother's revelation teaches her that there is no other that she can count on, and her inexplicable irresponsibility in the death of Chicken Little convinces her that there is no self to count on either. Sula's psychic detachment exorcises her sense of responsibility for others and sanctions the exploration of "her own thoughts and emotions, giving them full reign, feeling no obligation to please anybody."[104] The biting sarcasm that she expresses on her deathbed regarding what needs to happen before the community will "love" her is understandable. If Sula has not been "good" enough to garner maternal favor, she certainly will not receive the approbation of community members who shun her as "the devil in their midst."[105]

In the tightly knit Bottom community, "one finds perhaps the most paradoxical areas of African life." Corporate life makes every member "dangerously naked in the sight of other members."[106] Anonymity and ruthless individualism in an African traditional community, Mbiti maintains, are impossible:

Everybody knows everybody else; a person cannot be individualistic, but only corporate. Every form of pain, misfortune, sorrow or suffering; every illness and sickness; every death whether of an old man or of the infant child; every failure of the crop in the fields, of hunting in the wilderness or of fishing in the waters; every bad omen or dream; these and all the other manifestations of evil that man experiences are blamed on somebody in the corporate society. Natural explanations may indeed be found, but mystical explanations must also be given. People create scapegoats for their sorrow.[107]

And Nel creates a scapegoat in Sula to absolve Jude of deliberate acts of moral evil, marital infidelity and familial desertion, which destroy their marriage. Nel abnegates Jude's potential for evil. Sula takes him from her; he does not willfully leave her and their three children. Nel places the burden of betrayal on Sula and not on Jude, wanting to know why their friendship did not foreclose Sula's sexual liaison with her husband. Sula's counter that if they were good friends Nel should have recovered from the betrayal raises two salient conjugal differences between African traditional and Western cultures. The first is that polygyny, an accepted practice in early African cultures of a man having more than one wife at one time, is sanctioned in some African societies even today; whereas in the West, monogyny prevails.[108] Under a different cultural contract, "Sula and Nel might have been able to share Jude amicably."[109] Second and "more germane," as Gay Wilentz asserts, "is the incident's relation to the Western notion that conjugal relationships are the most important in human action." In many African cultures blood kinship and some types of relational ties not based on blood exceed marital ties. Wilentz states that "According to [anthropologist] Niara Sudarkasa, African-based societies often emphasize consanguinal [*sic*] relations over conjugal [. . . and] that these extended family networks, because of the African American experience in slavery and afterwards, also included communal . . . 'significant others,' such as friends, related by neither kinship nor marriage." In this light, we may also consider Nel to have betrayed Sula.[110]

Sula's last words to Nel, spoken to provoke Nel's and the reader's interrogation of fixed, absolute notions of good and evil, stress the social constructions of those absolutes and Nel's wholly Westernized perception of them:

> She opened the door and heard Sula's low whisper.
> "Hey, girl." Nel paused and turned her head but not enough to see her.
> "How you know?" Sula asked.
> "Know what?" Nel still wouldn't look at her.
> "About who was good. How you know it was you?"
> "What you mean?"
> "I mean maybe it wasn't you. Maybe it was me."[111]

Nel expects her beneficence toward Sula to be rewarded in kind, whereas Sula's traditional, experiential, and philosophical insight concludes that good may as easily be rewarded ambivalently with evil or indifference. Since "[b]eing good to somebody is just like being mean to somebody. Risky. You don't get nothing for it."[112] Sula's question of "who was good" insinuates that the discrimination of Nel's consciousness, the judgment of her ego, grounded in the cultural and the subjective, is the sole and insubstantial arbiter of good and evil. Furthermore, Sula's idea of the concept of goodness is unfixed since acts of good and evil are an inescapable part of human nature and, therefore, of her own personality as well as Nel's. One may be deemed good, or evil, as easily and legitimately as the next person.

The same potential for moral wrong that Nel denies in Jude she also denies in herself. Nel is unable to admit that nothing separates her morally or ethically from Sula. They appear polar opposites but personify, as Wilentz posits, the "African concept of the interrelatedness of ostensible opposites."[113] The two form a collective personality, a unified whole, a balance of the feminine and the masculine principles. Moments in the narrative point out their complementary dialectical natures and reciprocal elemental forces. Cut off from her New Orleans and Voodoo cultural roots, Nel is ordered, middle-class, Western assimilated, communally oriented, and conventional, whereas Sula is disordered, class defiant, Africanist, egocentric, and experimental. Nel imagines a passive, feminized self "lying on a flowered bed tangled in her own hair, waiting for some fiery prince." Sula figures herself as active and masculine, galloping princely "through her own mind on a gray-and-white horse tasting sugar and smelling roses in full view of a someone who shared both the taste and the speed."[114] In stressful moments, the Chicken Little episode for example, Nel is composed; Sula is discomposed. The two enter into a metaphorical, playful, marriage of the Marassa Twins, the expression in Voudoun of an individual's twinned nature that is depicted as children at play. Upon hearing that her mother does not like her, Sula severs emotional ties with her parent and cleaves to Nel. The offspring of their consummated union, figured in the conjugal earth-digging play scene of "1922," is Chicken Little, the "issue" of the male-female Marassa-Trois.[115] His inverted birth, death in a watery womb/tomb, binds them "always," as Shadrack's priestly pronouncement at their figurative nuptials preordains. They will never be separated into a competitive, conflicting dualism. They are a balance and in "Voudoun one *and* one make three."[116]

A quarter-century after Sula's death, Eva agitates Nel's acceptance of the moral complementarity between Sula and herself: "You. Sula. What's the difference? ... Just alike. Both of you. Never was a difference between you."[117] The comparison comes on the heels of Eva's accusation that Nel killed Chicken Little. Eva mysteriously knows that Nel, actively interested, "watched" Chicken Little drown. Unable to repress her guilt over the "joyful stimulation" and the "contentment" that "washed over her enjoyment" after "the water closed peacefully" over Chicken Little's body, Nel ponders the psychic dissonance between the pleasure she felt at that moment and the horror of death that she should have felt. She had enjoyed human misfortune and loss. She questions the "good feeling she had had when Chicken's hands slipped. She hadn't wondered about that in years. 'Why didn't I feel bad when it happened? How come it felt so good to see him fall?'"[118]

In Jungian terms, Nel's conscious discrimination forms the psychological entity called "the shadow" – "a portion of the natural whole self that the ego calls bad, or evil, for reasons of shame, social pressure, family and societal attitudes about certain aspects of human nature."[119] Nel suppresses her shadow since to be conscious of it involves recognition of the evil aspects of her personality. Unable to own her evil side, she projects it onto Sula. Sula is guilty of Chicken Little's drowning and silence about it; she was present but not responsible. She passively saw what happened. She did not actively and joyfully watch. In African traditional terms, however, Nel is out of touch with the totality of her self. She is imbalanced.

If one judges the two women as complementary halves of a unified whole, as a Marassa, more precisely Sula *is* the shadow of Nel, her lawless self completely disembodied (as another character) from the lawful self. Nel's self-affirming goodness mirrors the town's response to Sula. Her good self must be asserted to temper and survive the evil self's assault on the acceptable side of the whole. Sula is a scapegoat, a reification of Nel's and the community's self-assessment of themselves as moral and ethical. Sula is the necessary means for achieving equilibrium in the Bottom of Medallion, a town whose name and inversion of bottom and top signify the reversible, abutting heads of a single coin. Sula's evil keeps the community unified and thriving.

But Sula is not wholly evil – an absolute destroyer of accepted social structure – and, following the morality governing an African traditional worldview, the Bottom should pardon her once her evil is in abeyance. Bockie explains the community's responsibility to forgive a wayward member:

Any ndoki suspected of harming others is disliked or hated at the time [s]he is harming. But when [s]he is at peace, that is, when no one is sick, dying, or experiencing misfortune, the community more or less forgets [... her] wrong doing and welcomes [... her back] into the family like any other member. Like any other nonevil ndoki, [s]he is to be loved and cared for as if [s]he had a clean record.[120]

China, "the most rambunctious whore in the town," has a biracial son, living proof that she had sexual relations with a white man, but her certain

breach of interracial taboo does not fingerprint her for all time as communally unforgivable. The Bottom "turned out in numbers to put the fallen
sister away."[121] The same community women turn out for Sula's mother
at her death. The women whose husbands Hannah had slept with weep for
her "burned hair and wrinkled breast as though they themselves had been
her lover."[122] But communal amnesty does not come for Sula.

In her final days, Sula's possessive mating with Ajax exacts a decline in
her worthy of village commiseration. Because "concepts of health are far
more social and cultural than biological," within African thought it is not
uncommon to believe in psychosomatic disorder or that the situation
causes the sickness and not that the sickness causes the situation.[123] The
impetus for Sula's illness is never disclosed textually, but the situation
leading up to it and the psychic dis-ease that she experiences as a result are.
When Ajax leaves her because she begins to suffocate him emotionally,
either excessive graveyard love catapults her into a languishing illness or the
progressive wasting away of her body validates spiritual warfare, a counter-
assault against her invisible powers. And when she passes on, no one comes
to identify Sula's body. The closed coffin stuns Nel, the single mourner at
Sula's graveside, while only an unafraid few hover at the edge of the
cemetery to witness "the burial of a witch."[124] A "witch is buried without
any ceremony, and if it is a barren woman, all unmarried persons and those
who have no children must keep away from the corpse lest they are infested
by the same tragedy."[125]

The Bottom does not pardon Sula because the disconnection with Africa
that an American orientation causes displaces the appropriate response to a
witch whose moral evil is in abeyance. Furthermore, equal parts fear of her
invisible powers and gall at her arrogance keep them at a distance. Sula
remains up to the last a paragon of ruthless individualism – an excessive
reliance on self that is intolerable to an African sensibility. Nel believes Sula
to be too prideful, while in fact she is self-absorption personified.

EVA PEACE – SULA'S NDOKI PREDECESSOR

Because kindoki, African witchcraft, is almost exclusively unilinear in its
patrilineal and matrilineal descents, fathers transmit the practice of kindoki
to their sons, and mothers to their daughters, pre-and post-natally. The
witchcraft of men may lie dormant their entire lives, but the extraordinary
powers of women are thought to be activated at least once and are more
virulent than male powers. Occasionally, still following a familial trajectory, an ndoki initiates in early childhood a relative whose reasoning

powers are underdeveloped or an older child whose mind communal values already shape,[126] but for the most part one can say that kindoki is an inherited art or "like a craft, . . . may continue in one family."[127]

Eva Peace, Sula's grandmother and matriarch of the Peace household, has intersecting ndoki and loa traits, holdovers from an African past and (un)consciousness, which underscores Voudoun's role in sanctioning the morality of incinerating her son, Plum, a malevolent act that to the Western mind is irreconcilable with maternal care. As human dispenser of harming and protecting kindoki, Eva is Sula's ndoki predecessor. Her survivalist savvy and mother wit allow her to support her children, Hannah, Pearl, and Plum, without a husband, in the direst of straits. Left cold, hungry, and penniless when BoyBoy deserts the family, Eva leaves her children with a neighbor for eighteen months and returns without a leg but with money and the wherewithal to insure her family's survival and prosperity. Proving herself not the average or ordinary person can be attributed to the exercise of unique power or "good kindoki."[128] Her attainment of economic success through unaccountable and possibly excessive means such as self-mutilation, placing her leg in the path of an oncoming train for example, conversely hints at harming kindoki. Once married but now manless, Eva is not a sexual threat to the residents of the Bottom. She bequeaths manlove to her daughters but despite "a flock of gentlemen callers . . . she did not participate in the act of love."[129] The bird imagery attached to Eva and the heron-like manner in which she swoops down on great folded wings on crutches from her bedroom to set Plum on fire further her alignment as a traditional witch. Birds are symbolic signs of witches, and people from Gabon, Cameroon, and Nigeria in particular believe that witches have an external soul that they deposit in animals who are their familiars.[130]

Eva's burning of the hairs that collect in her comb signifies her active taking of precaution against becoming the victim of sympathetic or contagious magic, magic based on the idea that there is no clear line dividing matter and spirit, the founding doctrine of Vodun. A "material object retained its spiritual connection to its original source even though physically separated, that is, it kept a sympathetic relationship."[131] In a Voudoun ceremony a houngan or mambo (priest or priestess) practices sympathetic manipulation, often against witches. Moreover, his or her use of the hair and nail clippings of a hounsi, a Voudoun initiate, to reconstruct his or her gros-bon-ange (soul/psyche), exemplifies the sympathetic nexus between the physical and the metaphysical. In American Voodoo, however, the popular imagination conflates the traditional priest(ess) with the witch and

witchcraft American-style, the use of magical control and palpable apparatus to cause misfortune. Eva does not manipulate misfortune by performing rituals, uttering spells, and concocting medicines with the hair of
others, but carefully disposes properly of her own fallen hairs. Burning
one's hairs to prevent them from falling into the wrong hands or a bird
taking them to build a nest is a practice to which some African Americans
adhere even today. "In the latter case, it is feared that the owner of the hair
will thereafter have chronic headaches."[132] Eva's precaution points to the
belief that a single hair from her head can be manipulated to cause her
bodily or material misfortune regardless of her physical distance from the
hair and the person conducting the manipulation. Her aggressive search for
a misplaced comb only moments before seeing her daughter Hannah
burning in the yard below her bedroom window temporarily raises suspicion that sympathetic manipulation may have caused Hannah's misfortune, since to the traditional mind there are no accidents.

Complicating the plot, a compelling case can be made for Eva's direct
culpability in the burning of Hannah. If Eva is Sula's ndoki forerunner,
she, watching her daughter from above, literally has a psychic motive for
the involuntary flitting of harmful witchcraft-substance onto Hannah. The
day before, Hannah, wondering aloud, questions Eva about loving Plum,
Pearl, and herself and her motive for killing Plum. Eva charges Hannah
with "evil wonderin'".[133] And long after Hannah has left the room, Eva's
psychic energy remains fixed on Plum, as Sula's "dark thoughts" similarly
precede Chicken Little's death. In both cases, turbulent psychic energy has
been roused to lash out unconsciously.

Eva is easily read as Eve, the first mother of the Old Testament who has
supernatural or divine qualities, and the details of her house fit within a
Christian frame. Impractically located for a person with one leg, Eva,
creator and sovereign of her home, resides on the third floor or "third
heaven" of her house with many rooms at 7 Carpenter's Road. "Directing
the lives of her children, friends, strays, and a constant stream of boarders"
from her high seat, she receives men who ascend to her throne to worship at
her foot.[134] The address of the house is significant. Seven is considered
God's perfect number, while carpentry was the trade of Joseph, the human
father of Jesus. BoyBoy, Plum's father, is also a carpenter; hence the name
of the road bears the trade of BoyBoy and his employer of many years ago
and reinforces the idea that on this road a builder or creator resides. But
Morrison invokes a Voudoun attachment to the domestic, matriarchal site
by placing four sickle – crescent-branched – pear trees forming a peristyle
or sacred Voudoun precinct in the yard of 7 Carpenter's Road. The

smallest of the four trees takes on a negative valence in opposition to the other three. The pea-green-dressed mistress of BoyBoy leans on it when he comes to visit Eva after his desertion of the family. The woman's laughter sets off Eva's eternal hatred of Boyboy, and the interlocking crescent-branched pear trees are structural signifiers by which to interpret the alternative cosmology affecting Eva's worldview and by which she and her household should be interpreted.

The invocation of a Voudoun peristyle outside Eva's house nullifies the textual interpretation of the deweys, the three young boys she adopts, as exclusively Christian. "A trinity with a plural name,"[135] the unchanging, interchangeable, inseparable Afro-, Anglo-, and Chicano-descended deweys, whose bodies are not recovered from the tunnel disaster and, therefore, seemingly transcend death, are three persons functioning as one. They speak with one voice, think with one mind, and maintain a mysterious aloofness. Despite their differences in age, size, and coloring, they cannot be individually distinguished even by one of their mothers. Accenting their connectedness is a moment in which they play chain-gang: they tie their shoelaces together to forge an unbroken link.[136] To make meaning of their presence, a Christian Trinity application is feasible but triadic symbology also abounds in Voudoun. First, there is the Divine Trinity of les Morts, les Mystères, and les Marassa; second, in Voudoun three rivers converge at the vertical axis of the cross; third, serviteurs pour three libations at the entrance of the circular peristyle; and fourth, one spirit with three names – Baron Samedi (Zombie), Baron Cimitère (Cemetery), and Baron Croix (Cross) – heads the dreaded Petro (Haitian) loa phalanx that has great prominence and importance within its sacred precinct of worship. Eva's three adopted sons, the deweys whose lives water claims, and a fourth, her only begotten son, Plum, whom she sacrifices by fire, inform Eva's maternal and moral ambivalence since she responds with divine precision to protecting and harming the latter according to the proper propitiation he bestows upon her.

In keeping with Morrison's commitment to producing fiction that is identifiably Black, the dewey trio bears a closer reciprocity to the interchangeable dancing duo Nagoa and Noaga in *The Radiance of the King* (*Le Regard du roi*, 1954) by Camara Laye, the Upper Guinea writer that Morrison credits with influencing her writing enormously.[137] An in-depth inspection of Laye's twins and Morrison's triplets engages a discussion of the Marassa, the Divine Twins in Vodun and Voudoun, and the Marassa-Trois in Haitian myth. Maya Deren's *Divine Horsemen: Voodoo Gods of Haiti* (1970) supplies an explication of the Marassa's worship and its cosmic significance:

The Worship of the Marassa, the Divine Twins, is a celebration of man's twinned nature, half matter, half metaphysical; half mortal, half immortal; half human, half divine . . . In Voudoun songs, there still exist vestigial references to the ancient African myths of origin. The word Silibo (and the loa Gran' Silibo) which is sometimes mentioned in songs, is the African Dahomean word for a *tohwiyo*, a founder of an ancient sib; the Dahomean tohwiyos are considered to be the offspring of one human and one supernatural parent. Today the Marassa are said to be the first children of God and their feast has, in some cases, been assimilated to Christmas, itself a celebration of a holy child, offspring of one human and one supernatural parent. The sense of firstness, newness, beginning, innocence – in sum, the sense of the childhood of the race, is preserved in the fact that the Marassa are still conceived of as children, and when they possess a person, they play at marbles and other children's games. The food destined for them can later be offered only to children.[138]

Like Laye's playful, mischievous Nagoa and Noaga, Morrison's deweys are eternal children. Never growing taller than forty-eight inches, four feet, they are a Marassa unity, essentially one, and "whatever disease or accident besets one . . . is understood to threaten the other."[139] They are like the plat-Marassa, the food plate offered to the Divine Twins that consists of two clay bowls joined together because the fate of one is the fate of the other. All three deweys' drowning at a single event, the collapse of the river tunnel, and the Bottom's failure to recover any of their bodies indicate their commonly tied fate. Since "[t]heir violent separation may lead to disaster[, . . . e]very effort is made to have all their important activities . . . occur simultaneously."[140] Eva insists that Mr. Buckland Reed place the deweys of descending ages in the same grade at school. Remaining a unity despite differences, the Marassa represents the aboriginal cohesiveness of the races.

Haitian myth extends the Marassa of the Divine Twins to a "constellation of three," the Marassa-Trois, invoked as Marassa-Dossu-Dossa (Dewsō-Dew-sä). Three, a prime number whose only positive divisors are one and itself, affirms totality and the cosmic unity. The vever, a symbol drawn in flour or ashes at the base of a tree or cross in service to a loa, when dedicated to the Marassa-Dossu-Dossa is "a figure of three" and its food plate consists of "three small earthen bowls joined to a single head."[141] The game of the deweys tying their shoelaces together in chain-gang fashion mimics the design of the plate and the concept of the Marassa-Trois. The third element, the issue, which is understood as the offspring of the male and female twins and affirms multiplicity and unity, is another way in which Haitians conceptualize the Marassa-Dossu-Dossa. The relationship of segments is important. The Marassa "are not to be separated into competitive, conflicting dualism. In Voudoun, one *and* one make three."[142]

If the deweys are cosmic unity and balance, then Plum is an opposing and offending fourth and the Christian representation of Eva and her seemingly immoral maternal action assumes a pre-biblical neutral valence. Her maternal ambivalence compares with the traditional ambivalence of the loa of the Vodun pantheon despite her direct correspondence with Eve, the first mother of Judeo-Christianity, whose name translates as "life." Eva's mediations of the crises related to Plum illustrate the benevolent-malevolent balance and protecting-harming potential pervasive in African cosmologies. As creator-protector of an infant Plum, Eva, when warm water and castor oil prove ineffective, manually unlocks her son's bowels, thereby preserving his life. Yet the life-giving Eva transmogrifies into a life-taking mother when a grown, shell-shocked, heroin-addicted Plum, deteriorating into the infantile dependent he was at birth, threatens to return to her womb. As is done time and again in Haiti, serviteurs of the loa juxtapose the visual representation of gods of the Voudoun pantheon with visual representations and characteristics of the Christian virgins and saints of Catholicism. For example, "St. Patrick, in the act of sending the serpents into the sea, is Damballah, the great serpent deity – since there are serpents in the picture."[143] Eve of Judeo-Christian belief corresponds with Ayizan, the loa of the psychic womb of the race and parental entrance into the world. Eva's later defense to Hannah that Plum wanted to crawl back into her womb ostensibly echoes Nicodemus's misunderstanding of Christian rebirth as a man literally entering a second time into his mother's womb and Christ's clarification of the figurative rebirth by water and spirit.[144] Eva's "baptism" of Plum with kerosene and fire as he lies in bed hallucinating on heroin and her celebration of a symbolic Eucharist before his sacrifice by sipping from a glass of blood-tinged water (Plum's reservoir for cleaning his heroin syringe that she mistakes for soda pop) frame the Christian reading. From a Christian perspective, Eva, a mere mortal, lacks moral justification for killing her son. But a morally ambivalent Eva/Ayizan, drawing from an African traditional cosmology, has cosmic grounds.

Trudier Harris observes that "In deciding that her son Plum would be better off dead, Eva recognizes no authority, no morality except herself," and in doing so "Eva is a slap in the face to all traditional [Western] matriarchs, for there is no [Christian] God-centered morality informing her actions." I have inserted Western and Christian to stress that Harris's assessment is not all-encompassing and Eva's actions foreground an alternative religious ethos. Eva is free to "love, hate, create, conquer, and kill, with responsibility and accountability only to herself. She is free to be moral if she wishes, amoral if it pleases her, and immoral if necessary." Eva "inverts notions of right and wrong, thereby standing morality on its head and identifying with the folkways that defy *absoluteness* in behavior."[145] Eva personifies ambivalent power and the neutralization of absolute good, evil, and morality.

Morrison neutralizes the Africanist reader's moral censure of Eva's action given the psychological deterioration of Plum, which precludes his proper relation to Eva. What in other circumstances would be determined moral evil, undeserved harm, brought about by human agency, the work of the ndoki, may be read alternatively as metaphysical evil, a maternal creator's necessary killing sacrifice or euthanizing of her creation. Eva eliminates what offends her, and Plum's heroin addiction offends her. Eva becomes the vengeful African divinity who has not received the proper propitiation from the life she has created. Harris explains:

[T]he effrontery of his misuse of his life is sufficient for her to take it. She rewards those who serve her well; she casts aside those who do not. That is the distinction between her murder of Plum and her risking of her own life to save Hannah's. Hannah, Eva's oldest child, has served her mother well; after her husband's death, she had moved back into Eva's house "prepared to take care of it and her mother forever" . . . She has also accepted the "manlove" bequeathed to her and has carried out, vicariously, the sexual activity to which Eva may allude but from which she has been restrained by infirmity and inclination. Thus shaped in the image of the goddess and responsive to her wishes, Hannah earns Eva's greatest sacrifice.[146]

Requiring appeasement, a divinized Eva, who descends from the uppermost level of her home to end ritualistically by fire the life of her only son whom she refuses a second entrance into her womb, resembles Ayizan of the Voudoun pantheon. The preeminent ancestral loa of the psychic womb of the race and parental entrance to the world, Ayizan intervenes on behalf of her progeny. When Plum misuses his life, he ceases to salute Eva/Ayizan. Plum's fictional state compares with the real-life situation of a serviteur whose service to his loa and care for himself disintegrates. Deren states that the serviteur ceases

to salute that in man which knows and serves divinity; it is to say that if a man should ever deny this [divinity] in himself, neglect its development, corrupt or suspend its activity in the service of the loa, then there would be no loa, his cosmos would be without soul, man would cease to be man and, only as an animal, along with the other merely animal forms of life, would become once more part of an amoral mass of organic matter, part of the purposeless inevitabilities moving on the purposeless momentum of original creation.[147]

Plum does not develop his own divinity or honor the divinity external to him. The fifth biblical commandment, "[H]onor thy father and thy mother that thy days may be long upon the land thy God giveth thee," which Eva later quotes, conflates with traditional thought. She expects to be honored and the unencumbered continuation of Plum's life is evidence of that honor.[148] Demonstrating dishonor, Plum deserves his sacrifice. His life is purposeless. Sula knows that Eva's Ayizan powers do not end with Plum's sacrifice. Fearing the same consequence, burning, for dishonoring Eva, she locks her bedroom door at night.

As the spiritual maternal principle, Ayizan/Eva controls the rites of spiritual birth. In the Voudoun ceremony of bruler-zin, the initiate stretches out on a bed where he receives an anointment with purifying oil that cleanses his personal past. Ayizan exorcises evil from the innocent who regresses to infancy. Before setting her only son afire, Eva gathers a chuckling Plum up in her arms, rocking him back and forth and remembering when he dropped water onto her bosom while she bathed him as a baby. Fire must touch Plum's soul, the soul of the initiate in the rite of bruler-zin, before the deceased descends into the waters of the afterworld. Fire is essential to regenerating the initiate's or, in this case, Plum's life spirit.[149]

Viewing Morrison's matriarchal Peace households as the "embodiment of African female power" and the "essence of womanhood," Ayoade Joy Asekun affirms Eva's ambivalent power:

Eva within a Yoruba perception, accordingly, has the female power of creativity – a power which can be distorted for destructive ends. If this be the case, should Eva's killing of her son Plum be viewed indifferently as a reflection of the antithesis of her female power to create, or as Barbara Christian describes it, as a "ritual killing inspired by love"? Morrison impedes our judgment of infanticide, as a taboo act, in absolute terms of good or evil – which if viewed within a Yoruba system of thought can be viewed with neutrality as reflective of the normative female power dialectic of creativity and destruction. This action is also expressive of Eva's dual female personality. Her killing of Plum is not malevolent; in fact, it is ritualistic. The imagery of her pouring kerosene over Plum is analogous [to] an African ritual blessing.[150]

Asekun identifies "the normative female power dialectic of creativity and destruction" that she alludes to in the passage above as the fused binarism of the Yoruba female principle – the positive procreative "ase," the life force that gives expression to everything and can be good and evil, and the "aje," the negative destructive force of the witch. "*Ase* facilitates creativity, and as women are the vessels of procreation, their powers are thought to be potent and can be distorted for evil ends."[151] An important ase undercurrent and caveat to consider is that from a traditional view, death is not an ending but rather a transference to another but not distinctly separate sphere. For example, in *Beloved* Sethe's maternal/moral killing of the crawling-already? girl (later called Beloved) and attempted sacrifice of her other three children to put them somewhere they cannot be dirtied by slavery turn on the same normative creative/destructive dialectic.[152] Keeping in mind the transference of Plum's spirit to another place dulls the "evil" edge to Eva's death-dealing. If Eva has in fact overstepped her creative/destructive jurisdiction, the argument that Hannah's death, a perfect judgment,[153] punishes her for playing God with Plum's life dovetails with African traditional belief since it negates accidental causality and privileges a retributive cause and effect.

Eva undoubtedly has harming as well as protecting potentials that set her apart as not the average or ordinary person. The retention of traditional beliefs that she exemplifies in the Peace household and that her neighbors exemplify in the Bottom grounds the designation of Sula as a witch of African ilk. Set apart from the valley and European-American culture of greater Medallion, the Bottom hill community in which the Peaces reside is racially and geographically isolated. The traditional beliefs its members carry subliminally are not wholly indistinct from and do not openly conflict with the Christian beliefs that overshadow their lives and active consciousnesses. The religious worldview formed from an amalgamation of African traditional beliefs substantiates Sula's credentials as the moral evil that the Bottom must nonviolently bring under subjection.

BELOVED – NDOKI KIA DIA (SOUL/PSYCHE-EATING WITCH)

In *Beloved* the title character's infestation of 124 Bluestone Road, a road whose name implies an interest in keeping out evil,[154] takes two sequentially discrete ontological forms and phases: living-dead ghostly spirit and living witchly flesh. The forms delimit first the apparitional activity of the crawling-already? girl whom Sethe, her mother, kills, and then the (re)incarnated body that the crawling-already? girl takes as Beloved, the sacrificed daughter who returns to avenge the foreshortening of her earthly life. In the latter phase the fully grown, fleshed Beloved passes from a being akin to the Ibo ogbanje or the Yoruba abiku, a spirit-child who reincarnates in human form to be with its mother; to dual manifestations of

Dahomean/Haitian Erzulie, the loa of boundless emotion and ambivalent sexual morality; to the morally evil Kongo ndokia kia dia, soul/psyche-eating witch. The text discursively draws a demarcation between the spirit of the crawling-already? girl and Beloved, the incarnated flesh-consuming ndoki whose hunger for Sethe's undivided attention and love is insatiable. The appearances of the ogbanje/abiku, the Erzulie manifestations, and the ndoki kia dia alongside the textual subscriptions of the Kongo Yowa ground the interpretations of Beloved's characters as inextricably Black, reinforcing West and Central African traditional ways of being and knowing.

The ghostly spirit phase begins with the onset of paranormal activity at 124 Bluestone Road approximately seven years after Sethe successfully slashes the throat of the crawling-already? girl, her older infant daughter, rather than remand her to slavery. Sethe's surviving daughter, Denver, hears the baby ghost of her sister crawling up the stairs of 124. It ends more than a decade later with the arrival of Paul D, a former Sweet Home slave, to the former Bluestone Road way station on the outskirts of Cincinnati, Ohio, and his confrontation with and driving away of the spirit's presence. Sethe and her younger daughter Denver, born during her mother's escape from Sweet Home, confide to the newly arrived Paul D that the spirit of the crawling-already? girl was "[n]ot evil, just sad," then "lonely and rebuked," and finally "mad, maybe."[55] Once he exorcises the house of the pitching and undulating red light that signifies the spirit's presence, Sethe and Denver, who initially resist a man in their home, accept Paul D and relax into a new life together. They inaugurate their new beginning with a carnival outing, a social emersion that for almost two decades was unimaginable given, the 124 women's longstanding excommunication from the Black community.

Colored Thursday, the Jim Crow carnival day set aside for people of African ancestry, initiates the second phase of Beloved: her witchly flesh (re)incarnation. The extreme exoticism at the carnival – One-Ton Lady, Arabian Nights Dancer, Abu Snake Charmer, Midget and Giant, Two-Headed Man, and Wild African Savage – affirms opposites and negates absolutes of nature and physical normalcy.[56] The carnival, the word itself calling forth the indulgence of flesh before privileging the spiritual, presages the advent of a fleshed being that challenges human categorization. While the hand-linked trio amuses itself at the carnival, a fully fleshed evil fourth, a grown and dressed Beloved with lineless skin and infantile behavior, walks out of the stream near 124 Bluestone Road, sits on a tree stump in front of the former way station, and awaits the return of its inhabitants. The site of her reincarnated emergence, a stream, is noteworthy since it is a common gathering place for West African spirits and witches, and her resting place outside the former way station, on the circle of an amputated tree, one of the first veiled signages of the cross and circle of Voudoun that appears in the novel, implies the intersection of the spirit and flesh planes, the fusion of ghostly spirit and witchly flesh.[157] Months later, when Sethe deduces the true identity of the reincarnated Beloved, she rationalizes that "Paul D ran her off so she had no choice but to come back to me in the flesh."[158] Conversely, when Paul D, with the aid of the Underground Railroad river conductor Stamp Paid, learns that Beloved's death came at the hands of Sethe, he ponders the ghost-to-witch transfiguration in 124 Bluestone Road and Sethe's unfazed response to it: "The ghost in the house didn't bother her for the very same reason a room-and-board witch with new shoes was welcome."[159] Whether in the form of spirit or in the form of flesh, boundless maternal love, self-recrimination, and her returned daughter's accusation that she breached motherlove compromise Sethe's resistance to Beloved's moral malevolence.

The spirit manifestation of the crawling-already? girl during the first phase of her return does not terrorize Sethe, Baby Suggs – Sethe's mother-in-law, or a grown-up Denver for they recognize her with a healthy balance of fear and affection as their deceased infant kin. A familiar adult spirit discomposes them as it would their African forebears, but they would fear bodily harm from an unrecognized, disquieted spirit unrelated to them. Visitation from their dead is not as "fearsome as those of another family, who would not be bound by ties of kinship to respect those they meet."[160] Baby Suggs's suspicion that her eight children, who were taken or chased away by slavers and are now probably dead, are "worrying somebody's house into evil"[161] speaks to the traumatizing effect that unrecognized spirits and the living-dead have on the living unrelated to them. Those who remain at 124 (Sethe's sons, Howard and Buglar, flee) and know the spirit in the house interpret the ghost of the crawling-already? girl not as evil or mad, whereas outsiders firmly concede that "an evil thing looking for more" haunts the former way station.[162] While the crawling-already? girl's haunting of 124 Bluestone Road is relatively benign, Beloved in witchly flesh turns malevolent.

Most West and Central African traditional peoples believe firmly in reincarnation, the passage of the soul from one body to another or, as Geoffrey Parrinder asserts, the "appearance of a person again upon the earth in a human body."[163] The retention of the Kongo cosmogram and the ring shout kept alive in the Black Atlantic diaspora the certainty of the indestructibility and circularity of the human soul. Therefore Sethe passes on the belief to Denver that nothing ever dies. In traditional cultures familiar physiognomy, unique skin colorations, and incisions such as the cut on Beloved's throat identify children as reincarnated family members, the living-dead who are not in any way the ancestors, and those who are perceived as such.[164] Family members mark the bodies of stillborns and the deceased young with stylized cuts in order to recognize them when they return as the newly born. Remnants of these ontological survivals explain why Sethe interprets Beloved's throat scar as physical evidence of the crawling-already? girl's reincarnation, and the news among the colored women emphasizing "Sethe's dead daughter, the one whose throat she cut, had come back to fix her," goes uncontested.[165]

The nature of the returned Beloved is at once both the ogbanje/abiku spirit-child who reincarnates, returning from a contiguous world, to be with its mother and bifurcated manifestations of the Voudoun loa of love, Erzulie, who is both infant and woman and is "as important as the loa of the elemental cosmic forces and even more beloved."[166] Failing to reconstitute in human form through physical rebirth, the crawling-already? girl returns through a metaphysical route to the world of the living. In Ibo culture the ogbanje "refers to the iconoclast, the one who runs back and forth from one realm of existence to another ... It also refers to the mystical, unsettled condition of simultaneously existing in several spheres. Conceptually, the power inherent in the ogbanje erases natural and artificial boundaries that are drawn to systematize the cosmos."[167] In Yoruba culture the abiku is the child that dies in infancy, reenters its mother's womb, and is reborn, only to die again. "The abiku child returns to earth usually because of mother-love; it is drawn by the deep evocative desire of its mother,"[168] which in Beloved's case is Sethe's "too thick" love.[169] Beloved's love is equally too thick and her infantile traits – excessive feeling; insatiable craving for sweets and drink; inexhaustible love of dancing and wearing ribbons, beads, and beautiful clothes and unchecked carnal appetite – suspend her personality between two Erzulie identities. She has the fused characteristics of Erzulie Freida, the loa of the benevolent Rada rites of the Voudoun pantheon that originated in Dahomey, and Erzulie Ge-Rouge (Red Eyed), the Haitian-created loa of the malevolent Petro phalanx. Haitians added Erzulie Ge-Rouge to the Petro pantheon not from evil motives but from rage against the inhumanities and displacement they suffered under slavery when slave owners broke up husbands from wives and families at will. The crawling-already? girl's death is the climax of the Sweet Home slave master's, (schoolteacher's) attempt to transport Sethe and her children back to slavery in the South, terminating their reunion in the free North with Baby Suggs, the only consanguineal relation they know. Beloved rages at her mother's extravagant method of displacing her, ending her earthly existence, to thwart her slavemaster's attempt to reclaim them.

The outward appearance of Beloved and her physical and emotional needs are not at variance with the loa Erzulie. In Voudoun it is not uncommon for loa to have the eyes of a newborn and to eat, drink, and desire carnal pleasures like their human counterparts. Appearing at the former way station from a nearby creek on Thursday, the sacred day of Erzulie whose personification is a water snake, Beloved as Erzulie Ge-Rouge assumes in 124 Bluestone Road the attributes of the tragic goddess of love. Drawings depict Erzulie Ge-Rouge in the fetal position "with her knees drawn up, the fists clenched, the jaw rigid and the tears streaming from her tight-shut eyes; she is the cosmic tantrum." She laments the shortness of life and the limitations of love. Her volatile fits of anger are not of a spoiled child but of a cosmic innocence that "cannot understand and *will* not understand – why accident should ever befall what is cherished, or why death should ever come to the beloved."[170] Once Sethe discerns that Beloved and the daughter she killed are one and the same, she cannot pacify Beloved's escalating demands for answers to why she took her life and for daily reaffirmations of her maternal devotion. In a combination of rage and despair, "Beloved slammed things, wiped the table clean of plates, threw salt on the floor, broke a windowpane."[171] When Sethe's efforts to reassure Beloved of her love fail, she seeks to win her reincarnated daughter's forgiveness by plying her with ribbons, bright dresses with blue (Erzulie's color) stripes, – jewelry, beads, lace but nothing can answer Beloved's stream of tears and accusations. Exacting vengeance upon those who betray her in love is a central characteristic of Erzulie's personality, and it is for this reason that Beloved, like her loa counterpart, is feared as much as loved.

Beloved's carnal fixing of Paul D is an anomalous, reckless and immoral act of a young woman coming of age and experimenting with her sexuality, unless read within the context of Erzulie Ge-Rouge's alter ego, Erzulie Freida/Maîtresse (Mistress), "whose love is so strong and binding that it cannot tolerate a rival[... The] most jealous female spirit," she destroys marital and romantic relationships. Erzulie Freida/Maîtresse suffers no compunction when she calls a husband away from his wife or an unmarried man away from his mortal lover, as Beloved calls Paul D away from Sethe, foreclosing the potential for their marriage.[172] A woman "will gain no husband if an altar to Erzulie is in her house" since "[h]er jealousy delights in frustrating all plans and hopes" of a woman seeking male companionship in love.[173] Inviting Beloved to stay at 124 Bluestone Road[174] signifies Sethe's devotion to Erzulie Freida/ Maîtresse whose effect on men is irresistible. The most powerful loa, Damballah, conceded to Erzulie Frieda's call, and other men braved the decline of their health and luck before bowing to her summons. Paul D's mere mortal resistance is no match for Erzulie/Beloved.

Paul D's movements from Sethe's bed, to the rocker, to Baby Suggs's bed, to the storeroom, and finally to the cold house follow the typical removal of a reclamé, a man the amorous loa calls to her service, from a love competitor. What begins as an inexplicable stirring or dream whose demand is unfathomable to Paul D leads to his broken will and Beloved's expectation that he will renounce the mortal Sethe. The reclamé Paul D must prepare a bedchamber, "The Erzulie Room," for Erzulie Freida/Maîtresse and himself exclusively, and Paul D does so in the cold house, a shed separated from the main house. Repeating "Red heart," Paul D shouts at the height of sensual pleasure his devotion to his Mistress Erzulie/Beloved whose loa symbol is the pierced red heart of valentine shape.[175] The pitching, undulating red light signifying the presence of the sad, lonely, and mad ghostly spirit of the crawling-already? girl becomes the red-eyed, red-hearted Beloved denoting her witchly flesh. In Haitian worship Erzulie's vever, a flour drawing featuring a valentine heart (see figure 2), is pierced through its center by the poteau-mitan, the vertical, metaphysical axis, perfectly dividing its left and right sides into mirrored halves. The heart's vertical axis intersects with the Kongo Yowa suspended above it.

Like the mating mount of the turtles on which she transfixes, Erzulie/ Beloved mounts, and spiritually possesses, a serviteur who goes from coquettish to crying himself to sleep. The nocturnal, carnal appetite that the Erzuliean Beloved directs toward Paul D explains only in part why she is critically misread as a sexual demon of Western ilk; it does not account for the physical wasting that Sethe, the recipient of Beloved's rage and despair, suffers.

In "Figurations of Rape and the Supernatural in *Beloved*," Pamela E. Barnett argues that the "character Beloved is not just the ghost of Sethe's dead child; she is a succubus, a female demon and nightmare figure that sexually assaults male sleepers and drains them of semen." Her argument extends Beloved to the embodiment of the vampire figure, "another sexualized figure that drains a vital fluid[, which] was incorporated into African American folklore in the form of shape shifting witches who 'ride'

Figure 2. Vever for Erzulie (valentine heart).

their terrified victims in the night."[176] Despite Barnett's reluctance to
accept Richard M. Dorson's assertion in *American Folklore* (1972) that
"the shape shifting witches who straddle their victim in bed are English
not African creations,"[177] she posits a connection between haunting and
rape that invigorates Beloved as the Western-imaged succubus figure. Her
argument that Morrison figures sexual violence as "eating one's victim up"
falls short of grounding Morrison's figuring of Beloved as the African
traditional witch who performs kindoki kia dia, flesh or soul/psyche-eating
witchcraft, as the dominant trope of the novel. It is generally affirmed
among many traditional groups that spirits and disincarnated humans suck
their victims' blood like vampires and give men sexual dreams like the
succubi of the Middle Ages. The belief in the ndoki who performs kindoki
kia dia, metaphysical anthropophagism, and who also drinks blood pervades almost every group. The predominant trope of "eating" in the novel
is cannibalizing spiritual eating, Beloved's figurative consumption of
Sethe's soul/psyche that physically diminishes her flesh.[178] The text's
numerous veiled allusions to Voudoun and the indivisibility of spirit and
flesh, Voudoun's defining doctrine, solidify Beloved's consumption of Sethe
as retaliations for Sethe's severing of her spirit from her flesh. Morally

evil, Beloved slowly destroys the emotional and sexual relationship Sethe has with Paul D and her own mother-daughter relationship with Sethe as she slowly consumes Sethe psychically and physically, visiting a wasting dis-ease upon her body that will culminate in her demise if it continues.

When paired with the noun kindoki meaning "witchcraft," the Kikongo verb "dia," meaning "to eat," describes the ndoki's mystical eating of a victim behind closed doors at night while everyone is asleep.[179] Impelled by rage, fear, and hatred of her victim, the ndoki is merciless since she does not know how to forgive. One of the victim's own, a family member or close friend, the ndoki "eats" slowly over time, and the eating of the victim's flesh is incorporeal, spiritual, and symbolical. The witch invisibly attacks the victim's soul/psyche, the inner source of his or her life and vitality. Stealing and eating the soul/psyche, the witch devours her victim "gradually so that a wasting disease is the outward sign of soul/psyche destruction taking place."[180] The words soul and psyche must be conjoined because to use only soul to describe the gros-bon-ange or esprit in Voudoun, the essence of Sethe that Beloved consumes, would misrepresent the essence of the body's animating force. The words do not have "moral and mystical connotations" commonly associated with the soul in Christianity:

[The] sense of gros-bon-ange or esprit, which is understood, in Voudoun, as the invisible, non-material *self* or character of an individual, as distinguished from his physical body[, translates more precisely as] ... the word "psyche," as it is used in modern psychology [and] conveys some aspects of the Voudoun gros-bon-ange much more accurately than the word "soul."[181]

Therefore, invisible power consumes the invisible nonmaterial self-producing visible material consequences.

Beloved approaches Sethe at night as she slides into sleep with "[a] touch no heavier than a feather but loaded, nevertheless, with desire."[182] But unlike the attacks that vampires and succubi launch exclusively at night, Beloved's cannibalistic consumption of Sethe is not exclusively nocturnal. In daylight she invisibly attacks Sethe's neck in the clearing using psychic power. Beloved is a waking and sleeping horror that spiritually strangles Sethe's inner life force causing her to emaciate physically toward death. Sethe decreases as Beloved increases. "The bigger Beloved got, the smaller Sethe became; the brighter Beloved's eye, the more those eyes that used never to look away became slits of sleeplessness ... She sat in the chair licking her lips like a chastised child while Beloved ate up her life, took it, swelled up with it, grew taller on it."[183] Because she is one of the victim's own, Beloved demands excessive, absolute devotion from Sethe, whose crime stems from ambivalent powers. Infantilism and fear subvert Beloved's rational processing of Sethe's creative and destructive maternal powers. Her mother's objective in killing the crawling-already? girl, and attempting to take the lives of Denver, Howard, and Buglar is not death. She is exemplifying, as Morrison maintains, "a person determined to be responsible."[184] Her plan is to remove them, herself included, to the afterworld of the living-dead ancestors to be with her mother, Ma'am. Sethe has not acted immorally. She has not done what enslaved women before her have not done. Ella, a way station neighbor and the victim of "the lowest yet,"[185] permitted the deaths of the children that she birthed by father and son slavers who shackled and repeatedly raped her throughout her youth. And Sethe's own mother, whose enslavers impregnated her against her will, terminated the lives spawned by those unions. Mercilessly unforgiving and fearing her victim, Beloved pressures Sethe to redress her wrong, while the guilt of her own destructive excess consumes Sethe, gnawing away at her ability to function as an autonomous, responsible adult.

Western and traditional thought would both concur that the situation causes Sethe's dis-ease but would disagree with respect to the causing agent. To the Western mind, her guilt impacts on her physical wellbeing, diminishing her corporeal state. To the African traditional mind, however, an evil spirit incarnating the resentful Beloved motivates her to eat spiritually the soul/psyche of Sethe to nourish her own. The spirit's strength waxes while its victim's wanes.[186] Competition for Sethe's survival starts when the flesh between her forefinger and thumb becomes "as thin as china silk and there wasn't a piece of clothing in the house that didn't sag on her."[187] According to widespread traditional belief, a wasting disease is conclusive proof that an ndoki kia dia slowly ingests a person under psyche attack. Physical death results with the spiritual consumption of the victim's heart.

Inconclusive causality, however, surrounds the "basket-fat" stomach developing on Beloved. Under Ella's leadership, the thirty humming women who come to exorcise Beloved see a naked, beautiful "devil child" who "had taken the shape of a pregnant woman."[188] Beloved is either pregnant with the child of Paul D, or fat from feasting incorporeally on Sethe, or both. "Beloved animates her [... witchly] flesh with food but also with Sethe's life."[189]

The thirty humming women bring both "Christian faith" and "what they believed would work [– s]tuffed in apron pockets, strung around their necks, lying in the space between their breasts"[190] – to the former way station to liberate Sethe from the evil whipping her psychically and physically, and that evil, Beloved, seeks flight from their outrage. Among the Bakongo, "witchcraft accusation plays a significant role as sanction, and as symbol of the extent to which the members of a clan-section are linked to one another in times of distress ... Any evil ndoki accused of eating an indispensable member may be beaten to death if [s]he fails to seek safety in flight from community rage."[191] It is not compulsory for her to leave the village but she must back down. The women's use of what "would work" in addition to Christianity to subdue witchly flesh that has overstepped the boundary separating the metaphysical and physical worlds links the women to an "experiential communality" that points to their sharing of a guiding pre-Christian religious ethos through time and space that they express in common.[192] As cultural carriers living physically apart from the dominant, alien world from which they are racially segregated and cultur-ally insulated, the Cincinnati women who gather collectively concur that Beloved's psychic ravaging of Sethe is a threatening moral evil that they must neutralize with African traditional religious artifacts retained from the past.

CONSOLATA SOSA – NDOKI KIA DIA REVISITED

A false report of a posse of men gunning down a group of Brazilian nuns because the women practiced Candomblé, Vodun's survival featuring Yoruba and Fon beliefs in African-Brazilian culture, inspired Morrison's writing of *Paradise*. Learning that the incident never happened, Morrison states, "was irrelevant ... since it said much about institutional and unin-stitutional religion, and how close they are."[193] Morrison's loose reworking of the report into a narrative about a morally justified New World order's excision of evil in the form of a coven of witches treats old ideas, old situations. One of those old situations is the witch trials of Salem Village, Massachusetts, in 1692. At the center of the trials was the racially ambig-uous Tituba, a practitioner of Voodoo, a second Eve, who purportedly ignited the mass hysteria that invalidated the master narrative that America constructed of its founding as a prelapsarian epoch where freedom of religion and acceptance of difference were the orders of the day. Bernard Rosenthal's article "Dark Eve" addresses America's gendering as female and racing as nonwhite the corrupting communal/Caribbean evil that marked its national fall:

That the role of precipitating agent for this American fall should rest upon a woman is consistent with the [Eve-Edenic] archetype it perpetuates. That the woman should be dark reflects America's social engagement with the seemingly intractable problem of synthesizing a myth of national harmony with Indian wars and with slavery. The defeated groups in this war of color become merged into an ambiguously pigmented Tituba, at times "Indian" and at times "Negro." In a valuable survey of the racial representation of Tituba, Chadwick Hansen has shown how this [Carib] Indian woman emerged over the years as a half Indian, half black person, finally becoming entirely black in the hands of modern writers, from distinguished playwright to distinguished scholar.[194]

Whether "Indian" or "Negro," Tituba, Salem Village's dark Eve, the evil female spoiler of the Puritan New World Garden, brought chaos and death as did Eve of the Garden of Eden in Genesis. Tituba escaped execution but many whom her testimony incriminated in the New England witch-hunt did not. In the year following the trials, Puritan theocracy imprisoned more than a hundred of the accused and executed approximately nineteen, mostly women, on charges of witchcraft.[195]

Executed by a founding New World order patriarchy on charges of witchcraft, the "[b]odacious black Eves"[196] of the Convent in *Paradise* meet the prototype for the African traditional witch, the principal agent of moral evil typified by the New World Tituba. Consolata Sosa, Mavis Albright, Grace called Gigi, Seneca, and Pallas Truelove are racially ambiguous temptresses who in toto are held responsible for the social misfortunes occurring in Ruby, Oklahoma. They are targeted as the harbingers of original sin and death in the small southwestern town established in 1950 that is the result of a patriarchal quest proving Black manhood and founding Black nationhood. The utopian Ruby turns dystopian when the Convent women living too close in proximity, only seventeen miles outside its corporate limits, threaten its collective stability. Affecting its residents who are within the geographic arc of their power, the women allegedly destroy relationships and visit dis-ease and death on the people of the all-Black town that is isolated for ninety miles around from any other township. From the perspective of the Ruby patriarchy, the Convent women are the progenitors of moral evil, acts committed by one person against another that damage relationships. Before their arrival, Ruby was a "a town justifiably pleased with itself. It neither had nor needed a jail. No criminals had ever come from ... [this] town. And the one or two people who acted up, humiliated their families or threatened the town's view of itself were taken good care of."[197] Founded by the remainder of nine large African-American families fleeing sin, corruption, and interracial and intraracial persecution who formed an earlier all-Black settlement named Haven, Ruby is a twentieth-century New World order intent on getting right what the greater fallen nation it now insulates itself from got wrong.

It believes uncompromisingly in its morally superior exceptionalism and intends to remain by any means necessary a paradise uncorrupted by evil.

Proof that minimal miscegenation has occurred amid their ranks, the blue-black skins of the 8-rock Ruby families who take their name from a very deep level in the coal mines confirm their almost genetically undiluted African ancestry. Yet the senior 8-rock residents and their families dismiss their ties to the continent. The first name of an Old Testament prophet who had visions and a corrupted French Louisiana last name erase Ruby's founding patriarch Zechariah Morgan's African name Kofi, an appellative of Hausa origin. His French slave surname and Louisiana background indicate that his African forebears in all likelihood crossed the Atlantic from Africa's western shore by way of the French Caribbean.[198] Soane Morgan, married to the grandson of Zechariah Morgan, knows nothing about Africa. She once gave seventy-five cents to a missionary society; otherwise, she has no interest in Africa or its people. Ruby's schoolteacher, Pat Best – whose 8-rock father, Roger Best, chose a light-complexioned outsider for his bride and whose own fair skin testifies to his spousal choice – admits to Richard Misner, one of Ruby's three ministers, that Africa means nothing to her. The natural constituent elements that are the bedrock of traditional belief have been displaced by the scientific elements of the periodic table that she teaches to her students. The older citizenry in general scoffs at Ruby's young people, whose black consciousnesses in 1976 have been raised by the Black Power and Civil Rights movements of the preceding decade and who talk about Africans like neighbors or family.

In spite of Ruby's ignorance about Africa, its geographic organization mirrors the cross within a circle configuration imported from Kongo and Dahomey by way of the French Caribbean and Haiti in Voudoun. Ruby's houses do not have address numbers, and outsiders depend on insiders' local knowledge to navigate the town of five streets bearing the name of New Testament saints that cut across Central Street, which runs due north to the Convent seventeen miles away. At the center of Ruby (a name that calls forth the round, fiery gemstone) stands the circular Oven and beyond it in the southern hemisphere of the town is south country, an undeveloped area across a stream. The five streets in the northern hemisphere of Ruby, above the stream and to the east of Central Street, are in descending order St. Peter, St. Matthew, St. Mark, St. Luke, and St. John. To the west of Central Street and in descending, adjacent order are Cross Peter, Cross Matthew, Cross Mark, Cross Luke, and Cross John. The Kongo Yowa's subliminal imposition on a town that arises from an all-Black ordering[199] verifies that its residents are more closely tied to Africa than they are aware and that African traditional cosmological beliefs survive in their personal and collective (un)consciousnesses and to a degree govern their socio-religious thoughts and actions. The names of the Christian saints of the Gospels overwrite active primal remembrance of a West Africanist cosmology central to the Ruby residents. Because its citizens disremember and dismiss African religion and embrace Christianity – the tiny Ruby has three churches less than a mile distant from one another – individuals who once would have revered Consolata Sosa as a priestess now mark her as a witch, the harbinger of evil who, contrary to the traditional way of dealing with a witch that time has defamiliarized, must now be destroyed.

Everything that threatens Ruby comes from the independent Convent women who, living too close to the town for its comfort, are reputed to be the root of all evil and the disrupters of moral authority. Because traditional belief dictates that there are no accidents and all misfortunes have traceable agency, the townspeople of Ruby, like the Bottom community in *Sula*, must find causes or scapegoats for the misfortunes and outrages assaulting their town and corrupting their youth, who, from their perspective, have respect neither for self nor elders. Unconscious of the moral threat they represent, the Convent women are blamed for Ruby's birth defects, sexual immorality, and deterioration of relationships:

> Outrages that had been accumulating all along took shape as evidence. A mother was knocked down the stairs by her cold-eyed daughter. Four damaged infants were born in one family. Daughters refused to get out of bed. Brides disappeared on their honeymoons. Two brothers shot each other on New Year's Day. Trips to Demby for VD shots common. And what went on at the Oven these days was not to be believed [. . . T]he one thing that connected all these catastrophes was in the Convent. And in the Convent were those women.[200]

Bodacious black Eves, Consolata and her four boarders reside in a mansion turned convent turned coven that seemingly floats "dark and malevolently disconnected from God's earth" in mist that possibly obscures "witch tracks."[201] After living with Consolata for protracted periods of time, the boarding women participate in her ritualized practice outside of Christianity that an African (un)consciousness informs.

A Brazilian orphan brought to the United States by nuns, Consolata Sosa fuses her early exposure to Catholicism and Candomblé until she is nine years old. After Mary Magna, the nun who rescues her from the streets of Brazil, takes her to Oklahoma, Catholicism dominates the next four decades of her life. Consolata's unofficial rise as priestess or mãe de santo (mother of the saint) in the Convent once the Catholic sisters who initially occupied the mansion leave or die addresses the historical intersections of the institutional and uninstitutional religions. The coming together of Catholicism and Candomblé, and the later addition of Voudoun through her apprenticeship with Lone DuPres,[202] establishes the site of Consolata's body as the historical juxtaposing of the European and African religions and Catholicism's attempt to displace the African-derived religion. Consolata is the religious amalgamation and diasporic consequence of the arrival of Catholicism with the Portuguese on the continent of Africa in 1471; the Portuguese construction of the first slave castle at Elmina on the Gold Coast from 1482 to 1486; and the intensive importation of enslaved Africans to Brazil by Portugal in the sixteenth century. These events produced the African-Brazilian juxtaposing of Vodun with Catholicism and the rise of Candomblé.

Consolata's strong psychic leaning, developed under the instruction of Lone, who also fits the African traditional witch profile, supports her figuring as a "black Eve." Lone, a foundling like Consolata who is unmarried, childless, and suspected of anti-maternal acts, damaging four Ruby children, introduces Consolata to "stepping in."[203] Consolata, under her mentorship, psychically reunifies the spirit and flesh of the dying – first Scout Morgan when he flips his pick-up truck and later Mary Magna throughout her terminal illness – since the midwife in her eighties is too old to perform the reunification herself. After years of Catholic indoctrination and Mary Magna's cautioning, Consolata believes that the powers Lone exhibits come from witchcraft, which Lone "practiced." Once the "exhilaration was gone [from her own first stepping in, her act] . . . seemed nasty to her. Like devilment. Like evil craft."[204] Ashamed of her psychic power, she accuses Lone of casting a spell on her, but Lone denies the use of magical control or palpable apparatus, telling Consolata that she[, too,] is "gifted" and that she, Lone, "knew it from the start."[205] As the most direct spokesperson for privileging the foremost principal in Voudoun and Candomblé, the binding of spirit and flesh and not the elevation of spirit over flesh that Catholicism teaches, Lone cautions Consolata that Christian faith is not enough. "Sometimes folks need more [. . . W]e all need earth, air, water. Don't separate God from His elements. He created it all. You stuck on dividing Him from His works. Don't unbalance His world."[206]

Ascending to the role of mãe de santo, Consolata heads the Convent, now transformed into a woman-centered terreiro, a house of Candomblé, and her four female boarders assume the roles of filhas de santo (daughters/ devotees of the saint). Under her direction in the cellar of the Convent, the women lie naked in a circle (roda) of candles. Within the circle of fire, Consolata traces with white chalk and paint "templates" of their bodies in self-chosen poses of crosses: hands clasping shoulders, arms and legs flung wide apart, and a floater's pose.[207] Her tracings parallel the vevers in Voudoun, invocational symbols drawn in honor of the gods. As the continuing ritual grows more elaborate and as each of the four women positions herself in the circle, Consolata delivers a Candomblé/Voudoun-inspired message on the fusion of spirit and flesh that admonishes the women to "never break them in two. Never put one over the other."[208] As months pass, one of the women adds a "green cross on a field of white" to the etchings, completing divine drawings in white that are exegetically tied with the cross's physical and metaphysical intersection of spirit and flesh.[209] The cross-postured women in the feminine earthen space, balanced against the masculine fire-ringed circle with cross and outlines honoring them as the apotheosis of the intersection of spirit and flesh, respond to self-summoning. The sacred templates they shape in their own likenesses "*drew them* like magnets"[210] in accordance with the spirit-summoning that etchings drawn in honor of the gods of Candomblé and Voudoun produce.

Seventeen miles away, Ruby's ministers of institutionalized Protestant religions debate the manner in which the cross should be interpreted by the doctrinal beliefs handed down through the Methodist and Baptist churches, denominations that African Americans predominately affiliated themselves with during and after slavery.[211] Arguing that "God is not interested in you," Reverend Senior Pulliam, Ruby's Methodist minister, separates flesh and spirit, while Reverend Richard Misner, its Baptist minister steadfastly brandishing an oak cross, counters Pulliam's position with "God is you," and unifies spirit and flesh. Before the circle, the triangle, or the parallel, Misner's actions accede, the cross, the symbol of the intersection of spirit and flesh, was "the first sign any human anywhere had made: the vertical line; the horizontal one."[212] Given the Puritan outlook that shaped the founding of America and that Blacks accepted as their New World perspective, Misner's position is the minority view.

The patriarchs of Ruby believe that the Convent women "beat out snakes, the Depression, the tax man, and the railroad for sheer destructive power."[213] They preponderantly affix on the women of the Convent the responsibility for Ruby's moral evil and select European Americans' archetypical response to dealing with practitioners of witchcraft. Despite the subliminal African retentions shaping their traditional conception of evil, the nine Ruby gunmen who storm the Convent hunt the women out to destroy encroaching moral evil.

It is morally incumbent upon the intransigent men to take the lives of the unmarried and husband-estranged women whom they suspect engage in the "sly torture of children" and "revolting sex," activities customarily attached to the ndoki.[214] Past and present actions and facts known and unknown by the men sanction their labeling the women anti-maternal. First, during a summer trip to the Higgledy Piggledy to buy wieners, Mavis Albright leaves Merle and Pearl, her newborn twins, in the family's mint-green Cadillac with the windows closed. The infants die of heatstroke. Second, the Convent women give sanctuary to Arnette Fleetwood who wants to abort the baby she conceived before she and K. D. Smith, the son of the deceased woman for whom the town is named, are to be married. Punching her stomach to cause a miscarriage, Arnette delivers an infant that survives only a few days. And most compelling, considered by the men as "[m]ore like witches" than bitches,[215] the maternally compromised women, indisputably from the men's perspective, have the power to strike victims, particularly young ones, within close range. Sweetie Fleetwood's four children in Ruby hover perpetually at death's door, and a baby, along with its parents, freezes to death within walking distance of the Convent.

Furthering their ndoki status, the Convent women are deemed sexual predators and threats. The four boarders, sans Consolata and underwear, enact a Jezebel show at the wedding of Arnette and K. D. The men and women of Ruby morally censure the women's scandalous behavior but nevertheless watch them, enthralled. The men condemn the women's vile sexuality, neglecting to admit their own carnal indulgences with them. K. D. and his uncle Deacon Morgan have in the recent and distant past had affairs with Gigi and Consolata respectively. To distance themselves from their own sexual transgressions, the men of Ruby, however, insinuate that copulation other than heterosexual fornication and adultery takes place among the women. The sex that "revolts" them is lesbian sex.[216] It is true that before taking sanctuary in the Convent, a wealthy Norma Keene Fox in Wichita hired Seneca for sexual services. But the Ruby men's knowledge of the women's intimate lives before their arrival at the Convent and their day-to-day interactions within its walls are limited and purely speculative. They make the inferential leap that the women are lesbians when Pallas is spotted clinging to Seneca shortly after the women leave the Smith-Fleetwood wedding reception. Marriage and procreation are the most revered roles for women in Ruby; therefore, to the Ruby men, the Convent women living not only without husbands but "kissing on themselves"[217] form an unholy, anti-male, anti-maternal, anti-reproductive alliance. Their sexual (mis)conduct in general incites charges of rebellion against patriarchal authority, with the lesbian sex they allegedly perform being the most seditious.

The depiction of Consolata's cannibalism conjoins traits of Western vampirism with the African eating bewitchment of kindoki kia dia discussed above in conjunction with Beloved.[218] Consolata captures Deacon's sexual appetite briefly, but he ends the extramarital affair on the day her biting and licking of blood from his lip repulses him. Citing metaphorical cannibalism, she states that the impulse was involuntary, since she was uninterested in eating him; she was hungry for her own flesh. Before her sexual liaison with him, she has lived a spiritual life that has cut her off from her flesh. Reuniting with the stream of life and the body is a spiritual imperative for Consolata, but a spiritual imperative detached from cultural understanding and communal acceptance appears pagan and malevolent, a threat to established order and tradition and a defining act of witchcraft.

The flesh-starved Consolata and her coven are linked implicitly with the three skeletons found not far from their front door.[219] The fleshless remains are evidence that the practitioners of kindoki kia dia are not far away. In addition to Consolata, two of the women have psychologically driven preoccupations with flesh-eating and bloodletting, but they lack Consolata's exceptional psychic power to reunify spirit and flesh that positions her as not being an ordinary person. Mavis has a recurring dream of a lion cub intent on gnawing the "juicy bites" of her throat. Compliantly, "she willingly lets her head fall back, clearing the way" and in turn, she enjoys "pounding" Gigi's flesh during a fight, and "biting was exhilarating, just as cooking was."[220] A self-mutilator and consumer, Seneca finds psychological release in the "blood work" of streets, lanes, and alleys that she cuts into her arm.[221] Yet Consolata's resuscitations of Scout Morgan and Mary Magna situate her differently from the others. Dislodged from an Africanist worldview that Consolata's ability to step in (re)centers in the text if not in their consciousness, Ruby's residents speculate that Consolata, like Lone DuPres, "practices" what they interpret as witchcraft.

Living the first years of her life in a concentrated, African-Brazilian, diasporic population where Candomblé flourished, and passing the next forty years devoted to Catholic practices not unlike those of Candomblé, Consolata Sosa retains, in sublimated form, many of her West African traditional beliefs and practices. The nun-run Convent in Oklahoma, bearing a striking resemblance to a female-run house of Candomblé, strengthens the resilience of the African-based religion. Failing to comprehend her intertwining of the institutional and uninstitutional religions, her Ruby counterparts proclaim her witchery responsible for their moral decline. The distortion of the commandment on the round Oven that sits at the center of Ruby summarizes the major impact that spatial dispossession, the passing of time, and the conversion to Christianity has had in overwriting the personal and collective (un)consciousnesses of Americans of African ancestry. Founder Zechariah Morgan built the Oven at Haven, an earlier settlement, forging the words on its lip, and his grandsons carefully dismantled the commandment-bearing Oven and transported it to Ruby. Because of the loss of some of its lettering and flawed human memory, the Oven's written charge regarding the relational intersection of the human and the divine can no longer be definitively known.

***

Inspired by the reality that despite being Bible people, her family did not limit its understanding of the world "only through Christian theology,"[222] Morrison's novels collectively press for the recognition in African-American culture and life of a cosmology obscured by Christian domination. She manipulates Christian images and the Western reader's Christian worldview to expose subliminal West and Central African traditional perceptions of the "universal" concepts of good, evil, and morality that African Americans attach to a Christian face but, in fact, have pre-Christian provenance.

In concert with an African traditional monistic theodicy that invalidates absolute binaries and a puritanical understanding of good and evil, Morrison's Africanist conception of moral evil fuses with good at every ontological level. The retention of this view, even in its waning state, offers proof that the personal and collective (un)consciousnesses of twentieth- and twenty-first-century African America retain African survivals that transcended the Middle Passage. Morrison has asserted that the nonabsolutist, traditional way in which black people deal with evil accounts "for one of the reasons it's difficult for them to organize long-term political wars against other people" and "for their generosity and acceptance of all sorts of things."[223] If her assertion is true, then decisive literary and real-life investigations into and analyses of Black people's communality of responses to crime, punishment, notions of justice, and many other attendant concepts may lend understanding to and acceptance of African Americans' disparate way of knowing, being, and mediating social conflicts and roles.

Inscribed on the physical landscapes and character representations of *Sula*, *Beloved*, and *Paradise*, the vaguely visible Kongo Yowa serves as a subtle reminder that West and Central African traditional beliefs amalgamated in the Caribbean and brought to the mainland of North America presently influence African Americans' religious beliefs and practices in ways of which African Americans are unaware. Some trivialize or discourage discussion of these African beliefs, but many still grant them a respect and power that seems contradictory to their twenty-first-century Christian enlightenment.

4

Kanda: living elders, the ancestral presence, and the ancestor as foundation

To us [of European descent,] the idea of ancestral priority has just no meaning, but to ... older African men and women in the backland villages, life from day to day and, we might legitimately say, from moment to moment, has no meaning at all apart from ancestral presence and ancestral power.

T. Cullen Young, "The Idea of God in Northern Nyasaland (Malawi)"[1]

[I]t seems to me interesting to evaluate Black literature on what the writer does with the presence of an ancestor. Which is to say a grandfather as in Ralph Ellison, or a grandmother as in Toni Cade Bambara, or a healer as in Bambara or Henry Dumas. There is always an elder there. And these ancestors are not just parents, they are sort of timeless people whose relationships to the characters are benevolent, instructive, and protective, and they provide a certain kind of wisdom.

Toni Morrison, "Rootedness: The Ancestor as Foundation"[2]

According to Toni Morrison, the presence of an ancestor, a defining continuum in Black art and an identifiable quality of Blackness, drew troubled responses from some of the most gifted African-American writers of the twentieth century. Richard Wright, she asserts, had "great difficulty" with conceptualizing the ancestor, while its presence or absence "confounded and disturbed" James Baldwin. An interrogation of ancestral representation in contemporary African-American fiction revealed to her that "[i]t was the absence of an ancestor that was frightening, that was threatening, and it caused huge destruction and disarray in the work itself." In both urban and rural settings, "the presence or absence of that figure" determined the principal character's success or happiness. She concluded that in contrast to mainstream Anglo literature where "contemplation of serene nature" or escape from a corrupt townscape ushered in solace, the "person who represented the ancestor" was the catalyst of comfort. "Whether the character was in Harlem or Arkansas, the point was there, this timelessness was there, this person who represented this ancestor."[3]

81

The "concept of an ancestor not necessarily as a parent but as an abiding, interested, benevolent, guiding presence … not quite like saints but having the same access,"[4] is unquestionably an African retention that initially wended its way diasporically into African-American life. Reverence for the wise, timeless presence survived seamlessly as a cultural fixture in American slave communities and African-American free life under the veil of Judeo-Christian doctrine. The fifth biblical commandment to honor one's father and mother, and by extension all elders, resonated with West and Central African traditional practice that also required surviving members of the lineage to continue the veneration of elders after their earthly lives had ended.

With the consecutive publication of *Song of Solomon* (1977), *Tar Baby* (1981), and *Beloved* (1987), Morrison fashioned a trilogy that contains literal and symbolic, physical and metaphysical delineations of ancestorship that have traceable West and Central African provenance. Just as Morrison proclaims that *Sula* (1973) is "all about" the question of evil and Black people's counter-Christian conception of it,[5] *Song of Solomon* is all about ancestor reclamation, recovering from the African past the guiding force whose presence determines even now the success or failure of African-American survival in the New World. Affirming that the core objective of *Beloved* is to revive the memory of the disremembered African ancestor, Morrison spoke of her fifth novel "as a prayer, a memorial, a fixing ceremony for those who did not survive the Middle Passage and whose names we did not know."[6] Dedicated "[t]o the sixty million and more," an estimate of the number of enslaved Africans who perished en route to the Americas and from the genealogies of their descendants, *Beloved*, as the late literary scholar Barbara Christian astutely articulated, *is* an African ancestral worship.[7] It is important to note that Christian reluctantly uses the word "worship" for fear of forwarding the inaccurate yet entrenched belief in the West that African traditional cultures worship the ancestor as they would the Supreme Being. While readers of these works keep in mind that the ancestor must be regarded in a concrete sense, the ancestor's presence must also be read as a metaphorical appeal to African Americans not to become rugged individualists who lose connection with one another and with those who served, prayed, protested, fought, and died for their social and political advancement.

If one views *Song of Solomon* as the twentieth-century reclamation of dispossessed and disremembered ancestors and *Beloved* as a memorial for ancestors from before the mid nineteenth century who were lost and forgotten, then the narrative of *Tar Baby* marks the liminal site of imminent New World ancestral attrition and retention. Sequentially, the plots and settings of the novels substructure a regressive temporal and spatial trajectory that maps the historical conveyance of ancestorship to the New World. Christian maintains that after Milkman, the protagonist of *Song of Solomon*, discovers his oldest ancestor, Solomon, the flying African in the land of Shalimar, Virginia, Morrison was "stopped in her tracks. For in order to get back to Africa [to reconnect ancestrally], she had to confront the Middle Passage, [...] the dividing line between being African and being African American,"[8] which she does in *Beloved*. But not before, I contend, stopping off, by way of the Caribbean, *Tar Baby*'s setting, at the crossroads of African-American ancestral culture and the site where slave ships docked as their first port of call in the early period of the slave trade before proceeding to the American coast. For Africans whose voyage ended in the Caribbean, and for those who were acclimatized there before being brought to America's mainland, island disembarkation signaled not only the end of the Middle Passage but also the end of their national and familial identities. Slave traders separated familial and tribal members to decrease the possibility of insurrection, and slave owners bought and sold Africans disregarding their relational ties and thereby forwarding identity erasure. Island disembarkation signified the end of Africans knowing and being known by their kin, a process of patronymic, matronymic, and tribal disremembrance that moved concurrently backward and forward between Africa and America by way of a myriad intermediate Caribbean spaces. But their arrival and enslavement in the Caribbean also gave rise to an amalgamation of African ancestral beliefs in Voudoun that passed into the New World materialized as the cross within a circle and performed as the ring shout. *Beloved*, *Song of Solomon*, and *Tar Baby* narrate more than the experiences of physical displacement by peoples of whole and part African descents. They address the psychological and religious reality of what it means for African Americans in the New World to be cut off from not only their living kin but also their dead kin, from knowing and calling their names, and from continuing their responsibility of reciprocity to them in the circle of life. These novels treat what has been genealogically forfeited but culturally retained in African-American life with respect to the ancestor in the interstices of spatial dispossession, temporal disconti-nuity, and familial disremembrance.

Throughout her fiction, but particularly in these three works, Morrison delineates the discrete roles and operations of the descending continuum of eldership known as kanda: the living-dead ancestor – the timeless people of West and Central African traditional cosmologies, the elders, and the junior members of a clan. Morrison's fiction relies on an ancestral presence, a hybrid role of the two socio-religious roles at the kanda apex, the living-dead ancestor followed by the elder, to mediate and naturalize the activities of the metaphysical in the physical realm. Individually and collectively, *Beloved*, *Song of Solomon*, and *Tar Baby* give fleeting insights into the "existence" of the living-dead ancestor through time as s/he recedes into the infinite past and subsequent disremembrance. Each of these narratives contains covert and overt allusions to West and Central African-based religious retentions in the New World and the survival of the most profound ancestral symbol, the Kongo Yowa, which pays homage to the living-dead ancestor, "the real source of earthly power and prestige."[9] Morrison's repeated use of this cosmographic design that had been preserved in Haiti's Voudoun and the United States's Voodoo in concrete and abstract ways in her fiction negates interpreting her narratives through a wholly Christian and therefore Western lens. Its textual persistence challenges the reader to unearth the African civilizations buried beneath Western domination.

THE ANCESTRAL PRESENCE — MEDIATOR OF THE TIMELESS ANCESTOR

While much criticism addresses the figure of the ancestor in Morrison's canon, scholastic interpretations have great difficulty in identifying the ancestor and vary on which character in each of her novels mediates its persona.[10] In *The Bluest Eye* (1970), depending on the criticism consulted, Mr. and Mrs. MacTeer, Aunt Jimmy, and the healer M'Dear are each cited as the ancestor. In *Sula* Shadrack, Eva Peace, and the title character vie for the distinction, as do Pilate Dead and Circe in *Song of Solomon*. The mother/sister/she in the yellow dress, Ondine, the swamp women, Son, Thérèse, Gideon, the blind horsemen of the Isle des Chevaliers, and the women of Eloe in *Tar Baby* receive competing endorsements, along with multiple claims in *Beloved*, *Jazz* (1992), and *Paradise* (1998). Scholars collectively proclaim the identity, constitutionality, and performativity of the African-derived figure in the face of obvious critical, cultural, and historical uncertainty.

Although unstable designations of the African ancestor are rampant in literature and literary scholarship, a crucial reason why Morrison's ancestor figures elude definitive detection is her writerly insistence on conflating traditional social and religious categories. In "Rootedness: The Ancestor as Foundation," Morrison states that Pilate is the ancestor in *Song of Solomon* and discusses the living-dead ancestor and the living elder as interchangeable identities. In doing so, she conjoins the identifying and identifiable constituents of two very discrete ontological subjectivities found in countless traditional cultures throughout the whole of Africa. Kanda illustrates the common African traditional socio-religious ladder of authority. Historians Sylvia R. Frey and Betty Wood explain:

As part of the community of the living and the dead, ancestors composed the apex of a "continuum of eldership" that extended from junior members of the lineage, to living elders, to ancestors and was known in the Kingdom of the Kongo as *kanda*. The hierarchical *kanda*, which in the sixteenth and seventeenth centuries was often headed by a *kanda* female, was organized on a continuum of relative age, each level of which derived its authority from the preceding rank or grade.[11]

Morrison's blurring of the living-dead ancestor and living elder as an inseparable entity naturalizes successive textual "reincarnations" of the incorporeal spirit ancestor by optionally camouflaging his or her representation in fleshed, human form. The resulting "ancestral presence," a hybrid of the living-dead ancestor and the living elder, mediates the ancestor proper, permitting simultaneity of absence and presence, of past and present, and of flesh and spirit. The hybridization of the roles forecloses repetitive supernatural figurings within a single novel, between consecutive novels, and throughout Morrison's canon. The wise and comforting ancestral presence, the living elder last with or closest to the ancestor with respect to age or affection, relays communications from the living-dead to junior members of the lineage and not infrequently transcends human capability not unlike the "passed on" ancestor and the ordinary spirit. The character functioning in the blended role may as mediator of the metaphysical and physical realms also function as the formal or informal priestess of her community.[12]

Having the capacity to "blend the acceptance of the supernatural and a profound rootedness in the real world at the same time with neither taking precedence over the other"[13] is an aesthetic quality of Black art that Morrison skillfully manipulates on a multiplicity of levels. In African traditional life, theologian and African sociologist John S. Mbiti states, "the spiritual universe is a unity with the physical, and ... these two intermingle and dovetail into each other so much that it is not easy, or even necessary, at times to draw the distinction or separate them."[14] Having the living-dead ancestor and the living elder perform as a unity by merging and diverging their ontological boundaries fuses the spiritual and physical universes. Pilate Dead and Jake (aka Macon Dead the first) illustrate the fusion of the two worlds in *Song of Solomon*. In the novel's 1960s present timeline, Pilate, the living elder is not the living-dead ancestor; she is the ancestral presence, the living elder chosen to give advice and solace to Milkman (aka Macon Foster Dead). The living-dead Jake, who instructs Pilate from beyond the veil of the afterworld, and his father Solomon, now the subject of myth, are the ancestors. Although Morrison mutually conjoins the two socio-religious roles at the apex of eldership, living characters, like living members of a tribal family, are not ancestors; that honor can only be conferred on those who have passed to the afterworld. Other ancestral presences – Nan, Sixo, and Baby Suggs in *Beloved* for example – are living bridges to the past and to those who have passed on and, as memory bearers, may be thought of as biomaterial memory. They enable active, ontological, timeless presence for the ancestors despite the ancestors' physical absence.

Africanist readers of Morrison's fiction are able to identify several salient exchanges that occur between the timeless ancestors who have transitioned to the afterworld and the living members of his clan. Traditional cultures that communicated with individuals no longer living in the earthly plane existed in the Sudanic empires – Ghana, Mali, Songhay – of the twelfth to the sixteenth centuries and the belief in posthumous communication survives in the worldview of traditional peoples who yet populate West and Central Africa. Those who arrived on the shores of the American South as human cargo during the transatlantic slave trade brought with them many individual and collective beliefs of reciprocity between the living-dead and the living that thrived despite familial dispersion and erasure. The sub-Saharan Fon, Mende, Akan, Ashanti, Gã, Ibo, and Yoruba, like the tribes of Kongo-Angola in Central Africa, communicate with defunct elders, the wise and aged of the clan, whose personalities are believed to have "passed on" – survived the death and decay of their earthly bodies and migrated to the afterworld. The fictional depiction that Morrison provides of Jake's posthumous communications with Pilate exemplifies this ancestor-elder exchange that occurs in real life. Because those who survive the ancestors consult them as oracles with the aid of sacred specialists, ritual priests, and mediums, Pilate's role, based on her ongoing exchanges with Jake, extends to priestess as well. Now, as in the past, the ancestors are for many Africans who embrace traditional concepts religious, supersensible powers that have, since the living-dead are closer to God, access to all past knowledge. The omniscience of Beloved, who is not the ancestor but who has first-hand knowledge of events that predate her because she has resided in the afterworld, typifies the living-dead's access to knowledge throughout time. Communication with those who have passed on, therefore, allows the living access to an endless storehouse of knowledge and events.

In return for ancestral beneficence, the living demonstrate respect for their ancestors by calling their names, by pouring libations for them and offering proper propitiations to them, by insuring they receive a proper burial, and by carrying out their pre- and post-mortem instructions. Shrines or sites of contact for ancestors may be constructed in homes, at graves, in elevated caves, on forested hills, on the banks of specific rivers, and in front of selected stones and geological formations. All the afore-mentioned sites of contact are reminiscent of the placements of Jake's remains as his bones are transported from Pennsylvania to Michigan and finally to Virginia. The memorial practices of the living insure ancestors' personal immortality, continued life in both the physical and spiritual worlds.[15] Death – absolute and permanent severance from the living – has yet to occur, but not in the future sense. Because time flows counter-clockwise, backward and not forward in traditional thought, death lies in the unspecified past.

Mainly consulting the living-dead ancestors on matters concerning the family, the living beseech ancestral ratification of marriages and the assur-ance of fertility. It is believed that the increase of the clan particularly interests the living-dead since, as inhabitants of the spirit world, they yearn for a viable way of crossing back into the mainstream of the living, effecting their own familial rebirth and earthly return as the fictional Beloved does. In cultures "[w]here the belief in reincarnation prevails, there is thought to be a constant going and coming between the two worlds; and where there is no such belief there is recognition that 'living' and 'dead' are linked in an indissoluble network by their *force vitale*."[16] The living, therefore, do not attribute childlessness or barrenness, one of the greatest curses, to ancestor retribution because they know that it blocks the channel of reincarnation, the return of the living-dead as the grandchildren of succeeding genera-tions. Living survivors generally ascribe procreative failures to "witches or to some inscrutable god."[17]

Living relatives and descendants regard the ancestral living-dead ambiv-alently, with both affection and fear. They "are wanted and yet not wanted."[18] They fondly remember those who have crossed over into the afterworld, but they do not relish spectral visits from them. Disturbing, posthumous visitations, mainly with the oldest living elders, may take place in order for the departed to resolve current family issues, to express dissatisfaction with improper burial, or to demonstrate unrest from pre- or post-mortem offenses.[19] For ancestors who no longer have surviving relatives who knew them in life and whose names subsequent generations have forgotten, their "appearances" cause fear and dread since no one recognizes them as family. The dying process of the living-dead is now complete as they no longer have personal immortality only collective immortality, anonymous subsumption into the spirit family.

Passing from the physical or earthly realm to the spiritual afterworld does not guarantee induction into ancestorship, nor, as Mbiti affirms, does ancestorship guarantee exclusive access to past knowledge or sole right to the realm of the living-dead:

[In Yoruba culture, for example,] not all people who have died become ancestors, or at least ancestors to whom any ritual attention is paid. Special qualities are required for there to be such ritual attention. The most important quality in a family ancestor is having lived a good life, and as a consequence, having achieved the state of *orum rere*, which literally means being in the "good heaven" . . . The next important quality is the attainment of a ripe old age, for this is a good indication that one has fulfilled one's destiny. Yet another quality is the possession of dutiful descendants who remember the ancestor with appreciation and are willing to continue to perform the ceremonies in his [or her] honor.[20]

To speak of everyone who has passed on as an ancestor is misleading and broadens the concept to encompass living-dead that it excludes, "since there are spirits and living-dead of children, brothers, sisters, barren wives and other members of the family who were not in any way the 'ancestor.'"[21] However, there is nothing to suggest that the unancestralized living-dead – the living-dead who have not lived a good life, are young, or do not have dutiful descendants to remember them and perform rituals in their honor – are barred from afterworld past or collective knowledge.

The above general overview is principally applicable to the family ancestor class whose veneration is based on a descent group, but it is not the only ancestral class. Tribal ancestors may at times intersect with family enclaves. Their names and feats are known through personal knowledge or oral tradition. A third class, divinized ancestors, has veneration links to local and national historical groups.

THE INFINITE PAST – BELOVED AS TIMELESS
LIVING-DEAD PARADIGM

The crawling-already? girl, later reincarnated through an inexplicable metaphysical channel into Beloved, is neither the ancestor nor the author-ially constructed ancestral presence in *Beloved* – her life is short, her destiny unfulfilled, and after her second and final severance from the living she is unremembered and unritualized. She is, however, the only Morrison character that has a traceable afterlife that maps the ontological movement of the living-dead through the backward, counterclockwise spatialization of African traditional time. Many readers of *Beloved* have difficulty accepting Morrison's blending of a neoslave narrative with what, by all accounts, appears to be the Western ghost story – the spirit of a victim of violent death haunts the resident(s) of a house that is socially and spatially isolated from its surrounding community. In actuality, the novel creatively presents a revised concept of death that draws centrally from an Africanist world-view that perceives death not as an "end" of life, a cessation of conscious-ness occurring at a fixed moment in time beyond which no vital activity extends, but as a dynamic process commencing in the present and spread-ing over a protracted period receding into the past. Fifteen years earlier in *Sula*, with the title character's passing and necessary river crossing of her spirit that ushers the living-dead into the afterworld, Morrison establishes a fleeting glimpse of "life" in the infinite past that traditional cultures steadfastly embrace. Transitioning from the living to the living-dead, Sula "thought, 'it didn't even hurt. Wait'll I tell Nel.'"[22] Albeit brief, her contiguous animation and posthumous consciousness inaugurate a cosmo-logical precedent for *Beloved*'s treatment of timeless people, the ancestor proper, in a timeless place, the afterworld, where all who have lived, their collective memories, their collective experiences, and every event – all of the past – are. "'Wait'll I tell Nel,'" the final reported thought of Sula, implies that the living-dead's communication with the living is still possible.

In some ancestor cultures the recently born are held to be the last in contact with the living-dead. Young children described as "old souls," possessing inexplicable wisdom in addition to characteristics or physical distinctions of a departed family member, are suspected of having knowl-edge beyond their years from exposure to the living-dead throughout time in the infinite past. Returning as an infantile adult, the reincarnated Beloved, a recent inhabitant of the afterworld, is the last to have direct contact with the ancestors and to have access to their collective memories and experiences of all of the past. The imposition of African traditional time, therefore, has enormous ramifications on the ancestors, the ancestral world, and the directional movement of human experience and existence.

While Western scholars praise Morrison's innovative modern/post-modern, nonlinear treatment of time, her representations are actually pre-modern, a recuperation of Africans' traditional perception of time that is cyclical rather than linear and has an infinite past rather than an infinite future as in Western discourse and ontology. An Africanist con-sciousness guides Morrison's predisposition to reify alternate ways of knowing and existing. Referencing all that has preceded the present moment from an Africanist perspective, Morrison contends, "It's infinite, the past. I suspect more infinite than the future."[23]

Mbiti explains that "The linear concept of time in [W]estern thought, with an indefinite past, present and infinite future, is practically foreign to African thinking. The future is virtually absent because events which lie in it have not taken place, they have not been realized and cannot, therefore, constitute time." Therefore, within the conceptual traditional frame, "time is a two-dimensional phenomenon, with a long *past*, a *present* and virtually *no future*."[24] Hence in many traditional societies there is no word for the distant future. Natural events that occur routinely calibrate an abbreviated and quantitatively inconstant future that extends no farther than the next cycle of seasons:

If, however, future events are certain to occur, or if they fall within the inevitable rhythm of nature, they at best constitute only *potential time*, not *actual time*. What is taking place now unfolds the future, but once an event has taken place, it is no longer in the future but in the present and the past. *Actual time* is therefore what is present and what is past. It moves "backward" rather than "forward"; and people set their minds not on future things, but chiefly on what has taken place.[25]

Mathematical moments and numerical calendars[26] mark Western time that is commodified, utilized, bought and sold. Events and phenomenon calendars[27] measure African time that, inversely, is created and produced. Mbiti asserts that the African makes as much time as he wishes; he is not a slave to it.[28] Simulating circularity, African time goes back and forth between past and present, merges past and present, and recounts past events in a present sense. Qualifying the African's orientation of time in this way after his visit to West Africa, Richard Wright notes in *Black Power* (1954) that "[T]he African did not strain to feel that which was not yet in existence ... His was a circular kind of time; the past had to be made like the present. One did not leave the past behind; one took it with one."[29] Making the past like the present, Morrison implements the Africanist conception of traditional time as an identifying and identifiable quality of Blackness. Her characters do not leave the past behind; they take it with them. Individuals relive and render past experiences and events in the present tense and in the present sense. In *Beloved* Sethe, who carries the trauma of her past ubiquitously in her present, relegates the future to no time. She instructs her daughter Denver, who wants to defer the prospect of a painful hair-combing until the next day, "Today is always here ... Tomorrow never."[30] The text of *Beloved* delimits the forward movement of time.

The timeline and tense structuring of *Beloved* move along a past-like-present, fluid nonlinearity. Its plot moves back and forth between past and present, lacing the two so inextricably that the past and present are coeval. The narrative situates the present at 124 Bluestone Road in Cincinnati, Ohio, in 1873; moves to events in the recent past, the main protagonist Sethe and her family's experiences in Cincinnati after 1855; and explains the culmination of events after 1855 with incidents in the later past, Sethe's earlier experiences on the Garners' Kentucky Sweet Home plantation before 1855. The narrative then leaves the later past for the far past, Sethe's childhood before 1849 and her arrival in Kentucky. Moving thereafter to the remote past and to an unspecified time, it records the lived experiences of Africans of the Middle Passage before 1808, the year the United States Continental Congress declared the transatlantic slave trade illegal. Denver's recitation of her birth to Beloved, a recitation she appropriates from Sethe's memory, and Sethe's memory of her escape from Sweet Home via the Underground Railroad and its aftermath are two instances in which Morrison dispenses with the imposition of Western time, posing past remembrances in the present tense. Morrison also suspends the West's past-tense rule governing present-time narration in the novel. She reports two events set in the narrative's present timeline – Beloved's temporary disappearance in the cold house and Sethe's time conflation of the earlier arrival of schoolteacher's posse with Mr. Bodwin's later visit – in the present tense. Moreover, the past is also concomitant with the present through inherited or genetic memory – "rememory" – since, as Sethe warns Denver, "nothing ever dies,"[31] and even persons who did not live through specific events of the past, sharing a collective unconsciousness, can revisit and be revisited by them. A synchronous past and present and the reincarnation of palpable, individual, and collective memories enable Sethe to wrap herself in a "timeless present" when Beloved returns from a "timeless place."[32] Privileging the above concurrent sequencing of time and consciousness is paramount to understanding the reciprocal commerce that the living-dead has with the living.

Sethe's cutting of the infant crawling-already? girl's throat, which precipitates her first traumatic earthly departure, and the Cincinnati, Ohio, women's part Christian part "what they believed would work"[33]oral exorcism of the fully fleshed twenty-year-old revenant Beloved, which hastens her second and final leave-taking, transition the first daughter of Halle and Sethe from the Sasa period of the present to the Zamani period of the past. Two Kiswahili terms,[34]Sasa and Zamani express the African conception of

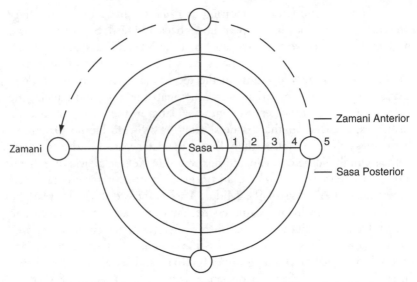

Figure 3. Sasa (the period of conscious living) and Zamani (the period of myth and pre-history). Passage from the Sasa to the Zamani takes four or five generations.[35]

time regression. I borrow them from Mbiti's scholarship to follow his strategy of avoiding confusion with Western thought associations that attend the English words "past," "present," and "future." Mathematically and numerically/quantitatively inconstant because events and not measured increments apportion it, the Sasa has its "own short future, a dynamic present, and an experienced [recent, far, and remote] past." It feeds, disappears into, or "'moves' backward" into the Zamani, the remote and unspecified past, "the graveyard of time" beyond which nothing can go, "the final storehouse for all phenomena and events, the ocean of time in which everything becomes absorbed into a reality that is neither after nor before." As the Sasa, the period of conscious living, flows back into the Zamani, "the period of myth" which dominates pre-history,[36] the two overlap. The posterior remote past of the former overlaps the anterior remote past of the latter (see figure 3). Passing into the afterworld removes a person *gradually* from the Sasa period of lived experiences, recognition, and personal immortality to the Zamani period of myth, disremembrance, and collective immortality. The passage is a gradual forgetting as living survivors disremember the individual's name and deeds or as they, too, join the afterworld assemblage, foreclosing the possible continuance of earthly remembrance.

Living in the present of the Sasa before her throat-cutting, the crawling-already? girl, after she passes on, continues to "live" in the recent past of the Sasa period, the period of recognition. Those who knew her in life carry memories of her and she has personal immortality. They recall her by name, "though not necessarily mentioning it."[37] They remember her personality, her character, and incidents of her life. When she reappears in the physical world, as spirit then flesh, Sethe and her sister Denver do not fear her. Death for Beloved has yet to occur in the unspecified past beyond which nothing can go, the Zamani.

The routed Beloved, crossing the river into the afterworld for the second time and with the passage of time and/or familial forgetfulness, sinks beyond the Sasa horizon into the Zamani when those alive no longer remember or deliberately forget her personally by name. And name recognition is of the utmost importance for the continuation of life in the afterworld. In her latter human/fleshed transfiguration, she tells the residents at 124 Bluestone Road that her name is Beloved, but the text never apprises the reader of the crawling-already? girl's given name. After her exorcism from the Cincinnati community, the final passages of the novel amplify the loneliness of the nameless and forgotten older daughter of Sethe: "Everybody knew what she was called, but nobody anywhere knew her name. Disremembered and unaccounted for, she cannot be lost because no one is looking for her, and even if they were, how can they call her if they don't know her name? Although she has claim, she is not claimed."[38]

Passage from the Sasa to the Zamani typically takes four or five generations, the lapse of time needed for the earthly recollection/recognition of an individual to dissipate in the complete sense. But "if the living- dead are suddenly forgotten, this means that they are cast out of the Sasa period, and are in effect excommunicated, their personal immortality is destroyed."[39] Beloved, quickly forgotten, completes the process of death at an accelerated rate, but she does not vanish out of existence. She enters into the state of collective immortality, "the state of the spirits who are no longer formal members of the human families."[40] Because of lost contact, if she appears to her living descendants they will neither recognize her physically nor call her name. Her appearance will cause fear and dread. The living may refer to her and may even mention her by name, in genealogies for instance, but it is an empty name reference or a name that is "more or less without a personality or at best with only a mythological personality built around fact and fiction."[41]

The timeless totality of Beloved's inherited or collective memory spans the present Sasa backward to lived experiences that predate her own contemporary consciousness. From the conscious living of her very short life as the crawling-already? girl, Beloved recalls the riveting sparkle of Sethe's "diamond" earrings, the lullaby Sethe composed to pacify her children, and the face of her mother "which is still her face, just as babies when they are around two, ... cannot yet see themselves as separate from their mother and thus see her face as their face."[42] From personally lived experiences before passing on from Sethe's cutting of her throat, to exposure to the experiences of the whole lived past where all is present, where "all of it is now ... it is always now ... there is no where [Beloved] stop[s]."[43]

Beloved's stream of collective (un)consciousness in the fourth section of the novel's second part is a threnody that laments the lived experiences of countless Africans who survived or succumbed to the inhumanity of the Middle Passage and now are among the living-dead. One of a multitude crouching and thrashing against chafing iron restraints in the hold of a rat-infested slave ship, she actively relives individually and collectively the lived pasts of those countless others alluded to in the novel's epigraph, "the sixty million or more" whose names we do not know and for whom the novel functions as a fixing ceremony. Like them, she is also too hungry to eat moldy, sea-green bread, too dehydrated to perspire or urinate. Individuals of European descent, "the men without skin,"[44] throw the bodies of the shackled who have corporeally expired from starvation and thirst into the sea, but before their removal, those who still "are trying to leave their bodies behind"[45] must stare into the immobile faces of those who have passed on. Beloved's access to the living-dead of the afterworld and the testimony she gives as/of one of the many captives who preferred death to the depraved conditions of a transatlantic slave ship crossing confirm the first-hand observations of Belinda Royall, a real-life survivor of the Middle Passage. Taken from the Volta River region of the northern Gold Coast in 1724 when she was approximately twelve years old and brought first to Antigua and then to Massachusetts where she lived most of her life, Royall recollected to an amanuensis her shock at "[s]cenes which her imagination had never conceived of, a floating world ... three hundred Africans in chains, suffering the most excruciating torment; and some of them rejoicing that the pangs of death came like a balm to their wounds."[46]

The more stunning details of the Middle Passage consciousness with which Morrison imbues Beloved's ancestral stream of collective (un)consciousness survives only in written form in a "consequential amount of descriptive material" in *The Interesting Narrative of the Life of Olaudah Equiano, or Gustavus Vassa, the African. Written by Himself* (1789). *The Interesting Narrative* covers incidents from Olaudah Equiano's abduction from what is now Nigeria, voyage across the Atlantic, arrival in Barbados, and time spent in Virginia where a British naval officer purchased him and took him to England. His narrative "stands alone and remains the classic first-hand account of the Middle Passage experience of Africans who were taken to Britain's New World colonies."[47] He relates the experience of living in a cramped, oppressively hot ship's hold filled with the dead and the dying:

[W]hen the ship we were in, had got in all her cargo, they made ready ... and we were all put under the deck ... The stench of the hold while we were on the coast was so intolerably loathsome, that it was dangerous to remain there for any time, and some of us had been permitted to stay on the deck for the fresh air; but now that the whole ship's cargo were confined together, it became absolutely pestilential. The closeness of the place, and the heat of the climate, added to the number in the ship, which was so crowded that each had scarcely room to turn himself, almost suffocated us. [... T]he air soon became unfit for respiration, from a variety of loathsome smells, and brought on a sickness among the slaves, of which many died ... This wretched situation was again aggravated by the galling [chafing] of the chains, now become insupportable, and the filth of the necessary tubs, into which the children often fell, and were almost suffocated. The shrieks of the women, and the groans of the dying, rendered the whole a scene of horror almost inconceivable.[48]

Historian Jerome Handler states that many of Equiano's Ibo countrymen "who were on the same ship that took him to Barbados, the first port of call, were sold on the island" and many, as noted above, died on the way. If these are Equiano's own experiences, his "narrative ... provides a unique case where the narrative of one individual can be viewed as collective testimony of the experiences of a particular shipload of Africans."[49] and authenticates the experiences that Morrison grafts onto Beloved as inextricably Black. If the narrative is a pastiche of others' experiences grafted onto Equiano's personal past, as critical debate now alleges, then ironically he, too, "relives," although quite differently from the fictional Beloved, the collective experiences of the living-dead ancestor with whom individuals of the African diaspora have lost personal contact.

Those who have kinship/tribal ties to and/or knew in life the crawling-already? girl – her maternal grandmother Ma'am and Ma'am's countrywoman Nan, Sweet Home's Sixo, and her paternal grandmother Baby Suggs – were, when alive, mediators of the ancestors, ancestral presences for her mother Sethe. Although the reader is uncertain of Nan's current status, three of the four, in the plot's present timeline, are now in the timeless place of the ancestors. As a living elder, each is active as the ancestral presence at specific sites and stages of Sethe's maturing. While Ma'am's body is the physical site of the sign of ancestral presence and power, Nan is the ancestral presence for Sethe during her formative years before Sweet Home. Sixo assumes the role at Sweet Home to assist a coming-of-age Sethe and to serve as the paradigm of African manhood for her and the Sweet Home enslaved men. And last, Baby Suggs picks up the ancestral presence mantle for the mature Sethe and her Cincinnati community. As ancestors, each is kept alive in the memories of Sethe, Paul D, Janey Wagon, Stamp Paid, and Patsy the Thirty-Mile Woman, among others, who survive them. African-born and Middle Passage survivors, they are generational bridges at the African and African-America crossroads. All four[50] characters know first-hand the horrors of being spoon-shackled in the bowels of a slave ship with a multitude of captives like Royall, over a three-month ocean voyage of more than 3,700 miles. The captain of each of their respective vessels would have judged the crossing a financial success if the death toll en route did not exceed one-third to one-half of the ship's human cargo.

NAN AND MA'AM: THE ANCESTRAL PRESENCE BEFORE SWEET HOME

Sethe's one-armed wet-nurse and surrogate mother, Nan, voices the past of Ma'am whose work in South Carolina or Louisiana indigo and rice fields from before dawn until after dusk restricts direct exchange between the young girl and her biological mother.[51] Nan's name is the abbreviation of "nana," a title of respect given to ancestors, grandparents, and chiefs that has it origin in the Akan language of West Africa, and of Naná, the divinized ancestor spirit of life and death of the Yoruba orishas.[52] She is the ancestral presence, the benevolent guide for Sethe before the young girl is sold away to Kentucky and Sweet Home. African-born, Nan tells Sethe in Ma'am's and her native language about their experiences on "the island" in the Caribbean, and before that, "the sea," during the transatlantic Middle Passage. In Ma'am's absence Nan reassures her countrywoman's daughter that her mother wanted her from conception. She explains that they "were taken up many times by the crew" during the passage on the sea but Ma'am never psychically acceded to her sexual violation or accepted the progeny of her rape: "She threw them all away but you. The one from the crew she threw away on the island. The others from more whites she also threw away. Without names, she threw them. You she gave the name of the Black man. She put her arms around him. The others she did not put her arms around. Never. Never."[53] The living elder who provides solace and is the literal and figurative giver of sustenance, Nan mediates the past and speaks as Africa to "small girl Sethe."[54] She is as necessary to Sethe's childhood maturing and survival under the system of slavery as Sixo and Baby Suggs are in her coming of age and adulthood. Sethe's biological mother can bridge past and present for her daughter but long hours of field labor, exhaustion after toil, and death by hanging eclipse her presence as comforter in both literal and figurative senses.

Textual clues to the spatial trajectory that the women follow move Ma'am and Nan backward from South Carolina or Louisiana, probably to the British or French Caribbean, where Ma'am discards a crew member's nameless spawn, and finally to West Africa and their native home and ancestral line. Sethe recalls her mother's back "stooping in a watery field in the place of her birth" in "Carolina maybe? Or was it Louisiana?"[55] Her memory's vacillation between Carolina and Louisiana may stem from Sethe's youth or her projection of Baby Suggs's past of working in Carolina rice fields onto Ma'am's past. A modicum of historical and textual evidence supports either location since both had the necessary wetlands for rice cultivation and planters in both states sought West Africans experienced in all facets of rice production.

When slave laborers quickly became the majority in the Carolina lowlands, uprisings and escapes occurred frequently. In locales where planters outnumbered their human chattel, corporal punishment, starvation, and mutilation proved effective in suppressing rebellions, but planter minority status incited uneasiness in the colonial British who settled on the death penalty as the best deterrent against insurrections. With a surplus of labor, the execution of a few insurgents would have minimal production and financial repercussions.[56] Attempting escape or participating in an insurrection is in all likelihood the cause of Ma'am's hanging. The potential for one or the other ostensibly looms in her mind when she forewarns Sethe that there might come a time when her daughter might not recognize her face. Her mother foresees a death, if either action is unsuccessful, that will distort her physically. A cross and circle on her ribcage under her breast will identify her body if her appearance is altered.

Western readers tend to interpret Ma'am's indelible cross and circle as a chattel marking that identifies her as the property of a specific slave owner or slave shipment, as it was the custom to sear with branding irons all human captives who had been gathered for exportation when overland caravans arrived at West African coastal forts. But the cross and circle insignia is an inconclusive clue to Ma'am's slave owner or to her place of origin. Indeterminacy surrounds its maker and its meaning. A nineteenth-century West African-born woman enslaved in either South Carolina or Louisiana where the American Voodoo or Haitian Voudoun versions of Dahomey's Vodun flourished as an amalgamation of different West and Central African tribal religions would certainly have an alternate interpretation of and reason for bearing the symbol. Ma'am's exposure to the geometric symbol would have been assured for "Kongo and Angola captives made up the majority culture among the slaves of New Orleans [. . . and] South Carolina."[57]

The crossroads – crossed, perpendicular right angles – is the most consistently represented figure in Voudoun ritual in the French Caribbean. In her *Divine Horsemen: Voodoo Gods of Haiti* (1970), Maya Deren, a mid-twentieth-century Voudoun initiate in Haiti, lists the Fula, Mandingo, Ashanti, Dahomean, Hausa, Yoruba, and Kongo as tribes that slave traffickers tore from their villages and took to Haiti, where they reconstituted a single religion that centralized the symbol.[58] A Voudoun adept would associate it with the Dahomean divinity Legba whose cross-roads symbol represented by a circle with a tree of the cross overlay signified the intersection between the two worlds – the visible mortal world and the invisible spiritual world that Legba mediates. The vertical axis of the cross and universe, Legba, loa of the crossroads is the means and avenue of communication between the two realms. Through him as the poteau-mitan or center-post the other loa, spirits considered divine horse-men, enter and possess their serviteurs. Direct West African, West Central African, and intermediate Caribbean exposure to the symbol would stabilize its meaning since all variations of Vodun and Voudoun petition the ancestors through cross-summoning and circle-gathering. In specific rites an individual stood within the symbol drawn on the earth and testified that s/he understood life as reciprocity between the living and living-dead, the "real sources of earthly power and prestige."[59] Substantial evidence exists for the importance of the ancestral function of the circle in West Africa as a whole, but the cross and circle symbol imported from the Kongo region "contributed disproportionately" to the Black Atlantic religious conscious-ness in the Western hemisphere "drawing West and Central Africa closer together culturally than they were previously thought to be." Historian Sterling Stuckey writes that "[t]he use of the circle for religious purposes in slavery was so consistent and profound that one could argue that it was what gave form and meaning to black religion and art. It is understandable that the circle became the chief symbol of heathenism for missionaries, black and white, leading them to seek either to alter it or eradicate it altogether."[60]

The breast covering the cross within a circle on Ma'am's body conceals the Kongo Yowa, the most important ancestral sign in Voudoun, the West African-based religion, transforming her body into the site of ancestral presence and power. Sethe calls her mother Ma'am, a contraction of the French "Madam"; however, the referent is also an abbreviation for "Maman," the courtesy title given to a Voudoun priestess and loa, or "Mambo," the title given to a Voudoun or Voodoo priestess. The common practice of calling a priestess "Maman" indicates that a serviteur expects the priestess to provide the protection a child "assumes of its parents" and that "the parent commands an authority and respect similar to that which is accorded the priest[ess] and the loa ... This interchangeable relationship reflects the universal tendency of children to regard their parents as gods and priest[esses]s."[61] The Mambo or Maman is the living elder on earth of the priest class that connects the living to the living-dead ancestor. Shortly after showing Sethe the cross and circle, Ma'am passes from the world of the living to the world of the living-dead. Encoded in the Kongo signage under Ma'am's breast is the way, the spiritual process, by which Sethe will "know" her mother, that is, have continuing knowledge of and access to her ancestrally after her severance from earthly life.

Because enslaved Africans throughout the American South were familiar with Voudoun and its attendant cross and circle symbolism, Ma'am and Nan's exposure to Voodoo/Voudoun/Vodun probably occurred in South Carolina or Louisiana, Barbados or the French Caribbean (Haiti, Dominica, Guadeloupe, and Martinique were the primary centers of Voudoun), or in West Africa. Textual ethnographic clues also point to a specific cultural region of West Africa as their place of origin. Their removal from their ancestral homeland along the banks of the Niger River in Mali, a primary African wet region known for the production of rice and millet, through the Caribbean to Louisiana or South Carolina where Voodoo flourished and whose regions were ideal for cultivating rice is very plausible. Slave traders transported many Malians experienced in rice cultivation to Louisiana, stopping briefly in the French Caribbean where some New Orleans planters met slave ships in Haiti and transferred their property to the mainland themselves.[62]

Sethe's memory preserves remnants of Ma'am's, Nan's, and thus her own African ancestral heritage. More than the language they spoke that she could not speak, Sethe remembers the women dancing the antelope. Bambaras (Bamanas), members of the dominant ethnic group of Mali whose name means "those that refused to be ruled" and whose ancestors are the Mandingos (Mandinkas) have the antelope as their cult animal. They celebrate their ancestry by dancing in male and female pairs with Chiwara figures, carved antelopes with long horns, to insure a prosperous harvest. The larger Chiwara, the male, represents the sun; the smaller with a young antelope on her back symbolizes mother earth. The two dancing together signify the balance needed for a successful harvest. Because of the creolization of cultures and customs, dancing the antelope does not require Ma'am to be a Bambara/Mandingo, though it is a fitting tribal affiliation for Ma'am given her implied unwillingness to be ruled and subsequent hanging.[63]

Years later, the recall of sights, sounds, and the rhythmic dance of an ancestral homeland from the time before Sweet Home remains with Sethe. Her living elders dancing the antelope long ago informs Sethe's imaginative envisaging of the swift-running African ruminant, "since she had never seen one,"[64] to describe her labor pains as she gives birth to the next generation of the women's descendants. Her children will function as human engrams by which they, Ma'am and Nan as ancestors, will be carried back into the mainstream of the living. The Kongo cosmogram replicated underneath Ma'am's breast, a place of nurturance, indicates that she understands the reciprocity between the living and the living-dead. After Ma'am passes on, Nan continues ancestral reciprocity by keeping Ma'am and Africa alive in Sethe's memory.

SIXO – THE ANCESTRAL PRESENCE AT SWEET HOME

The least adulterated ancestral presence, the indigo – blue-black – Sixo, who dances privately among the trees at night to insure that his bloodlines remain open, consciously chooses to live an African traditional past which requires him to reject an American present. African-born and intuiting that one's identity is bound to one's consciousness and language, he declines the offer of Mr. Garner, Sweet Home's liberal slave master, to teach him "to count on paper" and to read, suspecting "it would change his mind – make him forget things he shouldn't and memorize things he shouldn't."[65] Thereafter, he renounces speaking English altogether, declaring "there was no future in it."[66] Because Western "[t]ime never worked the way Sixo thought,"[67] he is forever out of sync with the temporality of the people who enslave him. Efforts to coordinate the precise measure of events required to cook potatoes perfectly overnight in an earth oven and to make time to be with Patsy, the woman he walks thirty miles to visit on an adjacent plantation, consistently go awry. Clearly, the Middle Passage conversion from African to African American does not pertain to Sixo. He will never be African American. The ancestral presence at Sweet Home, Sixo is a fusion of feminine nurturer and masculine paragon, bearer of intellectual wit and wisdom, and binder of the reciprocity between the living-dead and the living.

Associated with masculine fire and feminine earth and having a "flame-red tongue,"[68] Sixo, who experiments nightly with controlling fire in the earth and laughs victoriously during his own immolation, has an elementally balanced and dually gendered identity comparable to Esu, Mawu-Lisa, and many of the spirits, divinities, and trickster figures of West African cultures. Mastering the elements and withstanding trial by fire, he corresponds with the representation in Haitian literature of the spiritually adept Voudoun kanzo initiate that the loa protect.[69] And he, inversely, protects and nurtures. His maternal guidance proves invaluable to the newly arrived fourteen-year-old Sethe who is ill-equipped to handle the demands placed on a single Sweet Home house servant (and later on a young mother) who lacks culturally identified female counsel. A veritable store house of practical knowledge in the domestic sphere, the man above the Sweet Home men is "the biggest help"[70] to Sethe's rites of passage from girl to woman and woman to mother. One emergency, the realigning of her older son Howard's thumb, broken by a cow, denotes Sixo's surrogate mothering of Sethe's children and the comforting tutelage he brings her in the same capacity. To neutralize gender difference and sexual tension between them, Morrison carefully exempts Sethe from Sixo's sexual objectification by channeling his sexual energy entirely onto Patsy, the Thirty-Mile Woman. In touch with his feminine side, Sixo understands that the Thirty-Mile Woman is essential to his balance, his wholeness; she gathers the pieces of him together. He is the only Sweet Home enslaved man not paralyzed with sexual desire for Sethe during the year that she takes to select a husband from among Paul F, Paul A, Paul D, and Halle.

Assured of his African worldview, Sixo impresses Sethe with his freedom to be himself, to trust his instincts, his ways of knowing, and to draw upon his traditions for survival strategies in the New World. Sixo dismisses stroke as the cause of Mr. Garner's death and imposes his own interpretation. He determines that the Sweet Home owner who returns one evening slumped over his mare died not of a ruptured blood vessel but of "a shot in the ear put there by a jealous neighbor."[71] Never surrendering mentally or emotionally to his oppressors or their conception of death, he does not mourn Mr. Garner's passing like the others.

Unintimidated by Western intellect, Sixo improvises using West African oral folk culture to match wits with schoolteacher, Mr. Garner's brother-in-law and successor. Following the trickster strategy of Esu- or Anancy-modeled logic, he denies stealing a shoat as he brazenly eats it before the new Sweet Home master. He killed, butchered, cooked, and ate the pig only to improve schoolteacher's property, himself. Anancy (Anansi), the Twi word for spider, is the small black arachnoid of Ashanti fables that outwits formidable opponents and whose clever escapades were spread as Middle Passage retentions throughout the Caribbean and the Americas. The trickster strategist of a series of oral stories dealing with food shortage and acquisition, Anancy eats while others starve.[72]

Those who dominate Sixo's body – and they do so only in part because he roams freely at night – do not dominate his mind and spirit. Psychologically complacent, the other enslaved Sweet Home men do not have his militant daring to resist the institution of chattel slavery aggressively. The self-determined Sixo does not wear the shackles of a slave mentality. While the Pauls and Halle debate purchasing their freedom, Sixo is the first among them to learn of the Underground Railroad, to share with them its existence, and to decide to escape by its clandestine route.

Sixo is comparable to Brother, a towering Sweet Home sycamore tree under which he ritualistically sits at midday. Underneath Brother is the hole Sixo has dug and filled with twigs and rock to form his earth oven. The hole under the tree, the highest moment of the sun when he sits there, and the tree itself are analagous to the cross and circle of the Kongo Yowa. His presence at the horizontal and vertical axes of Brother at the noon solar point implies Sixo's spiritual groundedness – he sits at the crossroads of the living-dead and the living – at the peak of his maleness and strength on earth.[73] Sixo is an imposing, immovable figure firmly rooted in African spirituality and masculinity that sets the standard for African manhood. Years later, Paul D reminiscently compares Sixo with Brother: "Now *there* was a man, and *that* was a tree."[74] The manhood Mr. Garner confers on the Pauls and Halle pales in comparison to the manliness that Sixo's presence confirms. When Paul D "looks at himself through Garner's eyes, he sees one thing. Through Sixo's another. One makes him feel righteous. One makes him feel ashamed."[75]

Because the sycamore tree figures him as the gateway Gran Bois Legba who guards the mortal and immortal highway, Sixo's urgency to secure his place in the circle of life is consist with his Voudoun association. As he is a binder of the physical and metaphysical worlds, his belief in the reciprocity of life between the living and the living-dead ancestor, a mutual insurance of continuing life for one by the other in their respective spheres of existence, drives his determination to secure progeny. He urgently pursues procreation with a profundity unknown to the Pauls and Halle who have nonreproductive sexual relations with calves while waiting for the new girl's (Sethe's) selection of a husband that will resolve the issue of mating and producing offspring for only one of them. Walking to see the Thirty-Mile Woman with sexual consummation on his mind, Sixo, respectful of others' land and ancestors, asks permission of the Redmen's Presence to use the deserted stone lodge as his and Patsy's bridal chamber. He abandons its use, however, in his haste to insure that another man does not impregnate the "already fourteen and scheduled for somebody's arms"[76] Patsy and foreclose his own immediate guarantee of reciprocal life. During their flight to the Underground Railroad, Patsy and his unborn child, Seven-O, are his primary concerns. Pushing the pregnant Patsy into a creekbed when slave catchers draw near, he sacrifices himself as a decoy, running in the opposing direction to distract them from her and secure his unborn child's birth, freedom, and long earthly life as well as his own longevity in the afterworld.

Fearless of death because he has achieved progenitorial remembrance, the laughing Sixo claims the victory of personal immortality. He can now transition from the role of ancestral presence to the role of living-dead ancestor confident that he will remain alive in the afterworld. Unless he has a close relative and preferably a child "to remember him when he has physically died, then he is nobody and simply vanishes out of [the Sasa period of] human existence like a flame when it is extinguished."[77] Thus his calling out victoriously "Seven-O!" in the face of schoolteacher and his posse's thwarted attempt to burn him has literal and figurative implications. Sixo has generational continuity that transcends the Middle Passage. Five generations precede him and one follows. The Thirty-Mile Woman carries the child who, once it is born, will be his externalized physical continuation. Seven-O is the mortal cornerstone upon which his continued Sasa existence rests and is the first generation that will insure his father's personal immortality for five to seven generations to come.[78] Sixo has carried out his religious and ontological duty to marry and procreate since "[p]rocreation is the absolute way of insuring that a person is not cut off from personal immortality." And in African traditional communities, "marriage and procreation ... are a unity: without procreation marriage is incomplete."[79] One solidifies the other.

BABY SUGGS – THE ANCESTRAL PRESENCE IN CINCINNATI

Denver's speculation that Baby Suggs must be stopping her sister's spirit from returning to the physical world versus Sethe's opposing conjecture

that Baby Suggs, "on the other side, helped" Beloved to return to the realm
of the living illustrate that both daughter and mother view the deceased
Baby Suggs as the living-dead ancestor with vital agency in the afterworld.[80] Sethe expects to have herself the posthumous power that she
confers on her mother-in-law; she declares that she will protect Denver
while she is alive and when she "ain't."[81] Shortly after her arrival in
Cincinnati, Baby Suggs, holy, becomes the revered communal elder and
"unchurched preacher" who personifies African female power.[82] She
instructs the mature Sethe and the African-American community on the
outskirts of Cincinnati in spiritual survival strategies. Well into her sixties
and closest to the ancestors in eldership, Baby Suggs, the ancestral presence
for her granddaughter Denver and the Blacks who reside near her home, a
former way station, espouses a doctrine of self-love and self-determined
grace in the Clearing where her community gathers weekly for spiritual
edification that is counter to a Christian ethos. Her celebration of flesh
evokes the core doctrine of Vodun and Voudoun that does not relegate
flesh to a subordinate position to spirit but unifies them as coequals. She
and others celebrants gather to perform the ring shout, the circular dance
that physically forms the Kongo Yowa to connect their material selves with
the spiritual realm. Baby Suggs's unchurched role of issuing the Call to the
ring intensifies her performance with the Black community as elder,
ancestral presence, and uninstitutional priestess.[83]

The collapse of Baby Suggs's faith, love, imagination, and heart after
Sethe's Cincinnati arrival incapacitates her presence as the wise, comforting
elder. Balance in all things is a crucial African precept that must be upheld
in all circumstances lest destabilizing excess encroaches. Offsetting stabilizing balance, Baby Suggs's acquiescence to relentless white oppression leaves
her vulnerable to a debilitating melancholia. Living free in the North after
sixty years of bondage in the South, Baby Suggs makes a respected name for
herself as a cobbler, community servant, and Clearing caller. The loss of her
kin due to slavery, however, ultimately breaches the inner resolve that she
had believed inviolable. The excessiveness of white people demonstrates
that there is no free space, real or imagined, where they will not come to
dirty her existence. Because of whites not knowing when to stop, Baby
Suggs loses all of her eight children, including Halle who worked five years
of Sundays to free her. She loses a "husband" named Suggs with whom she
made a pact that whichever one of them got the chance would run for
freedom, and his chance came. When she is a free woman, a letter-writing
campaign to retrieve survivors of her scattered family produces no reun-
ions. After losing in a single day the support of the Cincinnati community

because of her excessive preparation of a feast and the life of a granddaughter at the hands of her intemperate daughter-in-law, Baby Suggs's earthly existence tumbles out of kilter and her heart constricts. In time, after her grandsons Howard and Buglar flee, a surfeit of emotion undercuts Baby Suggs's function as the balanced, benevolent ancestral presence.

Witnessing the killing of her grandchild like her real-life equivalent Mary Garner, the mother-in-law of the Kentucky fugitive slave Margaret Garner whose escape to Cincinnati and murder of her child were sensationalized in 1856, Baby Suggs, also like Mary Garner, is a religious woman who "could not approve or condemn" her daughter-in-law's "rough choice" of killing her child.[84] For Suggs, "[o]ne of the other might have saved her but beaten up by the claims of both, she went to bed. The whitefolks had tired her out at last."[85] Baby Suggs succumbs to an unrestrained malaise that is uncharacteristic of the stable profile of the ancestral mediator.

In a 1987 *Newsweek* interview, Morrison, confirming Baby Suggs's Middle Passage survivorship, states that she "came out of one of those slaveships,"[86] a revelation to many readers. With the exception of a single remark that Baby Suggs makes about massive Black drownings ("There's more of us they drowned than there is all of them ever lived from the start of time"), statements attributable to her throughout *Beloved* evince no definitive first-hand Middle Passage or Africa experiences.[87] It is plausible that she disremembers lived experiences from her very early youth before enslavement and cannot pass down stories of the sustaining force that made her survival in Carolina possible. Perhaps a failing active memory leaves her vulnerable. Notwithstanding her abdication as the balanced ancestral presence, Baby Suggs rallies as the vital living-dead ancestor, speaking from the afterworld to empower Denver, her last-known surviving grandchild, in whose hands her personal immortality rests. From the afterworld, Baby Suggs does not retract her last assessments of "whitepeople" being the "only bad luck in the world" and their not knowing "when to stop."[88] She reinforces it to dissolve all excuses for her granddaughter's inordinate reluctance to step into a racially hostile world:

Remembering ... her grandmother's last and final words, Denver stood on the porch in the sun and couldn't leave it. Her throat itched; her heart kicked – and then Baby Suggs laughed, clear as anything. "You mean I never told you nothing about Carolina? About your daddy? You don't remember nothing about how come I walk the way I do and about your mother's feet, not to speak of her back? I never told you all that? Is that why you can't walk down the steps? My Jesus my."

But you said there was no defense.
"There ain't."
Then what do I do?
"Know it, and go on out the yard. Go on."[89]

Baby Suggs knows from her own personal failing with excessive whites that the excesses of others must be counterbalanced. Her ancestral role is now to insure that the immoderation of whites does not claim her only remaining grandchild, who singly shoulders the responsibility of insuring all of their "lives" in the physical and metaphysical planes.

PILATE DEAD – ANCESTRAL MEDIATION
OF POSTHUMOUS EXCHANGE

Pilate Dead, the ancestral presence in *Song of Solomon*, guides her nephew Macon "Milkman" Dead's reclamation of the memory of Solomon, his paternal great-grandfather who is in danger of descending into the remote past beyond the graveyard of time. Solomon, the African-born enslaved ancestor who oral legend holds reputedly flew back to Africa of his own volition and power, is unknown by name and deed to his youngest son's branch two generations removed. A concatenated series of events – the peculiar institution of slavery, his flight, his wife's Ryna's insanity, a drunken Union soldier's error, the premature deaths of his youngest son Jake and daughter-in-law Singing Bird, Reconstruction, northern migration – and the vagaries of time preclude Solomon's grandchildren and great-grandchildren's knowledge of him, their "ancestor, ... [a] lithe young man with onyx skin and legs as straight as cane stalks, who had a name that was real. A name that was not a joke, nor a disguise, nor a brand name."[90] The consequence of forgetting their great-grandfather is the imminent death of the African ancestor, resulting, according to Mbiti's Kiswahili terminology in a foreshortened Sasa existence and immediate Zamani graveyard descent for Solomon. Dead, the surname that a drunken Union soldier registered in error for Solomon's son Jake, summarizes Milkman's and his unknown great-grandparents' present ontological status. As a Dead who humorously puns that he is already dead, Milkman is the living dead (no hyphen), a "zombie" whose walking-dead condition, Holly Fils-Aimé argues, is the "result of human action" and, therefore, is "a product of society and not a cosmology."[91] Pilate's communications and visitations with her living-dead father and her relay of his messages to the living dead Milkman provide her nephew with essential information from the past, making it possible for Solomon's junior lineage to rescue him from collective immortality, an anonymous subsumption into the spirit family.

Pilate's presence is necessary to direct Milkman, a product of twentieth-century bourgeois consumer culture who has explosive and exploitative relationships with members of his immediate and extended families. Contemptuous of his father Macon Dead and mother Ruth Foster Dead, insensitive to and meddlesome in the affairs of his sisters First Corinthians and Magdalene called Lena, and emotionally careless with his first cousin Hagar whom he discards after sexually conquering her, Milkman, in thirty-three years of living, has received material and emotional comfort and support from kith and kin but never contributed to the psychological and physical wellbeing of anyone inside or outside his Not Doctor Street home in Michigan. Set in motion by Pilate's guidance, Milkman's movement from "stupidity to epiphany"[92] frees him from the egoism, materialism, and ruthless individualism that weigh him down and bar him from the knowledge, pride, and reverence of family and community, past and present. He gains insight into the generations that preceded him, the names and deeds of people that make his privileged life possible. Ironically, it is a self-serving action – stealing Pilate's sack of bones and rocks that he and his accomplice Guitar Baines believe to be gold – that sets up the backward search into the past that ends in the discovery/recovery of Black gold, the name and tribe of Solomon, Milkman's link to Africa, the living-dead ancestor, and self-knowledge. Knowing who his ancestors are teaches him who he is and what personal adjustments are in order to bring his modern American individualism in alignment with his African traditional past that affirms communal/familial interconnectedness and continuity.

Inspired by Pilate's whetting his desire for gold, Michigan-born Milkman, inverting his family's northern migration, travels into the Deads' recent Southern past in Danville, Montour County, Pennsylvania, before visiting its far and remote southern past in Shalimar, Virginia, sites where his ancestors Jake and Solomon lived. Intrigued more by what is behind him – that which flows backward in time and space – than by what is ahead, Milkman is a prime candidate for ancestral recovery. Intuitively he fixates on actual time, what is present and what is past, not potential time, the future. As a young boy, whether looking backward as he rides in his father's Packard or turning in haste to see his sister Lena approaching from the rear before he finishes urinating or walking against a crowd of people and turning to see nothing but their backs and hat

[i]t was becoming a habit – this concentration on things behind him. Almost as though there were no future to be had. But if the future did not arrive, the present [the Sasa] did extend itself, and the uncomfortable little boy in the Packard went to school and at twelve met the boy . . . who would take him to the woman who had as much to do with his future as she had his past.[93]

As the elder force mediating the ancestral past, Pilate has a striking Africanist physiognomy and disposition. African features inherited from her father dismiss any doubt that the Deads are of direct African descent. An amalgam of binaries, Pilate, wearing a man's haircut, cap, and shoes, is androgynously gendered similarly to Sixo in *Beloved*, a reflection of the dual gendering and balancing of opposites that prevails in West African traditional thought. Male nurturing during her formative years makes her the "apogee . . . of the best of that which is female and the best of that which is male."[94] Physically defying the traces of time in the form of hairless, scarless, and wrinkleless skin belies her age of sixty-eight, empowering her towering frame with the flexibility of shape shifters and trickster figures of West African lore.

Pilate is the human manifestation of the tree of the crossroads Legba of Voudoun who mediates communication between the physical and metaphysical worlds. When Milkman first meets "the tall black tree" Pilate whose head is wrapped in black, he observes that "she was all angles . . . One foot pointed east [sunrise] and one pointed west [sunset]"[95] like roots spreading to either side of her in the earth. Her arboreal stature and feet alignment configure the intersection of the vertical and horizontal axes. To complete Pilate's affiliation as the sacred tree of the cross, the means and avenue of communication between the mortal and ancestral worlds, four huge pine trees stand at the back of her house,[96] and she perpetually smells of pine. Macon explains his sister's knowledge of the afterworld by informing his son that Pilate "can't teach you a thing you can use in this world. Maybe the next, but not this one."[97]

Pilate has a close supportive, posthumous communication with her living-dead father who instructs her from the afterworld.[98] In spite of his earthly death, she testifies to her father's personal immortality. Present with Macon when one of the land-greedy Butlers, their Montour County neighbors, shot him in the back of the head in order to expropriate his property, Pilate insists, "Ain't but three Deads alive." She and Macon are two. Her slain father is the third:[99]

"I saw Papa shot. Blown off a fence five feet into the air. I saw him wigglin on the ground, but not only did I not see him die. I seen him since he was shot . . . Macon seen him too. After he buried him, after he was blown off that fence. We both seen him. I see him still. He's helpful to me, real helpful. Tells me things I need to know ... It's a good feelin to know he's around. I tell you he's a person I can always rely on. I tell you somethin else. He's the *only* one."[100]

Although his words are spoken in jest, Reverend Cooper, the Danville minister whose stories immortalize Macon Dead, also testifies to his murdered neighbor's powers of resurrection: "Can't nobody keep him down! Not no Macon Dead! Not in this world! And not in the next!"[101] Seeing him since he was shot and interpreting his cryptic messages, Pilate is the only elder in Morrison's canon who, last with and closest to the ancestor when he was alive, has direct and repeated posthumous visits from the ancestral living-dead.

What appears to be a Christian analogue – the resurrection and post-humous visits of Macon Dead the first occurring on the third day following his death – takes on the subtleties of the pre-Christian four moments of the sun and the four constituent elements mapping, for Pilate and her brother, his personal immortality and the movements of the living-dead through time. After Pilate and Macon leave the big house sanctuary that the Butlers' servant Circe gives them and become lost in the Montour County woods in the black of midnight – the Yowa's highest point of a person's otherworldly strength – wind announces their father's specter walking in front of them. At sunrise, when "the sun was nearly a quarter way cross the sky," he appears again in the sunlight sitting on a tree stump and looking as though his face were underwater, allusions to the living-dead's spirit return by way of a vertical tree axis and submergence below the Kalunga line. Their resurrected father retreats from the sun into the woods. At intervals he reappears, staring past them at ponds, shading his eyes from the sun and looking at the valley floor. Right before sunset, after "the land itself, the only one [of the four elements] that they knew and knew intimately begins to terrorize them," their living-dead father beckons them into a hillside cave, a common shrine for the interment of deceased venerable elders.[102]

At sunset, the moment of the sun synonymous with the inevitable organic process of death, Macon Dead the first arrives at the cave where fishermen have improperly discarded his decomposing body. Seized by affection and fear, Macon and Pilate choose to follow his lead because his spiritual manifestation is recognizable; he looks like their father, and their father, they reason, would not hurt them. In time, he visits only Pilate, first uttering only "Sing" and then much later a second cryptic remark, "You just can't fly on off and leave a body."[103] She interprets both utterances wrongly because she does not know that "Sing" is her mother's name and the "body" she "just can't fly on off and leave" is her father's, not the remains of a man Macon stabs out of fear in the cave and for whose death she assumes joint responsibility. Pilate is the junior member of Jake's lineage who will act on his inscrutable utterances and for whom she will carry out his post-mortem instructions, because she intuitively understands ancestral alliance and obedience and has had experiences living on an island off the Virginia coast with a group of African Americans whose African-traditional beliefs and practices are less diluted.

Because Pilate's ancestral mediation misinterprets "Sing" as an action command and not her Indian mother's name that her father could not speak after she died in childbirth, Macon the first fails to secure Singing Bird's personal immortality, while his own afterworld survival is in equal jeopardy. Pilate, a newborn, and Macon, only four at the time of Singing Bird's death, were too young to remember her name and would respond with fear and dread at her unfamiliar face if she appeared before them. Ironically, Pilate does not wholly err in comprehending "Sing" as a literal command, for it is the singing of the Shalimar, Virginia, children that recuperates Jake's name and genealogy for the Deads and from death, from sinking beyond the Zamani horizon of the graveyard of time. At some point in the past, Pilate was exposed to Solomon's song but she or others have metamorphosed it into a blues complaint that substitutes "Sugarman" for the name of her paternal grandfather. Spoken as an averment but loaded with irony and prophecy, Singing Bird's observation is on the cusp of becoming true: "Macon Dead," the "new name would wipe out the past – wipe it all out."[104]

Of imminent concern is the familial/tribal disremembrance and Sasa deaths that threaten Solomon and Jake. Cut off from active access to their dead because of spatial dispossession and temporal discontinuity, Solomon's Michigan descendants do not know their grandfather's and great-grandfather's given names. Jake's posthumous visit to Pilate and declaration to her shortly after she gives birth to Reba signify his initiative from the afterworld to insure if not his wife's then his own personal immortality with successive generations. Macon Dead the first is still in the Sasa because his children recognize him, but his grandchildren have no memory of him; therefore his existence in the afterworld is heading rapidly toward the Zamani and collective immortality. Only two Deads who knew him in life survive, and distant acquaintances, friends such as Reverend Cooper in Danville, Pennsylvania, and Susan Byrd, his niece by marriage in Shalimar, Virginia, are approaching the ends of their own earthly existences. The elder of the remaining Deads, his son Macon, is too distracted with material acquisition to oversee spiritual affairs. The younger Pilate, balanced in both worlds, will dutifully oversee his proper burial and retention in the circle of life.

The stretch of earth that Jake makes his homeland converts from a material asset into a metaphysical liability since it figures in the termination of his living life and complicates his dead life.[105] The Butlers murder him for Lincoln's Heaven, a tract of land of about one hundred and fifty acres that has a wealth of oak and pine trees. At the moment of his murder, Jake is armed and sitting atop a fence guarding the entrance to Lincoln's Heaven. To the ancestors in death, as to the elders in life, land matters. Wrongfully and violently taken, the family land will not belong in perpetuity to Jake, now the ancestor. His failure to "pass it on"[106] deprives his children of its usage. Their expulsion from the place of his burial, a parcel of land far removed from his people in Virginia, prohibits their walking on his grave or the graves of other ancestors. To follow traditional burial custom would require his kin to return his body to his birth home.

In African consciousness there is a great reciprocity or unity between land or space and time. One is the coefficient of the other. Often one word serves for both, and content defines both. Geographical nearness matters most in space; experiential nearness, that which is in the Sasa, matters most in time. "For this reason," Mbiti points out, "Africans are particularly tied to the land, because it is a concrete expression of both their Zamani and their Sasa." As he explains:

The land provides them with the roots of existence, as well as binding them mystically to their departed. People walk on the graves of their forefathers, and it is feared that anything separating them from these ties will bring disaster to family and community life. To remove Africans by force from their land is an act of such great injustice that no foreigner can fathom it. Even when people voluntarily leave their homes in the countryside and go to live or work in the cities, there is a fundamental severing of ties which cannot be repaired and which often creates psychological problems [with] which urban life cannot as yet cope.[107]

A consequence of his life and his land being grievously taken from him and his children being unjustly dispossessed of his property, Jake's earthly displacement and unrest in the afterworld is a metaphor for Africans' forced removal as enslaved persons from their homelands and involuntary transportation to America. His children's deprivation of a landed birthright and their existential angst in the New World where they are unpropertied mirror many African Americans' dispossession past and present. Macon Dead's relentless, excessive acquisition of property is his material way of paying loving homage to the life of Macon Dead the first as well as psychically recouping the land that the rapacious Butlers ruthlessly stole.

Dissatisfaction with an improper burial in a place that will forever estrange him from his descendants and ancestors impels the living-dead Jake to seek Pilate's conveyance to Shalimar. Only sixteen and burying his father in haste, Macon piles rocks on his shallow grave near a creek in Lincoln's Heaven. Three months later, fishermen deposit the washed-up body in nearby Hunters Cave, the same hillside cave in which Macon and the twelve-year-old Pilate discover small bags of gold and the man Macon stabs. The living-dead Jake appears to Pilate three years later, just after she gives birth to Reba, the next generation upon which his personal mortality depends, asserting that Pilate cannot abdicate responsibility for an elder who has passed on.

Misinterpreting his statement and believing it her moral obligation to gather the physical remains of the man Macon stabbed and for whose death she felt responsible, Pilate returns to the hillside cave, collecting, however, the fishermen's deposit, the physical remains of her father. Piecing together details that time has obscured, Milkman deduces the truth that the bones mixed with rocks that Pilate suspends from the ceiling of her bedroom in a green sack and references as her "inheritance" and "Mr. Solomon" belong to her father. The living-dead Jake agitates for return to his birth home, Shalimar, where he will be near living relatives responsible for his sustenance in the afterworld and where he will be among a host of ancestors.

In many African cultures home burial is a fetish. George Thomas Basden, in *Among the Ibos of Nigeria* (1931), writes that "The desire of every Ibo man and woman is to die in their own town or, at least, to be buried within its precincts ... In case of death occurring at a distance, ... the brethren will bring the body home for burial."[108] William Bosman's *A New and Accurate Description of the Coast of Guinea* (1754) similarly reports that "Negroes are strangely fond of being buried in their own Country; so that if any Person dies out of it, they frequently bring his Corps [*sic*] home to be buried."[109] C. K. Meek, enlisting observations gathered in Nigeria, provides insight into the importance of home burial for Africans:

When a man dies at a distance from his home his body is always taken back, when possible, to his home, wrapped up in mats covered by a cloth and placed on a bier or cradle, which is carried on the shoulders of his relatives. The reason assigned for this is that the dead must not be severed from the company of other ancestors – they should be buried close to their living descendants on whom they are dependent for nourishment. Moreover, it is important that the ritual traditional to the kindred should be carried out accurately. This cannot be done by strangers.[110]

Return of the entire body is not necessary. "Among the Egbas [Ibos] and various tribes of the Congo family," for example, "various small parts of the body are brought home to be reinterred."[111] At present, the preference for home burial prevails in African-American culture and many African Americans still strive to meet the time-honored custom.

Ironically, and in lieu of returning her father's earthly remains to an unknown birth home for proper burial, the moss-green sack holding Jake's bones inside Pilate's Africanist Darling Street dwelling[112] is a traditional shrine or site of contact and containment for the ancestor that a responsible elder of a tribe is charged with overseeing. Such shrines for contact with ancestors may be erected in homes, at graves, in elevated caves, on forested hills, on the banks of specific rivers, and in front of certain stones or geological formations.[113]

The green sack, the "inheritance" suspended in Pilate's bedroom, is a well-known Northern Kongo reliquary called a kimbi (the Kikongo word for corpse, coffin, and hawk), a repository or receptacle for the body, bone, hair, nail parings, or ashes of a venerable person or martyr. A kimbi is a smaller version of what is known in ethnographic studies as a niombo, a bundle of blankets or a huge human figure made of cloth holding the smoke-dried body or bones of an important individual, a chief or a person of great wealth. Contained or captured within, the nkuyu, the spirit of the individual, animates the kimbi to guard a local group. The name of the person passed on to the afterworld and his or her relationship to surviving kinspeople in need of protection particularize the kimbi force. An ancestor exclusively animates a muzidi, a smaller spiritual container that an nganga, a sacred specialist, prepares. Individuals "eagerly prepare" these animated spirit containers "and keep them in the houses where they sleep or in special storage places. They think that having a[n] nkuyu guarantees the body against dangers by protecting it and sacralizing it and the life of the person."[114] Macon the first's life as a strong, protective husband and father confirms his venerability; his death at the hand of an assassin while bravely guarding his home confers his martyrdom. His heroic conduct during his living life has made him worthy of a kimbi in his living-dead life, and despite Pilate's active knowledge that she has fashioned him one, his spirit container hangs where she sleeps.

Pilate's role to give presence to the absent living-dead extends beyond Jake to other members of her clan. The green-and-white shoe box containing Hagar's hair that Pilate presents to Milkman after his cousin's earthly life ends and that he takes to his Not Doctor Street bedroom, is a second figuring of a kimbi sans the nkuyu, a nonanimated body-relic ark.

Childless, Hagar has no one to insure her living-dead life and personal immortality in the afterworld now that she has prematurely passed from her living one. Milkman's carelessness with Hagar's emotions and idle wish that she kill herself make his first cousin his "inheritance," his responsibility in the reciprocity of life. The hair-filled shoe box – bearing the commercial slogan "Thank heaven for little Joyce heels,"[115] as an allusion to the afterworld cosmology at play in the body-relic ark – is Morrison's twentieth-century adaptation of the kimbi that requires "a basket, a bag, or carrying sling" to transport and protect the body relic inside.[116]

Because an animated, closed spirit container discharges the nkuyu once it is opened, Pilate's untying the kimbi sack atop Solomon's Leap at Jake's home burial emits his nkuyu: "a deep sigh escaped from the sack and the wind turned chill. Ginger, a spicy sugared ginger spell, enveloped them.[117] Pilate laid the bones carefully into the small grave ... 'Should we put a rock or a cross on it?' Milkman asked. Pilate shook her head."[118] Packing the earth around Jake's bones, Milkman and Pilate insure that this time their ancestor is buried permanently. A second revivification of the discharged spirit from the kimbi is now impossible.[119] Pilate's ambiguous headshake, yet another participatory moment when the reader/listener collaborates imaginatively with the author, may confirm that a cross is no longer necessary since the spirit of Macon Dead the first, now properly interred, will not vertically descend again into the mortal plane.

The reciprocity between Pilate, the ancestral presence, and Jake, the ancestor, reflects the African traditional exchange that occurs between the designated living elder and her living-dead kin in the familial matrix.

SOLOMON – THE FLYING AFRICAN TRIBAL ANCESTOR

Enslaved Africans who flew back to their mother continent are the closest relational ties African Americans have to a tribal ancestry. They bear the tribal prestige of ancestors who at times may intersect with family enclaves and whose names and feats are known through personal knowledge or oral tradition. The subject of mythology and oral histories, the superhuman feats and incantations of flying Africans survive in African-American lore in transcribed sources. In *Drums and Shadows: Survival Studies Among the Georgia Coastal Negroes* (1940) and "All God's Chillen Had Wings" in *Doctor to the Dead* (1946), South Carolinian Prince Sneed of White Bluff and Caesar Grant of John's Island retell, respectively, their grandfathers' accounts of African men, women, and children flying away.

Geographically and culturally isolated from the American mainland, the residents of the coastal islands of Georgia and South Carolina retained their ancestral links to Africa in less adulterated form than their mainland counterparts well into the twentieth century. At more than "sixty-odd years" of age, Prince Sneed contributed his oral report to the Slave Narrative Collection of the Federal Writers' Project during the 1930s:

"Muh gran say ole man Waldburg down on St. Catherine own some slabes wut wuzn climatize an he wuk um hahd an one day dey wuz hoein in duh fiel an duh dribuh come out an two ub um wuz unuh a tree in duh shade, an duh hoes wuz wukin by demsef. Duh dribuh say "Wut dis?' and dey say, 'Kum buba yali kum buba tambe, Kum kunka yali kum kunka tambe,' quick like. Den dey rise off duh groun an fly away. Nobody ebuh see um no mo. Some say dey fly back tuh Africa. Muh gran see dat wid he own eye."[120]

At the outskirts of Savannah near White Bluff and Brownville, the formerly enslaved Tony William Delegal, a centenarian from Ogeecheetown, sang an African song in which select words phonetically match incantatory articulations recalled by Sneed's grandfather:

> Wa kum kum munin
> Kum baba yano
> Lai lai tambe
> Ashi boong a nomo
> Shi wali go
> Ashi quank[121]

The meanings of the African words in Sneed's recollection and Delegal's song are unknown. Reciting fragments of an unknown African language, the grandfather of Caesar Grant of John's Island told him of an elder who, about to be beaten, laughed in the faces of the slave master and slave driver and spoke words that triggered remembrance of how to fly in the other slaves working alongside him in the field:

And as he spoke to them they all remembered what they had forgotten, and recalled the power which once had been theirs. Then all the Negroes, old and new, stood up together; the old man raised his hands; and they all leaped up into the air with a great shout; and in a moment were gone, flying, like a flock of crows, over the field, over the fence, and over the top of the wood; and behind them flew the old man . . .

Where they went I do not know; I never was told. Nor what it was that the old man said . . . that I have forgotten. But as he went over the fence he made a sign in the master's face, and cried "Kuli-ba! Kuli-ba!" I don't know what that means.[122]

As with the Sneed story and the Delegal song, the origin and meaning of the old man's words are unknown.

Critically interpreted as a mythological reworking of the Greek Icarus who after escaping from Crete on wings made by his father Daedalus flew too close to the sun, Morrison's flying Solomon is based on an African tribal ancestral legacy, the oral stories and songs of Sneed, Delegal, Grant, and others that reclaim the belief that Africans could truly fly. Morrison drew upon the African-American myth of the flying African to shape the narrative of *Song of Solomon*:

[M]yths get forgotten. Or they may not have been looked at carefully. Let me give you an example: the flying myth in *Song of Solomon*. If it means Icarus to some readers, fine . . . But my meaning is specific: it is about black people who could fly. That was always part of the folklore of my life; flying was one of our gifts. I don't care how silly it may seem. It is everywhere – people used to talk about it, it's in the spirituals and gospels. Perhaps it was wishful thinking – escape, death, and all that. But suppose it wasn't. What might it mean? I tried to find out in *Song of Solomon*.[123]

After reading the personal accounts of enslaved Africans' descendants that repeatedly insisted that their grandparents witnessed seeing people from Africa in flight, Morrison embraced Africans who could fly as "a real thing":

[The story about flying Africans is] not so much . . . a legend but a given . . . Later on I read a lot of slave narratives, and I remember the interviewers asking these people who were children of slaves and have been slaves themselves, "have you ever heard of anybody who could fly?" and I was struck by the fact [that] . . . they kept saying things like, "well, I never saw it, but so and so saw it . . ." The flying thing was heavy and spiritual . . . I began to think about it as a real thing – like literally flying.[124]

In order to intertwine the "real thing" with myth and folk legend in *Song of Solomon*, Morrison combined the individual with the representative, personal family history with the oral histories of second-generation descendants of enslaved Africans. Morrison mixes fragmented memories of her own family history with African-born ancestors' oral accounts retrieved from the memories of their descendants. She adapts the first line, "Jake the only son of Solomon," that the Shalimar children sing in "a kind of ring-around-the rosy or Little Sally Walker game"[125] from a song that the Greenville, Alabama, branch of her family sang about John Solomon Willis, her maternal grandfather, and his first son, Green:

The song that my mother and aunts know starts out, "Green, the only son of Solomon." And then there are some funny words that I don't understand. It is a long sort of a children's song that I don't remember. But Green was the name of my grandfather's first son and it was a kind of genealogy that they were singing about. So I altered the words for *Song of Solomon*. These people were born in Greenville.[126]

The fictional Solomon, the ancestral founder of Solomon/Shalleemone/ Shalimar, Virginia, recaptures the fusion of a person's name with a place like the real-life Green of Greenville, Alabama.

The song of Solomon – three quatrains of *abab* rhyme and a fourth comprised of two couplets composing the first round, then a single *abab* quatrain and concluding couplet composing the second[127] – draws collectively from the interviews that descendants of enslaved Africans contributed to the Georgia Slave Narrative Collection. Each account contains a thematic riff on the absent ancestral patriarch, a departed or missing African father. A game version of the ring shout, consisting of the Kongo- and Dahomey- inspired circle dance and the accompanying song that the fictional Shalimar children perform in *Song of Solomon*, commemorates the name and deed of their founding patriarch and ancestor Solomon who fled American slavery by flying back to Africa. The father of twenty-one children by a single mother, Ryna, Solomon tries to carry his youngest son Jake with him back to Africa. Brushing against a tree, Jake slips from his father's arms to the plantation house below. Devastated by Solomon's unexpected departure, Ryna, convulsing on the ground, suffers an emotional breakdown that creates a need for the surrogate mother and Native-American neighbor, Heddy, to rear Jake.

In the center of the circle that eight or nine children form with a huge cedar in the background rearing up over their heads, a boy twirls around with outstretched "airplane" arms, his body configuring a cross, while the others recite the four quatrains of the song's first part. At the shout of "Jake!", the final word in the first round of play, the boy in the circle's center falls to the ground with one arm extended. If he points at no one, the first round starts again from the beginning, but if he points at another child, they all fall to their knees and sing the second round of the song. Ryna's plea to Solomon not to leave her comfortless in slavery is the subject of the single quatrain in the second part:

> O Solomon don't leave me here
> Cotton balls to choke me
> O Solomon don't leave me here
> Buckra's arms to yoke me[128]

The concluding couplet of the second round that the Shalimar children sing reveals the source of Pilate's "Sugarman" blues complaint introduced in the opening pages of the novel:

> Solomon done fly, Solomon done gone
> Solomon cut across the sky, Solomon gone home.[129]

Priscilla McCullough from near Darien, a contributor to the Georgia Slave Narrative Collection, tells a story her mother often repeated of African flight that involved the circle formation:

> Du slabes wuz out in duh fiel wukin. All ub a sudden dey git tuh gedduh an staht tuh moob roun in a ring. Roun dey go fastuhnfastuh. Den one by one dey riz up an take wing an fly lak a bud. Duh obuhseeuh heah duh noise an he come out an he see duh slabes riz up in duh eah an fly back tuh Africa.[130]

Unlike the Solomon story, return to Africa is not undertaken by a single patriarch but by a ringed group, and words of unknown meaning are not chanted.

The words of an unknown African language in lines two and four of each of the first three quatrains of the first round of Solomon's song directly mimic in assonantal form the utterances "Kum buba yali kum buba tambe" and "Kum kunka yali kum kunka tambe" of Prince Sneed's grandfather's account of Africans who rose off the ground and flew away, never to be seen again:

> Jake the only son of Solomon
> Come booba yalle, come booba tambee
> Whirled about and touched the sun
> Come konka yalle, come konka tambee
>
> Left that baby in a white man's house
> Come booba yalle, come booba tambee
> Heddy took him to a red man's house
> Come konka yalle, come konka tambee
>
> Black lady fell down on the ground
> Come booba yalle, come booba tambee
> Threw her body all around
> Come konka yalle, come konka tambee[131]

Following the quaternary three-plus-one pattern prevalent in Morrison's fiction, the fourth, coupleted quatrain, lacking lines constructed from an unknown African language departing from the earlier rhyme scheme, differs in narrative content. It catalogues the names of Solomon's progeny:

> Solomon and Ryna Belali Shalut
> Yaruba Medina Muhammet too.
> Nestor Kalina Saraka cake.
> Twenty-one children, the last one Jake![132]

Morrison here grafts together names she lifts from several Georgia coastal oral slave narratives of real-life people who "flew" off or were left behind. The enumeration of Solomon's scions recalls the names of the offspring of Belali Mohomet or Ben Ali Mohamet, a French-speaking Muslim enslaved on the Thomas Spalding Plantation on Sapelo Island in the early nineteenth century. Brought from Nassau in the French West Indies and before that "from the West Sudan or areas to the north," Mohomet left behind a thirteen-page journal written in corrupted Arabic dealing with "ablutions and the call to prayer." Anthropologist Joseph Greenberg took the journal on a field trip to West Africa in 1938 and found its contents to be Mahgreb-influenced excerpts from the *Risala*, "the product of a Malekite school of Islamic law. Prior to his removal from Africa, Mohomet, in all likelihood at the time a young student, had memorized portions of the *Risala's* text."[133] Katie Brown, his Sapelo Island descendant, attests that, as well as having a son of the same name, Belali Mohomet "had plenty daughtuhs, Magret, Bentoo, Chaalut, Medina, Yaruba, Fatima, an Hestuh." "Hestuh," whom Morrison mutates into "Nestor," made saraka cake of meal and honey and sometimes rice.[134] Mohomet does not fly away like his fictional counterpart, but he goes missing. The son of Belali Mohomet the second, Ben Sullivan of St. Simons Islands, whose African-born maternal grandmother was named Hettie, the probable inspiration for the Heddy of Solomon's song, recounts the story of his grandfather's disappearance: "Muh fathuh's fathuh come frum Africa too but wen muh fathuh Belali wuz a small young lad, muh granfathuh wehn tuh Dungeness on Cumberland Ilun tuh trade in slabes an nebuh wuz seen agen."[135] The "Kalina" of the song belongs to the oral history of another Sapelo Island family whose Ibo ancestors attempted to walk back across the Atlantic to West Africa. Abducted from their respective homes in Africa, Calina and Hannah, both Ibos, survived the Middle Passage, married "an hab twenny-one chillun."[136] Ousseynou Traore posits that Calina's appearance in the Solomon genealogy invokes the story of St. Simons's Ibo Landing, a point of arrival and departure comparable to Solomon's Leap in Morrison's novel. The Landing's oral history has it that once the Ibos' enslavers unloaded them from the slave ship, they immediately started back for home. Singing while they marched into the ocean, the Ibos drowned in their unflinching determination to return to Africa.[137]

Building on the theme of the missing patriarch but drawing from an oral history inverting the subject's gender, Morrison borrows the name Ryna from a narrative of maternal flight back to Africa. Rosa Grant of Possum Point near Darien, Georgia, tells the story of her great-grandmother

Theresa's flight that her grandmother Ryna witnessed and told to her as a child. Slavers had abducted Theresa and Ryna from their African home-land when mother and daughter went to get a closer look at a cloth of red, a color unknown to them, flying on the mast of a ship in the harbor. Weakened from the toil of slave-field labor in America, Theresa twirled around in circles, rose from the ground, and flew back to Africa. In response to her mother's abandonment of her, this Ryna's complaint was simply that she "alluz wish dat uh mothuh had teach uh how tuh fly. She try an try doin duh same way but she ain nebuh fly. She say she guess she jis wuzn bawn wid duh powuh."[138] Another Ryna, Ryna Johnson of St. Simons Island, testified to being afraid of an African she knew during her youth who boasted that all his "fambly in Africa could fly."[139]

Incorporating in her fiction numerous real-life testimonies of Africans flying, like Therese's flight back to Africa that her daughter Ryna wit-nessed, adds historical authenticity as well as tribal ancestral presence to *Song of Solomon*. Morrison is willing to take ownership for what passes as "superstition" in her own life and her fiction and to validate supernatural beliefs in African America that clash with Western pragmatism. Western pragmatism may discredit metaphysical phenomena by defining them as astral projections or dismissing them as aberrations of the mind when experiencing them in its own cultures. Morrison, however, chooses to use the relation that Black people have with those phenomena to enrich her work as identifiably Black.

MARY THÉRÈSE FOUCAULT – THE CARIBBEAN ANCESTRAL PRESENCE

The magic-breasted, broken-eyed, Caribbean native Mary Thérèse Foucault in *Tar Baby* is the ancestral presence at the crossroads of ancestral attrition and retention. With her assistance, Son (William Green) an undocumented African American who has a strong Africanist sensibility, must decide if replacing ancestral African traditional ideals and values with modern European-American values will be more empowering for a Black man in the twentieth century. The choice that confronts Son is whether to claim his ancestral, traditional past symbolized by Thérèse or abandon it.

Although she denies it for reasons of vanity – she does not want to admit her failing vision – Thérèse is a descendant of the mythical enslaved Africans who, as a fishermen's tale has it, were struck blind the moment they laid eyes on French-colonized Dominique in the seventeenth century.

While the island is a fictional creation, its name references St. Dominique (Saint Domingue), the pre-independence name for Haiti. Isle des Chevaliers (Island of the Horsemen),[140] a smaller island adjacent to Dominique that American candy heir Valerian Street purchased and then sold in plots to wealthy French buyers, bears the name of the marooned horsemen, timeless tribal ancestors[141] who still ride sightless in its hills. Gideon, Thérèse's nephew who has returned to Dominique from the United States to assume family responsibilities, tells the fishermen's tale to Son:

Their ship foundered and sank with Frenchmen, horses and slaves aboard. The blinded slaves could not see how or where to swim so they were at the mercy of the current and the tide. They floated and trod water and ended up on the island along with the horses that had swum ashore. Some of them were only partially blinded and were rescued later by the French, and returned to Queen of France and indenture. The others, totally blind, hid. The ones who came back had children who, as they got on into middle age, went blind too. What they saw, they saw with the eye of the mind, and that, of course, was not to be trusted. Thérèse, he said, was one such. He himself was not, since his mother and Thérèse had different fathers . . . [Those who hid rode] those horses . . . all over the hills. They learned to ride through the rain forest avoiding all sorts of trees and things. They race each other, and for sport they sleep with the swamp women in Sein de Veilles [*sic*].[142]

Thérèse, who wet-nursed hundreds of French babies in her youth and whose breasts, even though she is now well past sixty, still express milk, feeds the hidden-away Son before his presence at the Streets' estate, L'Arbe de la Croix (The Tree of the Cross), becomes known to its five occupants. Valerian Street, his wife Margaret, their servants Sydney and Ondine, and the servants' niece Jadine Childs are unaware that a Black intruder with Mau Mau hair lurks among them. Relying on a keenly developed sense of smell that compensates for her weak vision, Thérèse, the Streets' laundress, leaves avocados in the washhouse for the unidentified "horseman" from the hills whose presence she smells, but Son never finds the jade-colored fruit. Instead, he consumes chocolate stolen from the kitchen of the main house when Gideon, complicit with Thérèse, removes a pane from its pantry window so that the "rider" she smells might enter and be fed.[143]

Son's textual introduction depicts him as caught in a powerful, counterclockwise vortex in the Caribbean Sea. Coming from a communal practice that approves of doing things in time complicates his commitment to African ideals and activates his need for Thérèse's assistance when he falls in love with his cultural antithesis, fashion model Jadine, a product of ruthless individualism and Western linear temporality that requires things be done on time. Son must choose between remaining true to his tribal past or engaging in a modern present that has given rise to a capitalistic "making it" African American like Jadine who lacks the "ancient properties" to relate to the Black folk and to function within an Africanist corporate structure. The clash between Son and Jadine, therefore, is not a battle of the sexes but a culture war. Basing her assessment on Jadine's dismissive treatment of her and the other African-Caribbean natives, Thérèse knows that Son and Jadine do not share a common language or assumptions about Blackness, and Black is something Jadine chooses not to be.[144] The cultural dilemma of the novel arises for Son, the product of a strong African-American community, when he must decide to either "join the twentieth century as a kind of half-person like Jadine, or ... abandon it."[145] Selecting one over the other relinquishes the potential for balance, to sustain both a spiritually nurturing West African traditional past and a materially comfortable American present. "Because it is in her world view, it takes Thérèse to give [Son] a choice. She gives him this mystical choice between roaming around looking for Jadine [after Jadine rejects the tribal ways of Eloe, his Florida hometown, when he takes her there] and putting himself in danger that is not dignified, versus the possibility of joining these rather incredible men in the rain forest,"[146] embracing fully his African spirituality and past.

Morrison leaves open the choice that Son, under Thérèse's ancestral tutelage, makes but suggests which one he may choose. Returning from New York to Dominique and the smaller Isle des Chevaliers in pursuit of Jadine, Son risks having the near-blind Thérèse pilot him to L'Arbe de la Croix to find Jadine, who has fled New York earlier. Instead of landing the boat on the estate side of the island, Thérèse takes him to the far side, and once her talk about the horsemen ends, orders him to disembark. Son is reluctant to leave the boat and enter the rain forest, since approaching darkness obscures his vision. He poses an ambiguous question to Thérèse's command. His query, "Are you sure?," could mean "Are you sure *the men are there*?" since Thérèse has just been discussing the horsemen, or it could mean "Are you sure *this is the island*?" because he doubts her ability to see and the coastline of the island's far side is unfamiliar to him. She answers yes and tells him more about the blind horsemen, not the island. Son asks again if she is sure, but she does not answer or he does not hear her response. As he steps onto the shore, the trees step back and he runs lickety-split into the rain forest suggesting "a rabbit returning to the briar patch"[147] – the African primal world that the Caribbean island and his

Florida hometown (designed to invoke the first incorporated all African-American town of Eatonville, Florida) symbolize.

Thérèse, on the other hand, has no ancestral engagement with Jadine, whom she calls a "chippy" and a "fast ass," and counsels Son to forget her since she has forgotten her "ancient properties."[148] A product of white capitalism and Western intellectualism, Jadine has strayed so far outside the ancestral fold that, a cultural orphan as well as a literal one, she renders Thérèse, Gideon, and their domestic cohort, Alma Estée, socially invisible. Jadine disrespectfully calls the native island women out of their names, all are "Marys," and identifies Gideon only as a menial functionary, "Yardman." Analogous to the symbolism attached to Milkman in *Song of Solomon* as a white peacock, a male fowl that is genetically engineered and selectively bred only in captivity, Jadine, who is also called Jade, is an African American who has been carved from the white variation of the mineral. Multifaceted in meaning, her abbreviated name when read as a noun is applicable to a reprobate woman and a contemptuous name for a horse of inferior breeding. When read as a verb, jade means to become spiritless.[149] In sum, Jadine is a reprobate "white" child who, absent of spirit, does not know how to be an African daughter. Thérèse intuits that Jadine is beyond salvation, beyond familial, tribal, and cultural redemption. Jadine's cultural aloofness and intolerable egocentrism is predicated on a white solipsism that forecloses a corporate, reciprocal consciousness of giving back to those who have given to her, taking responsibility for her elders, and acknowledging and respecting the ancestors.

From Thérèse's standpoint, Jadine has imbibed the unnatural nurturing indifference of the European-American woman. Thérèse's principal curiosity about the United States is to confirm if "American women killed [aborted] their babies with their fingernails" – a concern that emanates in part from her internalized belief that the country's dominant capitalist culture violates even basic laws of nature for money. She asks Son if American women sell their babies behind park trees; and if doctors perform sex changes for gold that make it "not uncommon or strange to see people with both penises and breasts."[150] Both Margaret Street and Valerian's deceased first wife, who regularly visits him spectrally in the greenhouse, are examples of Thérèse's suspicion that American women indulge in torturing and killing the successive generation that they should nurture. Margaret stuck pins in the buttocks of her infant son Michael and burned him with cigarettes, while Valerian's first wife, "[i]n nine years of marriage ... had had two abortions and all she wanted to talk about during these [greenhouse] visits was how relieved she was that she'd had at least that foresight."[151] To Thérèse, Enfamil, the commercially produced formula that ended her wet-nursing service, "[s]ounds like murder and a bad reputation" but as the quintessential source of nurturance, her breasts continue to give milk.[152]

Thérèse's lactating, nurturing breasts solidify her status as the living elder closest to the ancestors and centralize her as the principal thesis of the recurring tar-breast imagery that poses Jadine as its antithesis. The image of an aged tar breast that opens the novel critiques the ecological imbalance that American and European violation of nature engenders. The construction of Isle des Chevaliers winter homes for the Streets and the French produces a metaphorical tar-lactating breast belonging to the ancient swamp women who mate with the blind horsemen. The island's rain forest river loses its course because of construction rerouting. It sat "in one place like a grandmother and became a swamp the Haitians called Sein de Vieilles. And witch's tit it was: a shriveled fogbound oval seeping with a thick black substance."[153] It is in Sein de Vieilles that Jadine later shuns the mythical swamp women's attempt to reclaim her.

Thérèse and an assemblage of living women (Son's Aunt Rose, his best friend Soldier's wife Ellen, Jadine's aunt by marriage Ondine, dog-ravaged Francine, and the woman in yellow) and living-dead women (Son's mother, his past wife Cheyenne, Cheyenne's mother Sally Brown, and Jadine's mother) bare their breasts to Jadine in a nocturnal vision that she has in Eloe. All knew how to nurture, to be daughters, to be soldier ants. "Pushing each other – nudging for space, they poured out of the dark like ants out of a hive."[154] The allusion to the breast-exposing women as thick black honey equates them with the sludgy stickiness of tar. Jadine retaliates by visually demonstrating that she, too, has breasts, but the women gathered in her turbulent thoughts disbelieve her. She is a cultural outsider to the tar-breast paradigm.

Morrison's selection of tar-breast imagery as a thematically galvanizing locus becomes clearer when one dusts off Tar Baby tales and takes a revisionist look at the African mythology behind the novel's title. The Tar Baby and Brer Rabbit tales that Joel Chandler Harris gathered and published have traceable roots in African spider and hare trickster stories from Nigeria to Angola that enslaved Africans brought to America and Europe and which later spread throughout the world. In *African Mythology* (1987) Geoffrey Parrinder records a Nigerian Hausa tale in which the spider steals groundnuts from his neighbor. When the neighbor discovers the theft, he fabricates the form of a girl made from the resin of the rubber tree as a trap for the dishonest spider:

When the Spider came along he saw the Rubber Girl, with a beautiful long neck and large breasts. He came up to her, put out a hand and touched her breast, and his hand was held fast by the sticky rubber. "Oh, you must want me badly," he said, and put his other hand on her other breast. The hand stuck tight, and he exclaimed, "you girls hold a man too tight. I will kick you." He did this and the rubber caught his foot. Then he was angry and called the Rubber Girl an illegitimate child of low parents, and kicked her with the other foot. That stuck too and he was clasped tight to her body. He tried butting with his head and that stuck also to the Rubber Girl. Then the neighbor, who was watching from a hiding place, saw the Spider securely held and gave thanks to God. He cut a pliable switch from a tree, warmed it in a fire, rubbed it with grease, and beat and beat the Spider till his back was raw.[155]

Although the Tar Baby story has many African and Western versions, a female-gendered lure, a resin that binds things, and feminized, maternal-ized sticky breasts (not sexualized ones as in the Rubber Girl tale above) are important aspects of the story which Morrison foregrounds in her novel. From prompting within the story, Jadine is easily read as the Tar Baby, Son as the Brer Rabbit who is stuck on her, and Valerian as the Farmer or Fox who fashions her. Nevertheless, the point of Morrison's narrative is that Jadine is not a Tar Baby; she is unable to hold very necessary communal and ancestral obligations together.[156] Morrison in an interview confirms that she had a very different tar paradigm in mind:

I use that old story because, despite its funny, happy ending, it used to frighten me. The story has a tar baby in it which is used by a white man to catch a rabbit. "Tar Baby" is also a name, like nigger, that white people call black children, black girls, as I recall. Tar seemed to me to be an odd thing to be in a Western story, and I found that there is a tar lady in African mythology. I started thinking about tar. At one time, a tar pit was a holy place, at least an important place, because tar was used to build things. It came naturally out of the earth; it held together things like Moses's little boat and the pyramids. For me, the tar baby came to mean the black woman who can hold things together, the story as a point of departure to history and prophecy.[157]

The ancestral swamp women who abide in Sein des Vieilles symbolize African women who know their "value, their exceptional femaleness" of holding things together. Jadine's fight to free herself from them when she becomes stuck in their "tar pit" perplexes the mythical women. The novel's narrative explains that "the first world of the world had been built with their sacred properties; that they alone could hold together the stones of pyramids and the rushes of Moses's crib; knowing their steady consistency, their pace of glaciers, their permanent embrace, they wondered at the girl's desperate struggle down below to be free, to be something other than they were."[158] Jadine has not forgotten her ancient properties; she has never known them. Both her parents died when she was very young and her Uncle Sydney and Aunt Ondine have been remiss in not educating her in the duties of a daughter. Ondine, who fails to be an ancestral presence in the life of her niece, reproaches herself for rearing Jadine to be clueless of her reciprocal social and familial responsibilities. Emotionally detached from any form of communal ownership, Jadine cannot sympathize with her patron Valerian when he recounts to her the saddest event of his life. She cannot find a common topic of interest to discuss with the "backward" women of Eloe, and is unwilling to reciprocate care for her living elders or to provide them with shelter in their declining years. To Sydney's query concerning Jadine's reliability in executing the most important service that one's closest surviving kin must provide for their relatives in African and African-American culture, overseeing their proper burial, Ondine responds, "I think we're going to have to bury ourselves."[159] Bereft of biological or surrogate parents and ignorant of her African past, Jadine snubs the Caribbean elder and ancestral presence who can educate her about herself. At the liminal site of New World ancestral attrition and retention, Jadine is cut off from herself as well as her living and dead kin.

A native of the Caribbean, the intermediate space of the Middle Passage and the crossroads of African and African-American culture and identity, the nurturing Thérèse knows the importance of holding things together, keeping ancient properties alive for successive generations of Black men and women. Her Caribbean nativity secures her position as the living, direct descendant and bridge to the living-dead tribal ancestors whose life or death rests on her ability to give them presence. Thérèse's appearance in *Tar Baby* resonates as a caution to "making it" African-American men and women not to sever themselves culturally from the "backward" people who give their lives meaning.

THE BLIND HORSEMEN AND SWAMP WOMEN – THE ANCESTOR TRANSFIGURED INTO A GOD

Morrison's inclusions of sentient plant life, bodies of water, and other material forms in nature on Isle des Chevaliers are not gestures at literary personification or the magical realism that Jorge Luis Borges and Gabriel García Márquez in South America, Günter Grass in Germany, and Italo Calvino and Umberto Eco in Italy popularized after World War II. Initially skeptical of the term but now indifferent to it, Morrison was first made aware of "magical realism" when she noticed its usage to describe a style of writing by Latin American men. She regarded the "label" as "evasive," as "a way of *not* talking about the politics . . . in the books." Applying the word "magical" seemed to *dilute* the realism legitimately "because there were these supernatural and unrealistic things, surreal things, going on in the text." Literary historians and literary critics' usage of the term "seemed to be a convenient way to skip again what was the truth in the art of certain writers." She also sensed that the word "magic," especially when applied to works treating discredited knowledge held by discredited people implied that those works lacked "intelligence."[160] Although discredited knowledge that Blacks embraced seemed unbelievable, Morrison felt it was impossible not to write about their knowledge as an authority and authentication of Blackness. *Tar Baby*'s sentient landscape addresses the knowledge that "while we watch the word, the world watches us . . . that the trees look back on us." Natural phenomena are choral witnesses to and commentators on human actions. Hence Morrison "puts all that on the surface of the novel in a way that is open to animism or anthropomorphism."[161] She personally qualifies her treatment of animism, stating that she "grew up in a house in which people . . . had some sweet, intimate connection with things that were not empirically verifiable."[162] She unabashedly admits that her "relationship to things other than human beings" informs her beliefs.[163]

The preponderance of African traditional religions and their diaspora mutations are grounded in the belief that nonmaterial "spirit" animates matter; therefore natural objects, natural phenomena, and the universe itself possess a consciousness. Originating from a number of sources, divinities and spirits of the natural elements animating trees, stones, and other material objects characterize animistic religions. Mbiti posits that "spirits in general belong to the ontological mode of existence between God and man. Broadly speaking, we can recognize two categories of spiritual beings: those which were created as such, and those which were once human beings. These can also be subdivided into divinities [or] associates of God, ordinary spirits and the living-dead." Divinities, whom God created as personifications of his activities, on rare occasion may once have been human national heroes that have been divinized. Ordinary spirits are the incorporeal essence of individuals who once lived but have descended below the horizon of the Zamani. They are depersonalized and have collective immortality. Some cultures, however, believe them to be a specially created "race" that reproduces itself. In either case, rarely do ordinary spirits appear to the living as the living-dead are prone to do at their own discretion. Generally, ordinary spirits make their appearance in folk stories. As there are exceptions in both the first two subdivisions, there are no hard and fast absolute classifications of animating spirits and their origins as one moves from culture to culture.[164]

In the French and formerly French-colonized Caribbean, the setting of *Tar Baby*, African-Caribbean natives retain some form of belief in animism alongside Catholicism that today more than four-fifths of the respective populations of Haiti, Dominica, Guadeloupe, and Martinique profess. Half the Catholics of these islands practice Voudoun, which is an animistic religion but falls short of being an orthodox animistic religion since it does not systematize its pantheon in terms of the four constituent elements – earth, water, fire, and air.[165] Deren explains the correspondence between the soul's/psyche's filling of the human vessel and the spirit-filling of the nonhuman vessel:

Just as the physical body of a man is a meaningless, material substance, devoid of judgement, will and morality, unless a soul infuses and animates it, so the universe would be but an amoral mass of organic matter, inevitably evolving on the initial momentum of original creation, were it not for the loa [Mystères, gods, or spirits] who direct it in paths of order, intelligence and benevolence. The loa are the souls of the cosmos.[166]

Spirits that have achieved a degree of divine elevation and cannot be remembered as human beings, the loa may reside *in* trees, stones, streams, and similar natural structures that serve as merely physical vessels for them and should in no way be interpreted as the spirits *of* the trees or the spirits *of* stones, and so forth. The animistic process, therefore, infuses the champion daisy trees that change from "serene" to "wild-eyed and yelling" in the face of ecological upheaval and the avocado tree standing by the road that suspects Jadine misuses the word "horseshit" and folds "its leaves tightly over its fruit" as it watches her go by. The process contextualizes the consciousness of the "[p]oor, insulted, brokenhearted river that exhausted, ill and grieving ... stop[s] just twenty leagues short of the sea."[167] Nature spirits, territorial divinities such as the swamp women, are for the most part ancestors who entered the Zamani so long ago that all ties to a lineage have dissolved and they now watch over all in a specific area. Their absorption into nature constitutes the indissoluble relationship between the living-dead and the land they inhabit.

The blind horsemen are not of the same spiritual order as the nature and water spirits discussed above since they have not been detached from the human family. Viewed concretely as men who were once human, the three-centuries-old horsemen have surviving descendants of which Mary

Thérèse Foucault is one. They are ancestors who have a historical past that has been swallowed whole by a mythical present. Now the subjects of myth, they move through a dynamic, ancestral evolution that in earlier times would result and in a certain sense has resulted in their divinization. Deren states that "Those who cannot remember create[, . . .] and in time, the ancestor becomes archetype. Where there was once a person, there is now a personage . . . What was once believed, is now believed in. He who was once respected is now revered. The ancestor has been transfigured into a god."[168] Therefore divinization "does not consist in the spiritualizing of matter" but the living descendants' "reclamation of the soul of the deceased from beneath the Kalunga line of the waters of the abyss" of the afterworld and time, the "retirer d'en bas de l'eau."[169]

Although the slaves who were struck blind the moment they saw Dominique in the last quarter of the seventeenth century are the fictional composite of Morrison's imagination, their movement from men to myth is easily hypothesized in real-life terms. Common in the West Indies in the seventeenth and eighteenth centuries, maroons, the real-life precedents for the blind horsemen, were fugitive enslaved Africans who fled to the hills and mountains of their respective islands to escape European enslavers. Because there are historical parallels between Haiti and the setting of *Tar Baby*, because the laborers who cleared the Isle des Chevaliers for winter homes and named Sein de Vieilles are Haitian, and because perhaps it is no coincidence that St. Dominique (Saint Domingue) was the former name of Haiti,[170] it is a rational hypothesis that Morrison drew upon the maroon history and mythology of Haiti, the first independent Black republic in the Western hemisphere:

The first slave-trade shipment to Haiti was in 1510. The first slave revolt recorded was in 1522, a mere twelve years later. The type of protest known in French as "marronage", running away into the hills, must have begun as early, if not even before. Haiti came under French rule in 1677, but it did not diminish the "marronage". It is recorded that in 1720 alone, a thousand Negroes gained their freedom in this manner; while by 1751 the number had grown to 3,500 . . . But almost no attention has been paid to the fact that, in those hills, they *must*, during the Spanish period, have encountered the Indians, who, being on home ground, would no less than the Negroes, have had recourse to such escape from the brutal massacres that characterized the Spanish colonization.[171]

The Indian women encountered in the hills are easily transformed into swamp women who mate with the marooned Africans struck blind. Ophthalmia (a generic name for trachoma, a disease of the eye that causes blindness and is exacerbated by unsanitary conditions) was and is common in Africa and the Middle East and often plagued the human cargo and crews of the Middle Passage. John Greenleaf Whittier's preface to his poem "The Slave-Ships" reclaims for modern readers the story of the French slave ship *Le Rodeur*'s bout with trachoma. All but one of its 160 West Africans destined for slave markets in the Americas and 22-man crew between Bonny, Nigeria, and Guadeloupe suffered blindness. And that last, sighted crewman, after safely steering the ship into Guadeloupe's port, contracted the disease three days later. To contain the outbreak during the voyage, the French threw thirty-six Africans overboard; insurance would recoup their loses. *Le Rodeur* hailed *El León*, a Spanish slave ship it encountered en route, but it could provide no assistance since all its crew were blind. The ships parted and *El León* was never heard from again. The respective incidents involving *Le Rodeur* and *El León* occurred in 1819 but ophthalmia was a constant scourge on slave ships throughout the slave trade era. One can therefore easily imagine how Caribbean lore surrounding visually impaired Africans bound for slavery who, against all odds, triumphantly freed themselves could be winnowed down to an affection for and fear of an immortal, marooned, blind race.

The mythical and mystical "blind horsemen" of Isle des Chevaliers call forth imagistically and assonantically the "divine horsemen" of Voudoun, the loa or spirits who reside in trees and have achieved divinization. Their temporary "possession" – displacement of the animating force of the physical body – mirrors spirits' permanent animation of nonhuman matter:

Under certain well-defined and ritualistically determined conditions the loa may temporarily displace the gros-bon-ange [the invisible nonmaterial self] of a living person and become the animating force of that physical body. This we know as "possession." In the terminology of Voudoun, it is said that the loa "mounts" a person, or that a person is "mounted" by the loa. The metaphor is drawn from a horse and his rider and the actions and events which result are the expression of the will of the rider . . . The function and purpose of such divine manifestation is the reassurance and the instruction of the community.[172]

Zora Neale Hurston's *Tell My Horse* (1938), a field collection of the politics, folk beliefs, and traditions of Jamaica and Haiti, states that in a Voudoun ceremony "[t]he person mounted does nothing of his [or her] own accord. He is the horse of the loa until the spirit departs." Whether through loa-mounting or feigned loa-mounting, Hurston noted that the "phrase 'Parlay cheval ou' ['Tell my horse'] was in daily, hourly use in Haiti."[173] In Voudoun the rider or divine horseman may be Legba, Ghede, or any other loa of the extensive religious pantheon. Morrison takes the adjectival

referent, "divine," alters it assonantically to "blind," and mythically personifies spirits who ride "horses," serviteurs, by reformulating them collectively as a quasi-loa subclass.

Jadine's encounter with the tree swamp women in the fifth chapter of
Tar Baby is a veiled Voudoun possession initiation that climaxes in a
divine/blind horseman attempting to mount Jadine who, in the position
of the horse and potential serviteur, will have none of it. She rejects the loa
swamp women who want to claim her as one of their own. Jadine's name
turns on multiple meanings, and "jade," defined as a spiritless horse of
inferior breeding, applies in an exact sense here because she is an adulterated form of a daughter of African descent who breaks the circle as serviteur
and nurturer by refusing to take care of her elders and ancestors and to be
"possessed" by a greater African consciousness. The tree Jadine passes as she
enters the ring of trees and the presence of the swamp women preface the
mounting initiation. But it is failed mounting. The rider (the swamp
women collectively) is unsuccessful at expressing its will through her.[174]

The serviteur in a Voudoun ceremony must first salute Legba who is a
tree stretching skyward, the keeper of the gate, guardian of the sacred Gran
Chemin (celestial arc of the sun's path), and the road leading from the
mortal world to the divine world. Not the most powerful loa, Legba
nevertheless is the most important one because he grants contact with the
other loa and hence opens the avenues for mounting. Because a serviteur
must first salute him, he is the guardian of the crossroads, the vertical axis of
the universe, the carrefour, *l'arbe de la croix*:

> For this reason the crossroads is the most important of all ritual figures, whether
> drawn in flour on flat ground, or traced in the air, the sign of the crossroads is
> always the juncture of the horizontal with the vertical, where communication
> between worlds is established, and the traffic of energies and forces between them
> is set up. Through the center-post [of a cross or tree at the entrance of a tree-ringed
> peristyle or constructed circle], the poteau-mitan, the gods enter. At its base, the
> vevers [sacred symbols] are drawn. Around the center-post all ritualistic move-
> ments and dance revolve.[175]

In the swamp scene in *Tar Baby*, "[y]oung trees" that "ringed and soared
above a wavy mossy floor" frame the swamp[176] that is analogous to a
hounfor peristyle of Voudoun ritual. With many paths of access but only
one main entrance marked by one or two trees for Legba directly inside, a
hounfor contains sacred precincts that include sacred trees encircled at
their base, an altar chamber, and a peristyle for ceremonial activities and
dances. A grove of trees may wall in the whole to provide "almost total
shade and create perspectives of deep green corridors."[177] After Son's

departure to get gasoline for the stalled jeep, Jadine, with charcoal and sketch pad in hand, seeks shelter from the sun by heading toward a cluster of trees to the left of the road. The "sly" shade tree cluster pleasantly surprises her:

There was hardly any color; just greens and browns because there was hardly any light and what light there was – a sentimental shaft of sunlight to the left – bunched the brown into deeper shadow. In the center under a roof of greens was a lawn of the same dark green the Dutchmen loved to use. The circle of trees looked like a standing rib of pork.

Attracted to the peristyle's mossy center lawn, Jadine takes only a few steps through its entrance before sinking to her knees in a tar substance. Similar to loa that may reside in trees,[178] the swamp women hang in the rafters of the encircling trees looking down as if in a quandary about descending through the poteau-mitan, the vertical axis of the gateway tree. Jadine encircles the tree's trunk with her arms to halt her sinking, and, as a strategy to extract herself from the black quicksand, considers lying horizontal, mapping her position on the horizontal axis, the visible, mortal world on earth. Had she lain on the ground, her reclined position would have been indicative of the hounsi (vodunsi), the Voudoun initiate who stretches out on mats after entering the peristyle as part of the initiation ritual.

Jadine elects to tighten "her arms around the tree and it swayed as though it wished to dance with her." Like a lover, she mirrors the tree's movements; "Sway when he sways and shiver with him too."[179] At one point, she wrenches one leg free and bends it enough to kneel while the other remains steadfastly lodged in the black sludge. When the gods enter and possess a serviteur, a shimmy-dance upon one leg with one knee bent takes place at the base of the tree. As a Voudoun initiate, Deren provides a compelling narration of the rooting, fixing, and wrenching loose of her left leg during her dance of possession that is comparable to the movements that Jadine executes.[180] Cardinal points; mirror imaging of both sides of the horizontal and/or vertical axis (of which the cross and circle most perfectly reflect); backward, east-to-west counterclockwise movements; and movements executed with the left hand, left leg, or to the left side are very important in the Voudoun ceremony and serviteurs must salute some loa in mirrored gestures. The shimmy that Jadine dances backward, reversing the tree movements, satisfies these required movements.

With Jadine's dress and approach to the grove of trees, Morrison subtly but succinctly implies her status as a potential initiate. Stepping outside of Western temporality, the watchless Jadine comes to the tree-ringed peristyle from the left side of the road dressed in an ambiguous peasant wedding dress of white, the symbolic color of Legba and the color a hounsi initiate wears to his or her spiritual birth when the houngan (the Fon word for a Voudoun priest), leads her to the sacred trees and introduces her to the familial divinities.[181]

The charcoal drawing of Son's face on the sketch pad that Jadine drops at the base of the tree on the peristyle lawn faces up at the swamp women in imitation of a vever, a sacred drawing designed with mirrored symmetry. According to ritual, in order to honor a loa, his or her symbol must be placed within the circle at the base of the vertical axis of the tree or cross. Son's linkage by the ancestral mediator Thérèse with the divine/blind horsemen, whom serviteurs draw vevers to honor, qualifies him as a legitimate recipient. The human face reflects the east-west, right-left symmetry that the vever design requires. Jadine, at the novel's end, also associates Son's prowess in lovemaking celestially to a "star," which is a vever design commonly drawn with flour or African flour (ashes). The star also conforms to the mirrored symmetry of the vever lace design. The design may take the form of a cross with an X overlay producing an eight-point design that contains the cardinal points and the compass points between them.[182] It may also take the celestial mapping of the hexagram that commonly represents the Star of David.

During the picnic scene preceding the swamp episode, Son becomes obsessed with first seeing and then touching Jadine's feet, which she hides under her peasant wedding skirt. Submitting to his request, she straightens her legs and holds her bare feet in the air. Like the hounsi of Voudoun initiation, Jadine must not allow her bare feet to touch the ground for fear that she will be spiritually mounted (possessed). Initiates being led to the sacred trees walk on mats that "are hurriedly gathered from behind and once more laid out in front" of them to foreclose premature or random mounting.[183] During the picnic lunch, when Jadine removes her shoes it allows the reader to step into one of Morrison's participatory "holes and spaces" and contribute imaginatively to the narrative. The shoes are most likely espadrilles with canvas uppers and rope soles that invoke the hemp mats used to protect Voudoun initiates against unwanted or premature loa possession. Nevertheless, with Son, Jadine submits to mounting. Son "puts his forefinger on her [bare] sole [a play on the word soul] and held it and held it and held it there."[184] Once she returns to L'Arbe de la Croix, Jadine reflects that the fingerprint on the sole of her foot proves that Son wants her – an ambiguity that plays on the idea of Son, the horseman-loa equivalent, wanting to possess her not only sexually but spiritually as well.

The picnic episode completes an earlier bedroom scene in which Son mounts Jadine's back in canine fashion but the gesture is rife with equine implications.

Jadine's symbolic dance in the swamp peristyle and the swamp women's attempt to claim her as a daughter is not her first encounter with the tree of the cross and circle ancestral cosmogram or her first rejection of its life-affirming reciprocity through kinship. In New York Jadine reflects sadly on a school ritual that she once observed of mothers and daughters, dressed in pastel skirts, holding hands, singing, and swaying in the afternoon light around a "towering brass beech – the biggest and oldest in the state" near a well on the north side of the campus.[185] Afternoon sun to the left or west of the tree's northern location replicates the cardinal point of the "sentimental shaft of light to the left" of the tree in the swamp scene. Motherless and holding the circle ritual in contempt, Jadine never joins the mother-daughter ring dance. She denies the importance and power of ritual to (re)connect her to those who are in the circle of life, living or dead.

***

A single image, North Carolina Mutual Life Insurance agent Robert Smith taking suicidal flight off the top of Mercy Hospital in *Song of Solomon*, encapsulates the reciprocal relationship between the living-dead and their living descendants in the African ancestral exchange operating in Morrison's novels. Morrison states that "The name of the insurance company is real, a well known black-owned company dependent on black clients,[186] and in its corporate name are 'life' and 'mutual'; *agent* being the necessary ingredient of what enables the relationship between them."[187] Smith, whose responsibility is to enable that relationship, has defaulted as the agent insuring mutual life. In fact, his clandestine membership with the Seven Days, a secret vigilante society that randomly executes in like manner a white person for every Black person whose white killer is never brought to justice, sets him apart as mutual death insurance agent.

The "secret" of the Seven Days, which restricts its membership roll to seven, is "time. To take the time, to last. Not to grow; that's dangerous because you might become known. They don't write their names in toilet stalls or brag to women. Time and silence. Those are their weapons, and they go on for-ever."[188] Ironically, Mutual Life Insurance agent Smith's affiliation with the society forecloses his going on forever, or being known by name and deed through time. He has vowed never to marry and never to have children, and without descendants to insure his personal immortality he will immediately sink beyond the horizon of the Sasa into the graveyard of the Zamani. Time is the weapon that will obliterate him. "More regular than the grim reaper" and already "heavily associated with illness and death"[189] in the consciousness of his clients, Smith has not insured himself against collective death. When the policyholders from whom he collects premiums forget he existed, his death will be complete. Smith's "suicide" is in fact not his leap off the roof of Mercy Hospital; it is his forgoing family and fatherhood to insure his remembrance through time. Passage from the Sasa to the Zamani takes four to five generations and according to Guitar Baines, the Sunday man for the Seven Days whose calculation is more generous, every person "is good for five to seven generations of heirs before they're bred out." Therefore, each time whites succeed in killing a Black, "they get rid of five to seven generations."[190] What is not factored into the Seven Days' rationale is that the personal sacrifice of each of them forgoing progeny results in the same generational erasures. Each member of the Seven Days has no mutual life insurance protection.

The trope of the mutual life insurance that the living-dead ancestor and his or her living lineage guarantee one another also extends to the two basic types of insurance coverage one may obtain in modern American life: term life insurance and whole life insurance. Term life insurance, a temporary insurance, covers a person against death for a limited time. Whole life insurance, a permanent insurance, does not have a fixed, limited duration and accrues value over time. The death of the individual covered determines its end, assuming that the policyholder continues to pay the premium. The term and coverage of African traditional mutual life insurance depends upon the time it takes for those remembering the living-dead to complete their life cycles on earth. As long as there is one descendant, one person alive paying the premium of remembering, the ancestor can expect whole life coverage that stretches across the generations contracted in the Sasa. If no one survives or remembers, the life or personal immortality of the passed-on ancestor rapidly sinks below the horizon of the Zamani into the collective graveyard of time.

The impetus for Morrison's treatment of the absent ancestor and the living elder who renders his or her presence as the benevolent guide straddling the African and American worlds and the metaphysical and physical realms to bring in both cases the former forward into the latter has an unsettling cautionary edge. Because her own informal education was greatly enriched by the generations before her, the Africanist presence that her grandparents and communal elders culturally embodied, Morrison sees clearly the cultural perils of the African and African-American past and its people appearing dead or irrelevant to the present generation. *Song of Solomon,*

Beloved, and *Tar Baby* stress the social and psychological disarray that ancestral loss effects when the living not only forget the passed-on who stretch backward and forward between past and present moments but also sever all ties with their heritage, their "DNA ... where you get your information, your cultural information."[191] These works compel the surviving junior lineage to remember those who have passed on since forfeiting the timeless connection forecasts mutual doom: "If we don't keep in touch with the ancestor," Morrison warns "we are, in fact, lost ... When you kill the ancestor you kill yourself [. . . N]ice things don't always happen to the totally self-reliant if there is no conscious historical connection."[192]

Prematurely buried because of forgetfulness and the vagaries of time and space, the passed-on ancestor, the real source of earthly power and prestige, lingers with uncertainty at the crossroads of retention or attrition in African-American life and culture. Morrison's substructural projection in her fiction of the ancestral sign of the Kongo Yowa preserved in Haiti's Voudoun, the most discernible African survival in the Western hemisphere, attempts to stem the encroaching extinction of a Black social, political, and religious consciousness in the American diaspora by bringing the African past forward to the American present.

5

Banganga: the specialists – medicine (wo)men and priest(esse)s

"Bard, physician, judge, and priest": the complex role of conjurer was filled by visionary men and women "of knowledge."

W. E. B. Du Bois, *The Souls of Black Folk*[1]

Nzungi! n'zungi-nzila	Man turns in the path,[*][1]
N'zungi! n'zungi-nzila	He merely turns in the path;
Banganga ban'e E ee!	The priests, the same.

Kongo Proverb[2]

As is true of fiction writers before her who depicted insightfully the complex array of African-American socio-religious roles, Toni Morrison includes among her representations characters that epitomize the banganga, sacred ritual specialists whose personages and practices reflect the identifiable qualities of the herbalist, diviner, medium, and priest of the West and Central African traditional world. According to African art historian Robert Farris Thompson, the ancient Kikongo word banganga survives in the African-Cuban world but not in the United States and not in Brazil where importation of enslaved Africans to the former Portuguese colony constituted the lion's share of human chattel brought to the Western hemisphere. Throughout the Americas, Europeans formulated terms for African medical and spiritual specialists during the transatlantic slave trade, and in the United States from the colonial period to the present the various African banganga, as Thompson establishes, were and still are called blanketly "conjurers":

Versions of some of the ritual authorities responsible for Kongo herbalistic healing and divination appeared in the Americas and served as avatars of Kongo and Angola lore in the New World. Kongo ritual experts in Cuba took the appropriate ancient name *banganga*; those in the United States were known largely as "conjurors" and "root-persons"; and others in Brazil were called *pae de santo* and *mae de santo*, names apparently originating in Yoruba worship – *babalorisha* and

* Path is also translatable as crossroads

137

iyalorisha, "father of the saint" and "mother of the saint." These ritual authorities were largely responsible for the dissemination of Kongo religious and artistic culture throughout the New World.[3]

In *The Religious Instruction of the Negroes in the United States* (1842), Charles C. Jones indicts "conjurers" in the American states as wielding undue influence over their African compatriots. Citing the 1822 insurrection in Charleston, South Carolina, of Denmark Vesey whose co-leader Gullah Jack, an African-born priest and doctor, equipped his men with protective charms to make them "invulnerable," Jones writes that "The superstitions brought from Africa have not been wholly laid aside. Ignorance and super-stition render them [peoples of African ancestry] easy dupes to their teachers, doctors, prophets, conjurers."[4] Although he declasses conjurers to con artists, Jones substantiates that the "superstitions" they and their adherents "brought from Africa" are Middle Passage survivals.

The bananga, the medicine women and men and priestesses and priests who became American-named and New World-fashioned conjurers, occu-pied, like their Old World predecessors, sacred overlapping offices devoted to preserving the physical and spiritual wellbeing of their communities. In much of the literary criticism devoted to the discussion of African tradi-tional specialists, scholars invoke the term conjurer as a collective signifier of the multiple roles that the nganga (singular of bananga) performs, drawing no discernible distinctions between the various offices. Buakasa Tulu Kia Mpansu defines the nganga as an interpreter whose primary role is to discern the source of sorcery and harming kindoki (witchcraft) that operate through words, objects, and dreams.[5] And in Swahili, a Bantu language like Kikongo, mganga, the equivalent of nganga, translates as doctor or philosopher, emphasizing the prestige the title confers.

African-American conjuring, past and present, encompasses healing, charm-making, divination, and sorcery – potion- and spell-crafting. Some of the earliest antebellum reports of secret healing and poisonings date to the 1720s in South Carolina.[6] Practices surrounding conjuring and medicine-making in the United States exhibit traceable West African traditional worship and healing practices of Kongo belief and Dahomean Vodun influence that coalesced in Haiti's Voudoun and were retained in American Voodoo. Despite its decline as ritualized worship and subse-quent rise as a system of magic and entertainment, Voodoo lasted in name if not in fact in New Orleans primarily because the elevated numbers of enslaved Africans that planters transported to Louisiana from Saint Domingue during the Haitian Revolution from 1791 to 1804 kept the

United States's strain of the religion alive. The hegemony of Catholicism in New Orleans, which easily juxtaposed with Voodoo, also contributed to the latter's continuation and defamiliarization. As early as the late nineteeth century, Albert J. Raboteau notes, "New Orleans became known as the capital of 'root work,' and voodoo, or hoodoo, came to be a synonym for conjuring and conjurers apart from the cultic context of its African-Haitian origins."[7] In the Caribbean the banganga of Africa, especially the priests and priestesses of Kongo and of Dahomey, fostered the survival of the worship culture. Assisted by island isolationism, Catholicism, the religion of the European master class, "was more conducive to the survival of African religion than was Protestan[t]ism."[8] Because Catholicism was also the dominant religion of Brazil, a parallel survival occurred in the African-Brazilian retention of Candomblé, Vodun's South American manifestation. A massive West and Central African enslaved population easily folded their traditional beliefs into the Catholicism of the Portuguese. In North America throughout the South, however, Protestant hegemony overwrote the ritual worship of Voodoo, and Black Baptist, African Methodist, and Pentecostal preachers emerged as the Christianized "priestly" power brokers in African-American communities.

Comparable in varying degrees to their Caribbean and Brazilian religious counterparts, the ritual specialists who inhabit Morrison's fictional American landscapes are ambiguously marked religious men and women whose Christian communities recognize them not in name but in deed as banganga, spiritual and material mediators: herbalists, mediums, diviners, and priests. A Caribbean native, Soaphead Church in *The Bluest Eye* (1970) epitomizes the fused-office ritual specialist whose areas of expertise survived the Middle Passage and passed into North American healing practices through Voudoun. "Reader, Adviser, and Interpreter of Dreams," Soaphead Church, a failed Anglican priest, is a synthesis of Christianity and West African tradition beliefs.[9] His affection for things because they resonate with human spiritual contact suggests religious values rooted in animism, the belief that spirit animates matter, while his epistle to God chastising Him for failing to provide a little Black girl with blue eyes approximates the intermediary role that the houngan, the Voudoun priest, performs to connect the loa, gods or spirits, with their serviteurs. Shadrack in *Sula* (1973) is Morrison's first figuring of the traditional priest whose loa traits indicate that a maît-tête, master spirit, of the Voudoun pantheon guides him in the institution of the psychosomatic method of healing. His portraiture subliminally and seamlessly forwards Morrison's stylistic prescription to write within the cultural purview of

Blackness drawn from identifiable African qualities of being and knowing. Shadrack's persona is a synthesis of the many manifestations of the Voudoun loa Ogoun, the divinity of war. His subscribed houngan-loa persona is prelude to the priestly representation of Pilate Dead in *Song of Solomon* (1977). A mambo or Voudoun priestess imbued with the qualities of Legba, the crossroads loa of the Voudoun pantheon, Pilate oversees the gateway to the spiritual plane. Four novels and twenty-one years later, Morrison shifts her depiction of the master loa of Voudoun to the orixás, gods, of Brazil's Candomblé, molding the character of Consolata Sosa in *Paradise* (1998) as a spirit-headed priestess or mãe de santo, mother of the saint. Officiating as a mãe de santo in an Oklahoma Convent, the equivalent of a terreiro or house of Candomblé, Consolata has the personality of Yemanjá, the orixá of the sea that governs women, childbirth, and axé (ase), the positive procreative female life force.

Along with Morrison's treatments of characters whose personalities are directly culled from Vodun influence are character meditations of specialists who articulate the primal founding doctrine of the African religion – the unity of flesh and spirit. The portrait of M'Dear as the Western hemisphere's manifestation of a West African traditional healer in *The Bluest Eye* (1970) gives way to the depiction of Circe, whose name invokes the circle imagery connected with African ancestral regeneration. She is the timeless medicinal priestess in *Song of Solomon* who assists in the reconnection of the fleshed world with the spirit world, the living Deads with the living-dead in the spiritual realm. Circe's placement in the narrative subtextually interrogates the Hellenic appropriation of select African divinities for exclusive inclusion in the Greek mythic pantheon. Continuing the exegesis of physical and metaphysical unity, Baby Suggs, the lay priestess/mambo in *Beloved* (1987), calls Cincinnati serviteurs to a Voudoun-inspired ring shout, the shuffling counterclockwise circle dance modeled on the four moments of the sun cosmogram. Her insistence that those assembled love their flesh reverberates with the principal tenet of Voudoun, the inseparability of flesh and spirit that mãe de santo Consolata Sosa reiterates in *Paradise*. Finally, medicine woman and priestess Lone DuPres counsels Consolata Sosa not to "separate God from His elements ... [from] His works."[10] The African traditionalist respects the tempering of opposites that typifies the intersection of God as Spirit and His fleshed creations.

The official priestly roles that Morrison's specialists exemplify are testaments to the traditional religions that enslaved West and Central Africans creolized into a single religion in the Caribbean, the crossroads of the

Middle Passage, and transported to North and South America. Those religious roles now abide in seen and unseen ways in peoples of African descent dispersed throughout the Americas of the Black Atlantic.

THE AMERICAS' HOUNGAN, MAMBO, PÃE DE SANTO, AND MÃE DE SANTO

The West and Central African traditional medicine women and men, the historical precedents for M'Dear, Soaphead Church, and Morrison's other specialists, may come from any background, any age group, and may have no official position outside of their professional duties of discerning people's needs. With powers conferred natally or obtained later by ingesting certain medicines, they can, according to John S. Mbiti, "harm or protect, kill or cure"[11] and may be adept at divination and witchcraft detection. Because they are taken to streams and taught the mysteries of various natural elements by others skilled in the medicinal arts, they are specialists in herbal remedies and the medicinal values of insects and other natural matter from which "the causes, cures, and the prevention of diseases and other forms of suffering" may be derived.[12]

"In African villages," Mbiti asserts, "disease and misfortune are religious experiences, and it requires a religious approach to deal with them."[13] Thus medicine women and men are doctors and ministers whose prescriptions are equally physical and spiritual/psychological. In addition to requiring a patient to consume powders and liquids, inhale vapors and smoke, or submit to massages or bleedings that incantation recitations may accompany, medicinal specialists may request the afflicted to act: sacrifice an animal, abstain from routine or common practices, observe strictly some taboo or avoid specific foods and persons. Because all "[s]uffering, misfortune, disease and accident" may be traced to some cause, that cause must be "counteracted, uprooted or punished." Medicine women and men provide rituals, prescriptions, and charms to prevent physical and metaphysical causation. The means by which they undertake to cure is of less importance than the cure itself.[14]

Two examples, from her early fiction, best illustrate Morrison's modern, loose adaptations of specialists' applying physical and psychological prescriptions to cure the afflicted. In her first novel, *The Bluest Eye*, the communal herbalist M'Dear prescribes the consumption of pot liquor, the juices from stewed vegetables and meats, as a physical cure for the cold in the womb of Aunt Jimmy, Cholly Breedlove's surrogate mother. When Aunt Jimmy dies while ostensibly on the road to recovery, women of the

Lorain, Ohio, community speculate that her unexpected demise is attributable to failing to abstain from restricted food: Essie Foster's peach cobbler. In *Sula*, Morrison's second novel, the afflicted, following the instructions of the specialist, must act to bring about her psychological healing. Soaphead Church requires Pecola to feed (and thereby unwittingly sacrifice) an animal to secure the cure of blue eyes she desperately desires to affirm her worthiness as a lovable and attractive human being. Her cure arrives by way of psychological deviation; Pecola's mental trauma at witnessing the dog die of convulsions delivers the blue eyes she requests.

African traditional mediums and diviners serve as time and communication portals for the living-dead ancestors and spirits. While in a sense they comprise subcategories of the medicinal specialists, mediums and diviners, in counterdistinction to medicine women and men who are strictly concerned with the physical and psychological healing of the living, officiate, as Mbiti confirms, in consultation with those who have passed on to the afterworld:

The spirits and divinities that possess mediums belong to the time period of the Zamani. By entering individuals in the Sasa period, they become our contemporaries. The state of mediumship is one of contemporizing the past, bringing into human history the "personality" of beings essentially beyond the horizon of the Sasa period. This phenomenon is, however, temporary, and the two time periods slip apart when the state of possession is ended.[15]

Therefore, and this is an important distinction, mediumship may be less about the communication between the living-dead and the living and more about the co-temporality of the past with the present. During possession, the temporary displacement of the soul or psyche by that of a spirit or divinity, mediums receive knowledge that is impossible for them personally or presently to know. In trance states they identify the locations of lost objects, committers of crimes, and threats of imminent dangers. Because mediums are psychically absent during the relay of information, they typically work with diviners who interpret the transmissions. Medicine women, men, and priests may occasionally fill the diviner role, and inversely, it is not uncommon for diviners or medicine women and men to act intermittently as mediums. With respect to gender, mediums are usually female, while diviners are typically male. With the personage of Pilate Dead, Morrison creatively evolves the role of the female medium who contemporizes the past with the present. Pilate, whose primary role is to assist in the ancestral reunion of the Deads, receives visits and interprets messages from her father, Jake, who has passed on to the afterworld.

Because there is no possession feature to her communication with the living-dead and because the communicant is not yet in the Zamani, Pilate is best typed as the living elder who gives presence to the absent living-dead ancestor and who must prevent Jake from descending into the Zamani graveyard of time. Nevertheless, she is the mediator and time portal between the living-dead and the living. Soaphead Church, whose primary role is to assist in psychological healing, exemplifies the wayward twentieth-century male diviner who professes to have the power to locate lost and stolen objects and alleviate misfortune.

Individuals who enter temples, shrines, groves, and convents to receive training in comprehending death and resurrection and to emerge with new personalities constitute another medium class. "The trainees are cut off, or killed, from the solidarity of ordinary society, when they enter their convents." They shave their heads and perform daily domestic chores. Because they have spirit and intuitive knowledge, people seek them out for private and public counsel.[16] The particulars of this class of specialist apply to the secluded women of the Convent in *Paradise* who, under the counsel of Consolata Sosa, not only comprehend death and resurrection but experience the unity first hand. After Ruby patriarchs shoot them, Consolata's initiates resurrect with shorn hair and altered personalities.

The priesthood tradition, found among the Yoruba, Ibo, Ewe, and other groups, is stronger in West Africa than in other parts of the continent.[17] Just as mediums are the intermediaries between the living-dead and the living, priests and priestesses function as intermediaries between divine spirits and the living. Associated with temples, shrines, and sacred groves, they receive training and initiation once they have set themselves apart from the communal mainstream. Priests and priestesses, who also operate as mediums, may serve in official capacities at sacrifices and other ceremonies, or they may be lay priests, individuals who routinely oversee communal rituals but do not bear the formal title of priest. Morrison's contingent of priestesses and priests is set apart from mainstream society and bears no formal appointment. Most reside in habitations – Shadrack's cottage across the river or Consolata's Convent seventeen miles away from Ruby, for example – set apart from larger communities near by. Often a grove of four trees or a four-columned structure symbolic of the sacred area of a Voudoun peristyle marking their priestliness stands in close proximity to their isolated domiciles.

The communal roles of the West African traditional priest and priestess survived the Middle Passage as the Caribbean houngan (from the Fon language – "houn" means "spirits" and "gan" means "chief") and mambo (the French transcription of the Carib-Indian term "ma," which means "great," and "boya" or "boii," which in its singular form means "snake" or "priest"). The houngan and mambo officiate over a hounfor, a sacred precinct or parish, where serviteurs come routinely for religious ceremonies. In Brazil the priest and priestess, pãe de santo and mãe de santo, head a terreiro or house of Candomblé, a sacred consecrated space. All are healers of physical and mental traumas and public servants of communal groups that in turn serve them. Because Voudoun and Candomblé are not centralized religions – they do not have a governing body at their apexes to which each hounfor or terreiro must report – priests and priestesses must rely on their ability to win the confidence and independent confirmation of each member of their society. And it is the member's confirmation that qualifies them for the religious post they hold. Collectively in Voudoun, for example, the members of the community determine who will be conferred with the asson (açon) in the ceremony of priestly investiture. In Maya Deren's exposure to Haitian Voudoun, only an individual elevated to the rank of priest is given the sacred instrument – a rattle with a small bell often attached – of divine power. She states that "It is the individual members of that community, acting upon their free initiative, who may adopt a man [or woman] as father [or mother], priest [or priestess] . . . and this adoption is neither absolute nor permanent. If he should fail to fulfill his manifold responsibilities, he can be abandoned. He retains his sacred rattle; but no one comes."[18] Here one must consider the representation of Shadrack who institutes in the Bottom the psychological ritual of confronting death once a year because of his own mental trauma encountered on the World War I battlefield. Every January third he rings a cowbell asson to draw to action those of his community whose confidence he has won.

Ritual and healing knowledge solidify the priest's or priestess's acceptance as the community's father or mother and that knowledge is very much predicated on rightly diagnosing dis-ease that stems from natural and physical disorder or from unnatural or "psychosomatic" disorder.[19] Herbal and ritual treatments are often given to combat organic and spiritual disturbance, with the latter ritual treatment being particularly important because the priest and priestess are intermediaries between the living and the spirits. With respect to the treatment of psychosomatic or psychic shock, these religious specialists may prescribe an action for the patient to complete as a physical therapeutic approach to healing psychic trauma.

To imprint her characters with identifiable Blackness, Morrison subliminally inscribes their personalities, particularly those of her priests and priestesses, with the traits of African-derived Vodun gods. It is a literary strategy that has traditional backing since in a Haitian Voudoun or Brazilian Candomblé ceremony the priest and priestess are the principal mediums through which the loa or orixás manifest themselves in the mortal realm. In Voudoun and Candomblé each spirit divinity has well-defined characteristics and associations that range from identifiable speech mannerisms and physical postures to signature vices, virtues, ritual objects, and sacred numbers. Devotional service to them may include wearing clothing of particular colors, offering them preferred foods, and observing sexual continence on days sacred to them. When a spirit possesses a medium, the voice of the medium may adjust to the divinity; she may crave special dishes or adopt a specific limp or gait. The personalities of personal or patron spirits – who offer guidance in times of need or may be consulted for any reason – are called maît-têtes, master spirits. Serving as a hounfor's loa-in-residence, a special guardian maît-tête attaches itself to a specific houngan. The spirit resides in the head of the priest(ess) or serviteur, manifesting itself in his or her behavior and character. Although there are seemingly countless families and manifestations of loa and orixás, some are popular though they never mount or possess a serviteur, while others present themselves frequently during possession rituals. Among the Haitian loa, Legba, Ghede, Damballah, Agwe, Ogoun, Erzulie, and Ayizan are among the most important, while the "twelve principal [Brazilian] orixás are Xangô, Og[o]un, Oxalá, Oxóssi, Omolu, Ossâim, Iroko, Yemanjá, Óxum, Iansã, Nanã, and Oxumarê."²⁰ Morrison subliminally inscribes prominent characters in her fiction with the traits of Legba, Ghede, Ogoun, Erzulie, Ayizan, Oxóssi, and Yemanjá. In the discussions below, the personalities of Ogoun, Legba, and Yemanjá are central to the personas of Morrison's representations of the houngan, mambo, and mãe de santo.

African traditional specialists – the healers, mediums, diviners, and priests in Morrison's fiction – are a cadre of communal practitioners who mobilize spiritual resources as well as material resources in practical and creative ways to address human physical and psychological dis-eases that assault individual, family, and tribal wellbeing. Members of the community regard them like other individuals with elevated religious status, such as twins or the mentally ill whose biological or psychological natures set them apart, with respect and religious awe.²¹ By and large, the sacred specialists, medicine (wo)men and priest(esse)s in African traditional life and in Morrison's fiction forward the religious life of their communities and are the "symbolic points of contact between the historical and spiritual worlds."²²

SOAPHEAD CHURCH – THE CARIBBEAN MEDIUM, DIVINER,
AND HOUNGAN

A "cinnamon-eyed West Indian with lightly browned skin,"[23] Elihue
Micah Whitcomb, (aka Soaphead Church) is a native of the Greater
Antilles – Cuba, Hispaniola (Haiti and the Dominican Republic),
Jamaica, and Puerto Rico – and an east-west fusion of cultures, beliefs,
and religious office specialties. A product of three-ancestries – a colonial
British patriarch and African Middle Passage matriarch of the nineteenth
century, and a half-Chinese birth mother[24] – he is a synthesis of an
Anglican priest and the African traditional priest despite his total leaning
toward Anglophilia and rejection of "all that suggested Africa."[25] As a
young man he entered an Anglican monastery and dallied with priesthood
but the Caribbean beliefs of Voudoun, his West Indies matrilineal inheritance, become his communal trade. Believing that "to name an evil was to
neutralize it if not annihilate it,"[26] he embraces the monistic view of evil as
a divine creation essential to the balance of good. Similarly, because evil
is an inescapable part of human nature and a necessary complement to
good, Soaphead Church's personality is a fusion of opposites, "an arab-
esque: intricate, symmetrical, balanced and tightly constructed." To temper his moral prudery he has "rare and keen sexual cravings" for little
girls.[27] Therefore he considers his immoral sexual predilection a "comfortable evil."[28]

West African animistic religions that infuse the physical with the metaphysical ground Soaphead Church's "fondness for things . . . a craving for
things humans had touched . . . [that retained t]he residue of the human
spirit smeared on inanimate objects."[29] In Voudoun nonmaterial spirit
animates matter in the same way that the gros-bon-ange, soul or psyche,
infuses the material flesh of the body, while divinity spirits animate trees,
stones, and other natural elements.[30] The houngan and mambo have the
power to summon *les Invisibles*, spirits, from the afterworld to manifest
themselves in the material dimension of the mortal world, and a govi or
nkisi (material vessel similar to the kimbi) is commonly used to lodge the
spirits after their return from the waters of the abyss beyond the Kalunga.[31]
Soaphead Church derives pleasure from contemplating "evidence of
human footsteps on the mat." He absorbs the smell of a quilt and wallows
"in the sweet certainty that many bodies had sweated, slept, dreamed, made
love, been ill, and even died under it."[32]

A brief devotion to Anglican monastic life cuts him off from the solidarity of ordinary society, sharpens his misanthropic proclivities, and results

in Soaphead Church's officiating as a New World houngan in Lorain, Ohio. Testifying that his priestly powers are natally inscribed, he affirms his position to clients as the intermediary between the spirit world and the living. After the abused Pecola Breedlove requests blue eyes and abruptly departs his residence, Soaphead Church addresses a letter to God, arrogantly proclaiming that while God was inattentive to her needs, he has played His role and done it well. "I gave her those blue eyes she wanted . . . I did what You did not, could not. Would not do . . . I played You. And it was a very good show!"[33] Most African traditional cultures view the Supreme Being as remote, too high above humans to be concerned with earthly affairs. Intermediate divinities and priests, ministering to the living, seek to remedy petitions concerning human physical and psychological dis-ease.

As self-appointed "caseworker" – "Reader, Adviser, and Interpreter of Dreams," Soaphead Church professes that he can show the sick the way to health, the role of the medicine man or herbalist, and locate lost and stolen articles, the role of the able medium and adept diviner. Claiming to be conversant with the spiritual world, he, as priest, can purportedly keep a baby's ghost and other spiritual visitors at bay, break the fixes of witches, and overcome the spells of sorcerers. And of utmost importance, Soaphead Church "respects the essential wisdom of the psychosomatic mechanism . . . [that the Voudoun priest employs] and uses it therapeutically." The therapeutic prescription he requires for the granting of Pecola Breedlove's blue eyes places the onus on the afflicted to effect her own healing. She must act, by giving Bob, his landlady's rheumy dog, a packet of meat laced with poison as an offering. Enlisting an unsuspecting carrier to deliver poison hidden in food, albeit to kill a dog, Soaphead Church shifts his role to sorcerer, the specialist who uses food, poison, and deception to destroy that which offends him.

The bi-religiosity that Soaphead Church exemplifies is equally apparent in the Lorain, Ohio, "people [who] led him into a profession designed to serve them." Because his Christian "clientele is already persuaded,"[34] the "experiential communality" that the group shares guiding its pre-Christian ethos[35] and the free initiative each of its members extends to him as the communal priest officiating over his or her dis-ease issues from institutional and uninstitutional religious valences. His Lorain clients may see his vocation as an extension of Christianity or as totally divorced from it. Their continued patronage of his services depends solely on his ability to maintain their trust. From his own background and perhaps from some of theirs, the sign of the cross that he makes over Pecola during her visit, for example, is ambiguously charged; it invokes simultaneously the cross of

Christ's Crucifixion from his Church of England training and the cross of the circle in Voudoun from the African traditional exposure of his Greater Antilles nativity. The first interpretation would be important to those of his clients who require Christian sanctioning of their "unorthodox" approach to physical and psychic healing. The second interpretation, though (un)known consciously by his African-American constituency, would be important to individuals in the African diaspora who openly embrace the African-centered ethos as their own. Some would clearly make a very definite separation between the two beliefs; others would simply regard the two as little more than different expressions of the same reality.

   Directed by more than Voodoo's decline in the United States as a ritualized worship and rise as a system of magic, Soaphead Church's remissness in his priestly role issues from his intemperate gravitation to the negative and not to the positive, to self-hatred and not to self-affirmation. For this reason, "he chose to remember Hamlet's abuse of Ophelia, but not Christ's love of Mary Magdalene; Hamlet's frivolous politics, but not Christ's serious anarchy. He noticed Gibbon's acidity, but not his tolerance . . . For all his exposure to the best minds of the Western world, he allowed only the narrowest interpretation to touch him."[36] Soaphead Church chooses to revere his colonial British patriarch whose claim to empire enslaved and extinguished countless African lives but not his African matriarch, the victim of his British grandfather's claim to empire. In fact, he wishes to exorcise Africa from both his genealogy and his body. His nickname, Soaphead, communally given to him because he uses soap as pomade to straighten his kinky hair, and the surname Church, suggesting the obfuscation of his African traditional beliefs by Judeo-Christianity, denotes his fragmented psyche. He is incapable of psychologically reconciling the oppositional complexities of his African, Asian, and European ancestries. Exploiting Pecola, at the nadir of her vulnerability, he is the New World spiritually and spatially dispossessed traditional priest who, though remaining close to his sacred African traditional roots, is unable to transcend his fractured New World identity.

SHADRACK – HOUNGAN AND WARRIOR OGOUN

Whereas the depiction of Soaphead Church establishes the historical continuum between the West Indian priest who sustained West African traditional beliefs and the communal reader and advisor who conjured in the United States, the representation of Shadrack, the West African priest figure in *Sula*, debuts the Morrison practice of subliminally inscribing her characters with the identifiable character traits of the Vodun gods as the African diaspora reconfigured them in the Western hemisphere. Vashti Crutcher Lewis explains that "in traditional African cultures," Shadrack would not be a pariah or a mystery since he represents "a profound rootedness in African cosmology."[37] Lewis asserts that the Bottom community shuns Shadrack because its historically disconnected residents do not recognize his African presence, his status "as a West African Water Priest who represents and speaks for a river god."[38] Unknown to his community, as well as to many readers of the novel, the persona of Shadrack, in addition to exemplifying the socio-religious role of the Voudoun houngan, synthesizes the many attributes of the loa Ogoun, the divinity of war, iron, and fire and the phallic principle whose symbol is the machete or saber. Depicted as the wounded warrior with outstretched hands, Ogoun resembles in body posture Christ taken from the cross. His feet, hands, and body are pierced and misshapen. Shadrack, like Ogoun, is the guardian of the hounfor because of his love of ritual and initiation.[39] His personality is an amalgamation of the family of Ogouns, the many manifestations of the Vodun spirit divinity as they have evolved over time and in various Western diasporic spaces.

"The Nigerian Ogoun who crossed the ocean from Africa was a figure in the same classic tradition as the Greek Zeus. He was a sky divinity, Lord of thunderbolt, of fire and of might. By logical extension he was patron of warriors and of the iron smiths, forgers of war-weapons."[40] In Voudoun "a collective creation" that "did not exact the abandonment of one tribal deity in favor of another . . ., the deity of the numerically dominant group absorbed the similar deities of the others; or the emphatic character of one tribe, such as the warlike qualities of the Nagos [Yorubans], gave their deities of war, Ogoun, preeminence over all representatives of that principle."[41] Thus, based on the basic African-descended Rada nation or rites, Shadrack is a creolization of many facets of the personality of Ogoun. To the Yoruba people of western Nigeria, Ogoun is Shangô (Xangô in Portuguese), the god of war. The thunder, wind, and lightning god of rivers and springs is the Dahomean Ogoun Shangô. Ogoun Badagris, associated with the moon, takes his name from the seacoast town in western Nigeria. Ogoun Bayé, the god of barriers and gateways, resembles Legba. Ogoun Balindjo or Ogoun Batala "is known as a healer. In this aspect he often shows particular concern for children."[42] Ogoun Panama takes his name from his custom of wearing hats. Ogoun Feraille, who is identified with St. Jacques, "impart[s] strength to a serviteur by slapping him firmly on the arms, the thighs and the back." He periodically shouts "By Thunder!" and is a conspicuous consumer of alcoholic spirits; he "spurts rum through his teeth in a fine spray, a gesture special to the Ogouns."[43] Ogoun Ge-Rouge, linked with fire, hotness, and the color red, is the Petro or Haitian amalgamation of the warrior god who metamorphoses into the politician St. Jacques. An intrinsic aspect of the loa Ogoun is that he may present himself directly – as the ancient hero warrior – or indirectly – as the personage of a modern or contemporary soldier.[44]

"Shadrack's divine nature results from his state of unconsciousness as a victim of shell-shock during World War I." This psychic event is important because "[i]n traditional West African culture when one has lain unconscious for many days, people believed that a person's spirit left the physical body and entered the ancestral world where he or she became an active participant."[45] The psychically altered soldier returns to Medallion and takes up residence in a riverbank shack to pursue the vocation of fisherman. Shortly after his return, he institutes and ritualizes an annual National Suicide Day, a celebration devised to implement a psychosomatic method of healing. Every January third, Shadrack, clanging a cowbell, his asson of priestly investiture, and dragging a hangman's rope, calls "the people together. Telling them that this was their only chance to kill themselves or each other"[46] to avoid the unexpectedness, the randomness of death. In the personage of the healer Ogouns, Balindjo and Batala, he prescribes the therapeutic ritual of action to assuage the psychic shock of death's uncertainty that first traumatizes him on the battlefield in France.

A cluster of textual signs subtly qualifies Shadrack's multiple Ogoun personas. In France shellfire and death rain on Shadrack's infantry as soon as it crosses a stream running along a field, a metaphorical Kalunga line dividing the hemispheres of the living and dead, which he and his comrades in arms have been marching along for several days. Under enemy attack, Shadrack "ran, bayonet fixed," a symbol of Ogoun's iron machete/saber phallus, "deep in the great sweep of men flying across this field."[47] Hence the phallic associations that attend his subsequent Medallion return – where he walks about with penis exposed, pees in front of women and girls, and uses a fish knife as his occupational machete to slash the days of the calendar – extend his phallic imaging begun on the European battlefield.[48] During the confrontation in France, Shadrack had hoped to feel the exhilaration or terror of war but he feels only "the bite of a nail in his boot, which pierced the ball of his foot."[49] His nail-pierced foot, combined with feet "clotted with pain" and an afflicted hand during his hospital recuperation in the United States,[50] contribute to an image of a wounded Ogoun with crucifixion wounds who survives, like Christ, crossing into death.

Allusions to the manifestations of Ogoun continue to define Shadrack after the shell-shocked World War I soldier returns to the United States and the Bottom. As he exits the grounds of the hospital, the surrounding trees convey some import to Shadrack's wellbeing, for he surveys their heads "tossing ruefully but harmlessly, since their trunks were rooted too deeply in the earth to threaten him."[51] All loa enter and exist by the gateway tree, and Shadrack, characterized as the gateway Ogoun Bayé, checking the disposition of the trees, takes the plunge into a potentially treacherous world. He heads for a gate by way of a low red building that bears the sacred color of Ge-Rouge Ogoun. Later, a planked bridge will be the "gateway" connector between Shadrack's Medallion riverbank cottage that "once belonged to his grandfather long time dead"[52] and the Bottom community in the hilly upper hemisphere of the town named for a circular medal with inscriptions. Not far from that plank connector is the peristyle of four leaf-locked trees that is the primary formation that a traditional priest oversees as central to his hounfor. The houngan mediating the living-dead and the living, he will have to cross the planked gateway spanning a metaphorical Kalunga line to pass up into the Bottom to call its residents to death with "a voice so full of authority and thunder" reminiscent of Ogoun Shangô, lord of the thunderbolt.[53] At the close of his first day of release from the hospital, Shadrack, incarcerated by the local authorities who suspect that he is mentally deranged, sleeps "more tranquil than the curve of eggs," a description that invokes the "cosmic egg" association attached to Ogoun Shangô.[54] Other manifestations and associations of Ogoun later explain Shadrack's inexplicable behavior: Shadrack's tipping his hat to Sula when he is not wearing one suggests Ogoun Panama, while his excessive, riotous drinking aligns him with Ogoun Feraille, the irreverent, conspicuous consumer of rum.

His battlefield and earlier post-World War I traumas trigger the ritual and lunar Ogouns to surface in Shadrack's persona, providing him with the incentive to institute the seemingly bizarre ritual of National Suicide Day, an annual psychological prescription for trauma caused by death. It is Ogoun's responsibility to guard the sacred precinct of his community, and it is his love of ritual and initiation that positions him as the most favored loa to serve in this capacity. "Like moonlight stealing under a window shade," the idea to begin National Suicide Day "insinuated itself" into the mind of Shadrack, and that flash of inspiration, which is likened to the stealth of lunar activity, the territorial agency of the moon-linked Ogoun Badagris, inspires the first ritualized suicide celebration. Similarly, after resigning himself on the night before the last National Suicide Day to the fact that the January third celebration would never accomplish its intent, Shadrack rationalizes that "He might as well sit forever on his riverbank and stare out of the window at the moon."[55]

Ritual practices maintain the socio-psychological wellbeing of a community and a positive balance of complementary forces. Shadrack's attempt to effect both in the Bottom blends the official communal duties of the houngan with the characteristics of Ogoun, a healer of trauma and founder of ritual and initiation. Shadrack relies on therapeutic action to resolve the unexpectedness of death and dying. "He knew the smell of death and was terrified of it, for he could not anticipate it ... [H]e hit on the notion that if one day a year were devoted to it, everyone could get it out of the way and the rest of the year could be safe and free."[56] As village priest with the loa Ogoun as his maît-tête, Shadrack, with a thunderous voice, crosses from "below" the river by walking across a planked bridge up into the "Bottom [and] down Carpenter's Road," the vertical axis of the town's geographical cross formation. The ritual implied here with respect to Voudoun is that Shadrack returns annually from below the waters, a direct parallel to the annual "retirer d'en bas de l'eau" in Voudoun, and moves along the vertical axis of Carpenter's Road to insinuate information about the nature of death into the Bottom and agitate for suspension of fearing it. The role of the houngan in general and Ogoun in particular is to officiate at rituals. He must remove barriers to the ritual process to insure its success as a healing mechanism.

Shadrack sounds an iron cowbell, the call to service, as a houngan would ring the asson. In the pre-colonial kingdom of Dahomey, only a king could confer the sacred asson but now conference can be undertaken by any established houngan of a hounfor. An instrument of power over the world of *les Invisibles*, only a priest can own and use it; otherwise, it has no power. Although now a cowbell, the asson rattle evolved from a calabash filled with bones, the equivalent of maracas, a form of which also appears in the mythology of the Arawak, the indigenous Indians of Haiti whose beliefs also shaped Voudoun.

Shadrack's ancient role is driven deep into the recesses of the Bottom community's collective unconscious. To accent its unconscious knowing, Morrison's projection of the cross and circle onto the geography of Medallion, an implied circle, is an encryption of the Kongo Yowa. The Bottom's tree-lined Carpenter's Road in the upper hemisphere of Medallion turns into Main Street in its lower hemisphere, where the citizens of European descent reside. The river bisects the town's diameter. Crossing the river into the lower hemisphere, select members of the Bottom, called by Shadrack, meet watery deaths.

Subverted West African traditional cosmologies guide the Bottom's beliefs, practices, and personalities. Morrison's merging of the priest persona with the traits of the loa is not at variance with the reality of intertwining the two in Voudoun. In Haiti the expression "'temperament mun, ce temperament loa-li' ('the character of a person is the character of his loa')" and the belief that "all major loa-principles are latent in everyone" prevail. "The reference to the sympathetic relationship between the character of a person and that of his loa relates to the maît-tête, the 'master of the head', or the loa which is dominant above all others in the psyche of an individual."[57] The priest especially is expected to have a dominant spirit guarding his hounfor that possesses and speaks through him and selects serviteurs.

PILATE DEAD – MAMBO AND CROSSROADS LEGBA

A crossroads figure, Pilate Dead is likened to a swaying willow tree whose feet point east and west.[58] Symbolized as the tree or vertical axis intersecting the mortal, horizontal plane whose maît-tête (master or head spirit) is the crossroads trickster and guardian Legba, Pilate is the communal mambo who mediates communication between the living-dead ancestors and the living Deads. Her association with a grove, four huge pine trees at the back of her house, marks the social roles that she performs as a Voodoo priestess in *Song of Solomon*. The shelter and guidance that she gives as an unrecognized mambo in her Michigan community were ordained at her naming at birth. Jake, her illiterate father, selected from the Bible a "group of letters that seemed to him strong and handsome; saw in them a large figure that looked like a tree hanging in some princely but protective way over a row of smaller trees."[59]

Bridging the spiritual and physical worlds, Pilate mediates the presence of the absent ancestor. In a general sense, she is the ancestral presence, the benevolent elder who gives the absent living-dead presence by mediating their clan's involvement in the physical realm. African-identified and a natural healer, she is medium and diviner by virtue of the fact that she mediates the communication of her father who appears posthumously to speak to her and she divines his messages. Pilate's spiritual contact with her passed-on father is essential for the resurrection of her grandfather Solomon's lineage and for rescuing it and him from premature collective death in the Zamani, the graveyard of time. Jake's cryptic "Sing. Sing" and "You just can't fly on off and leave a body"[60] culminate in the reclamation of the Deads' African and Indian patriarchal and matriarchal ancestral lines. Through Pilate's agency, the forgotten and lost of her family are remembered and found.

The intersection of the Deads' African and Indian ancestral histories[61] defines the bi-cultural religious personas with which Morrison imbues Pilate and Milkman and informs their spiritual bond. Because Spanish law sanctioned the enslavement of New World indigenous peoples who were suspected of practicing cannibalism, slave traders shipped Carib Indians to any island port where they could be sold as human chattel. Unknown numbers of Caribs were "carried in slave-ships to Haiti (Hispaniola) from every shore and atoll of the Caribbean,"[62] just as countless Africans were taken from the west coast of Africa to the Caribbean for the purpose of perpetual servitude. Many Africans fleeing slavery also sought refuge with Indians who had never known slavery but who had themselves sought refuge in the hills of the island. In response to their common Caribbean slave and maroon experiences, both dislocated groups banded together against a common enemy. Out of their alliance came the discovery that their religious beliefs were compatible with and susceptible to amalgamation. The amalgamated Voudoun divinities that issued from their common rage against displacement and enslavement are classified as Petro, the aggressive loa branch that originated in the Americas in contrast to the Rada branch, "the protective, guardian powers" whose origins are traceable to Dahomey. The Petro divinities are "'plus raide': more hard, more tough, more stern; less tolerant and forgiving, more practical and more demanding."[63]

Issuing from a lifeless womb after her Indian mother Singing Bird died during her birth, Pilate, born without a navel, is cut off from people early in life. Once individuals that she meets during her wanderings from place to place learn that she is navel-less, they part company with her. On discovering that she is without a navel, a root worker with whom Pilate apprentices and a group of migrant workers with whom she settles declare her unnatural and ask her to leave their camp. Only islanders off the coast of Virginia accept her into their community and one of them fathers her only child, Reba. Her reluctance to disclose her smooth, uninterrupted stomach even to him prompts her to decline marriage.

The Carib Indians interpolated into Voudoun the belief that an individual whose soul has fled or been stolen is a dead being and, therefore, lacks a navel, the anatomical sign of life. Ceremonially, the houngan at a serviteur's death liberates his or her gros-bon-ange (soul or psyche) and the maît-tête through the deceased's navel. Not having a navel symbolizes that Pilate is outside the mortal sphere and not the average communal member.

Because Pilate speaks with her father who has passed on, she is fearless of death and her physical association with the crossroads Legba, who mediates traffic between the physical and the metaphysical planes, implies that she is of both the living and the living-dead worlds. The green sack of bones that hangs in her bedroom, a Kongo reliquary known as a kimbi that houses the remains of a venerable or martyred person, is the priestly production of a sacred specialist. Moreover, the kimbi contains her father's nkuyu, Jake's animated spirit, which only an nganga can capture.[64] Metaphorically, as priestess, she unites the living dead Deads (Milkman, his father Macon, and Milkman's sisters Magdalene called Lena and First Corinthians) and the living-dead Deads (Solomon, his son Jake, and Jake's wife Singing Bird) who are threatened by ancestral extinction.

Although the above Voudoun connections demonstrate that along with Carib beliefs African traditional survivals covertly compose Pilate's character, overt nganga practices obtained as a root worker's apprentice on the island off Virginia's coast clarify her role as lay priestess. After reuniting with her brother Macon in Michigan, Pilate instructs her sister-in-law Ruth in the preparation of a greenish-gray rainwater mixture to slip into Macon's food to rekindle his sexual desire for her after ten years of abstaining from conjugal intimacy. To deter Macon from forcing Ruth to abort the baby (Milkman) she conceives after the rainwater potion is effective, a male Voodoo doll (a diaspora addition to Vodun) with a chicken bone between its legs and a red circle on its stomach appears in Macon's office. Tacitly, Pilate is responsible for the doll's construction and appearance. Macon, fearing that the sympathetic power of the doll will affect him, avoids touching it and destroys it with fire. Later, his repeated warnings to Milkman that Pilate is a snake who can drop her skin at will reifies her priestliness. In the Carib-Indian language, the word maboya, the name of the great Carib snake divinity, is similar to mambo (see above) and describes the wooden staff with which priests walk. The title of respect credits its recipient with being a "great snake," which conveys the same credentials of honor as "great priest."[65]

Pilate's role as Voudoun priest/priestess – an androgynous physical nature and a dominant male loa make her gender indeterminant – is best viewed in relief with Milkman's intersecting role as a la-place, a male apprentice and assistant to a houngan.[66] Interpreting her name, scholars cite Pilate's spiritual "piloting" of Milkman in his search for his ancestral forefathers, but they have heretofore lacked awareness of the socio-religious roles specific to Voudoun to apply the precise Africanist implications to Pilate and Milkman's "spiritual" partnership. Ritualistically, the la-place must perform his ceremonial role "backward," symbolizing the backward spatialization of time. He must execute all gestures from the left or with the left hemisphere of his body to emphasize this "mirroring" of backward temporality. Milkman's journey south mapping the inverted trajectory of his family's migration north, first to Danville, Pennsylvania, and then farther south and/or back with respect to time to Shalimar, Virginia, corresponds with the backward progression he makes to revitalize his familial lineage and recover his ancestral past. He metaphorically descends into the southern hemisphere of the cross and circle below the Kalunga line where those who have passed into the afterworld reside. From the moment he travels south and crosses the river to the hillside cave where his grandfather's bones were once deposited, his movements illustrate the regressive journey he takes into the land of the dead/Deads. The creek crossing, symbolically transitioning Milkman backward into the Sasa, shatters the forward west-to-east calibrated clockwise movement of Western temporality. Inspecting himself after falling in the creek, he looks at his "heavy, overdesigned" French gold Longines watch "to check the time. It ticked, but the face was splintered and the minute hand was bent." On his return to "[modern] civilization," he relies on the east-to-west counterclock-wise progress of the sun, consulting "the sky to gauge the hour."[67]

According to Deren, "When it is ritualistically necessary for the special guardian loa of a *hounfor* (parish) to be present, and if that loa has not become manifest by possessing someone, his presence may be represented ritually by the *la-place*."[68] Ceremonially, he, too, may have a special guardian master loa. The maît-tête or guardian loa that dominates and informs Milkman's character is Ghede, who is, fittingly, God of the Dead, "keeper of the cemetery, guardian of the past, of the history and heritage of the race ... Whoever would seek ancestral counsel or support must first address Ghede." He is the lord of resurrection, past, present, and future:[69]

This is the loa who, repository of all the knowledge of the dead, is wise beyond all the others. And if the souls of the dead enter the depths by the passage of which Ghede is guardian, the loa and the life force emerge from the same depth by the same road. Hence he is the Lord of Life as well as Death. His dance is the dance of copulation; in the chamber dedicated to his worship, the sculptured phallus may lie side by side with the three grave-diggers' tools [the pick-ax, the shovel, and the hoe]. His is the final appeal against death. He is the cosmic corpse which informs man of life. The cross is his symbol, for he is the axis both of the physical cycle of generation and the metaphysical cycle of resurrection.[70]

Milkman's gathering of the knowledge of the Deads resurrects them from the past to insure their present survival. Had he not chosen to become the repository and guardian of his family's history, the Deads would have perished in the Zamani. Milkman's quest for his African ancestral line is the final appeal against the collective death of his great-grandfather Solomon and grandfather Jake in the collective graveyard of time.

Both Legba, the master loa associated with Pilate, and Ghede, Milkman's master loa, are crossroads spirits who officiate over life and death. The tree of the cross is sacred to Legba; the cross is sacred to Ghede whose symbol is the cross on the tomb. Pilate, throughout *Song of Solomon*, physically bears the sign of the tree, and Milkman, carrying the grave-digger's shovel at the novel's end, questions her about placing a cross atop Jake's newly interred bones on Solomon's Leap. Because all Voudoun ceremonies begin with a salute to Legba and conclude with a salutation to Ghede, the novel begins with the presiding figure of Pilate singing at the death leap of Mutual Life Insurance agent Robert Smith and concludes with Milkman ascending to the priestly office that Pilate vacates at her death. In the role of the la-place, he sings her dirge before taking his own ambiguously codified life-death leap of uncertain flight at Solomon's Leap. The death of Singing Bird, Pilate's mother, precedes Pilate's birth, and the death of another bird, the blue-winged Robert Smith who takes flight from atop Mercy Hospital, precedes Milkman's delivery. Rumors spread after Milkman's birth that he was born with a caul, a placenta, over his face, presaging the possibility that he may be a seer and have the power to perceive the dead. And there is an exceptional quality about the visual countenance of both Pilate and Milkman. In contrast to Pilate whose single rudeness is staring others in the eyes, Milkman's "deep eyes" do not sustain the direct gaze of others.[71] His visual limitation is a physical ineptitude of the zombie, the living dead.

Pilate's lack of a navel intertwines her African and Indian ancestries just as Milkman's Ghede nature is an Indian interpolation that found its way into the African-descended Rada rites of Voudoun. Ghede is linguistically conflated with Baron Samedi or "zombie" – a living dead person whose soul/psyche has been stolen, leaving him a spiritless lump of flesh. "[V]arious Arawakan beliefs concerning *zemis* are precisely those of the *zombie* – the relation of the word is obvious; as it is equally obvious for zemi and Samedi." One could recognize the living dead of the Carib Indians "by the fact that the pupils of their eyes did not reflect: in Haiti, Ghede wears sun-glasses and the test of a real possession by Ghede is the ability of the possessed person to receive a sharp, burning liquid in the eyes without blinking."[72] Moreover, the living dead of the Carib Indians were known to walk about at night, and it is by way of Milkman's late-night perambu-lations that he spots his mother and follows her to the cemetery where her father, his maternal grandfather, is interred. Milkman leans on a tree at the cemetery's entrance and waits for his mother to return from its interior. Ghede is related to Baron Cimitière, the guardian of the cemetery who stands at its entrance.

A signature vice and physical deficit signify Milkman's abiding Ghede traits and provide more immediate clues to his intersection with Pilate's Voudoun priestliness. A substance addiction and a "burning defect" that impairs his physical posture tie Milkman's personality to the loa of death in the Voudoun pantheon. Milkman tries "to put a cigarette in his mouth every fifteen minutes" and his left leg is half an inch shorter than his right, giving him an affected gait.[73] Because Ghede is particularly fond of tobacco, a cigar or cigarette is one of his essential accoutrements.[74] When he manifests himself during possession, he crosses his right ankle on his left knee and smokes incessantly. To disguise the defect of his left leg, Milkman sits in mirror image of Ghede: "with his left ankle on his right knee, never the other way around. And he danced each new dance with a curious stiff-legged step that the girls loved and other boys eventually copied."[75] Like Erzulie and other loa of the Voudoun pantheon, Ghede loves to dance.

Ghede's dance is the dance of copulation, and his sign is the phallus accompanying the three gravediggers' tools: the pick-ax, the shovel, and the hoe. The ice pick, the Coalson skinning knife, and the butcher knife are the three gravediggers' tools with which Hagar threatens Milkman to avenge her unrequited, possessive graveyard love. Milkman loses the fear of death during her final attack with the butcher knife and determines that either Hagar or he must die. When Hagar is unable to execute the stabbing, he commands her to drive the phallic blade, fittingly, deep into her vagina. His life-threatening encounters with Hagar are not Milkman's only violent brushes with a knife that tacitly doubles as a phallus. In Solomon's store in Shalimar, Virginia, Milkman smiles when Saul, a town resident, threatens him with a knife after the two engage in dozens repartee on the topic of Milkman's penis. Saul slits Milkman's suit, face, and left hand, but Milkman emerges victorious with his manhood intact. With difficulty, the owner of the store leads Saul away, cut over the eye and cursing but with his "fervor gone."[76] George Eaton's research on Ghede identifies the divinity's possession of the phallic knife as an implement for beating people.[77]

Milkman's physical phallus, the "hog's gut that hangs down between [his] legs," has determined his power to decide the lives of the women in his family. His sister Magdalene called Lena charges that he has peed on First Corinthians, their mother Ruth, and her all his life.[78] And his urine is lethal. A four foot maple tree that as a boy he urinated on when it was a twig is dying prematurely, abnormally; green leaves in the midst of life are dropping from its branches. And like the tree, the three women are dying from patriarchal domination and dismissal. While serving up her accusation, Magdalene called Lena informs Milkman that he has not been favored, only tolerated, the customary treatment of Ghede by his serviteurs because of his alliance with death. She puts Milkman on notice that he is the line she will step across.[79] Ostensibly, Magdalene called Lena's calling him the "line" alludes to the line one figuratively draws when challenged by an adversary, but Milkman's identification with Ghede situates him below the Kalunga line depicted on the Kongo cosmogram in the region of the dead.

"Rising Sun," an allusion to the new moon, the time of Ghede's rites and Ghede himself, coincides with Hagar's ritualized attempts on Milkman's life and Milkman's nocturnal theft of Pilate's green sack. Hagar's monthly assault on Milkman with a phallic weapon has been "as regular as the new moon searched for the tide," and in an attempt to claim his life in a bar, an acquaintance named Moon assists Guitar in wrestling the knife from her.[80] Similarly, when Guitar and Milkman burgle Pilate's home "the moon came out and shone like a flashlight right into the room ... It hung heavy, hung green like the green of Easter Eggs left too long in the dye. And like Easter, it promised everything: the Risen Son and the heart's lone desire ... Guitar knelt down before it."[81] "Risen Son," troping on "Rising Sun," the pseudonym for Ghede, expresses resurrection in both Christian and Voudoun contexts, and in the latter instance reaches back to ancient Africa. One of the ancient names for Ghede is the bird of prey Khensou, a Theban divinity whose beaked-face head supports a full moon disk resting on a crescent. The Egyptians depicted a knife with a flint blade in the shape of a crescent moon, and thus the image imparts lunar symbolism. Khensou, like Ghede, is associated with knives.

Legba and Ghede, who are cosmically tied by the guardian of the crossroads Baron Carrefour, are spiritual companions, priest and apprentice, and the latter always follows the former. Milkman, as is true of the Legba-Ghede nexus, comes after Pilate, becoming what she once was. Ghede takes over Legba's duties and Milkman assumes Pilate's priestly role since they are mirror images of each other. Both are vagabond wanderers who typify their maît-têtes. A ragtag, hatted Pilate wanders the country with an infant Reba, while Milkman's roaming in Danville, Pennsylvania, reduces him to tatters; his hat, suit, shoes, and tie are ruined in his ancestral quest. Epitomizing the sun door, the "navel to the world,"[82] Legba/Pilate is the setting sun, the inverse of the rising sun or new moon Ghede in the cosmic mirror and as it is reflected in bodies of water. She also shares an affiliation with the phallus. Pilate wields a knife in the protection of Reba, placing its tip over the heart of her daughter's abuser and drawing blood. Her familiarization with Voodoo is uncontestable for it is her linkage with the Voodoo doll warning that she sends to her brother Macon threatening his phallus that indicates she is more than casually involved in or with the priesthood.

CIRCE – THE AFRICAN PRIESTESS

M'Dear in *The Bluest Eye* and Circe in *Song of Solomon* are both communal banganga who are timeless in age and sacred wisdom. Few of her Lorain, Ohio, community "could remember when M'Dear was not around"[83] and Morrison's Circe in her Danville, Pennsylvania, community is well beyond the years of the oldest old. Both intersect with the priestess model of the immortal Circe of *The Odyssey* who enters the Greek epic in book 10 to assist a lost Odysseus and exits the poem in book 12 along a tree-lined path. The compassionate healer, ideal domestic hostess, and medicinal artist, the classical Circe has tamed wolves and mountain lions that roam her grounds begging for table scraps like dogs. She carries a rhabdos, a wooden staff, and has knowledge of making mystical potions. One of her most important acts is advising Odysseus to go to the Underworld palace of Hades to seek counsel from the dead. While the classical Circe dispenses wisdom that resolves the past, her primary role is to give direction to the present moment.

"A skilled diagnostician, midwife, and herbalist, M'Dear towers over the preacher who accompanies her to the bedside of young Cholly Breedlove's ailing Aunt Jimmy. Four white knots of hair crown the circle of her head where she and the women of her day "had carried a world."[84] Her towering frame and the four knots invoke not only the four witches' knots of magic but also the Voudoun peristyle and the Kongo ancestral cosmogram of the four moments of the sun. More for communication than support, M'Dear walks with her own rhabdos, a hickory stick, which is a common accoutrement of Caribbean banganga, especially priestly figures. A mayombo, a stick that could magically beat any other stick, has the same linguistic formation as the Carib maboya.[85]

Similarly, Circe, who has served as midwife to the townspeople of Danville and three generations of Butlers and never lost a patient except Singing Bird, would be a "healer and deliverer" outside an Anglo-determined world.[86] Like her Hellenic counterpart, she is the ideal domestic provider, skilled in ancient medicinal arts such as prescribing cobwebs to staunch and heal Pilate's bleeding and infected pierced left ear, and counseling Milkman in the appeasement of the unburied dead. She surrounds herself with a pack of Weimaraners whose prefixes to their German names, Horst and Helmut for example, allude to the Egyptian and Greek gods Horus and Helios, associated with the sun. To Milkman, she reveals the names of Singing Bird and Jake, and the location of his grandfather's skeletal remains. The Circe of Morrison's narrative ensconces herself in the ill-gotten Butler mansion that has a four-columned portico bearing strong peristyle and priestess associations with the four intertwined trees in the backyard of Pilate's home in Michigan; to the four sickle-pear trees in Eva Peace's yard;[87] and to the four leaf-locked trees by Medallion's river near Shadrack's cottage.

The erotic responses that Cholly and Milkman have to the medicine women of their respective narratives demonstrate that both male characters unconsciously perceive their respective Circe figure as a sexual initiatrix, the prominent role held by the Grecian Circe as well. On the night of M'Dear's visit, a sleepy Cholly is aware "of being curled up in a chair, his hands tucked between his thighs. In a dream his penis changed into a long hickory stick, and the hands caressing it were the hands of M'Dear."[88] In all his dreams about witches, Milkman always awakes "with a scream and an erection. Now he had only the erection" when Circe, mistaking him for his father, greets him with an embrace in the decaying Butler mansion.[89] What starts in *The Bluest Eye* as a provocative, sexualized depiction of a medicinal expert who prescribes specific food, pot liquor, as a curative for an ailing womb progresses to the depiction of an erection-provoking sorceress/priestess named Circe in *Song of Solomon*. Her appearance highlights the historical reality that paralleling the later interpolation of Carib-Indian gods into the Haitian Voudoun pantheon, the Greeks interpolated many divinities appropriated from Africa into the Hellenic pantheon.

Herodotus and Diodorus, two classical authorities, insist that Greece owes its rites, religions, and gods to the Nile Valley civilizations of Egypt and Ethiopia. Herodotus, who maintained that classical religion has it roots in African cosmology, wrote that "almost all of the names of gods came into Greece from Egypt."[90] And, as several modern historians have asserted, there are common characteristics shared by East and West African divinities, suggesting that one influenced the other.[91] Memnon, Tithonus, Andromeda, Medea, Proteus, Phaeton, and Circe are a few of the divinities numbered among the Greek pantheon who are Ethiopian in origin and depiction. Homer, credited author of *The Iliad* and *The Odyssey*, references three times Olympian divinities' habits of feasting with the Ethiopians, and in book 4 of *The Odyssey*, it is proclaimed that in medicine, Egypt left the rest of the world behind.

Visual precedents for an African Circe as well as an African Circe trained in the priestly medicinal arts survive on fourth-century BC skyphoi in the Ashmolean Museum. The first, a two-handled vase, found in the sanctuary of Kabeiroi near Thebes, displays a pug-nosed, thick-lipped, black-silhouetted Circe mixing a potion in a horizontally handled cup identical to the skyphos design on which the scene appears. Depicted on a skyphos and with a skyphos in her hand, the African Circe appears on and holds a pre-Christian symbol of witchcraft, the cauldron, the concave vessel that signifies the womb and the site of (re)birth and (re)generation. Guardian of the womb in classical mythology, the mythical Circe informs M'Dear's representation as the diagnostician of the womb-afflicted Aunt Jimmy and Morrison's Circe as the priestess who will guard against the womb's reproduction. Circe in Morrison's text watched over the "[b]arren as a rock" Elizabeth Butler, the last of her covetous and murderous line, to insure the Butlers' extinction.[92]

The skyphos potion cup scene (see figure 4) validates an eroticized African Circe bearing the womb symbol. A nude Odysseus sporting an erect phallus "seems to recoil in terror as he holds his sword in one hand and the sheath [two additional phalli symbols] in the other."[93]

In another skyphos potion-cup scene, an African-phenotyped Circe stands "before the somewhat bedraggled Odysseus" offering him from a concave vessel the magic drink that will transform him into a swine. "Behind the hero is the loom of the enchantress and one of Odysseus's companions metamorphosed into a boar."[94] The tip of Odysseus's sheath discreetly shields from view the erect phallus that is fully visible in the first scene. A nude Odysseus with an erect penis in the presence of the time-honored African Circe parallels Milkman's phallic arousal in the embrace of a timeless African-American Circe. The reaction of Milkman's penis at her touch not only compounds his association with Ghede's phallic aspect but subversively reifies the porcine allusion that Magdalene called Lena attaches to her brother's penis: Milkman's "hog's gut" responds to the embrace of the priestess known for turning men into swine.

Song of Solomon's Circe is the only priest figure that Morrison gives a name recognized as Greek to call attention to her African ancestry and the Greeks' exclusive appropriation of the African god and priestess. The naming is an act of cultural excavation, of once again exposing the African palimpsest upon which Western culture superimposes itself. Reclaiming

Figure 4. African Circe and Odysseus on a Boeotian Kabeiric skyphos found in Thebes, fourth century BC. Black silhouette against a pale terracotta ground.

and not writing into nonexistence the cultural contributions of peoples whose histories and cultures early intersected, a practice evident in Morrison's inclusion in her fiction of Carib Indians', Native American Indians', and Amerindians' interpolations into African-American culture, is at the forefront of her literary aesthetic.

BABY SUGGS – AN UNCHURCHED MAMBO

In addition to indicating that she does not head a Christian congregation, Baby Suggs's designation as an "unchurched preacher" denotes that she may be considered a lay priest outside the doctrinal jurisdiction of the Judeo-Christian tradition. Visiting the pulpits of the "AME's and Baptists, Holinesses and Sanctifieds, the Church of the Redeemer and the Redeemed" in her Cincinnati community, the African-born Baby Suggs does not affiliate with any Christian denomination.[95] The pulpit, a tree-encircled "Clearing – a wide-open place cut deep in the woods nobody knew for what,"[96] in which she gives the "Call" every Saturday afternoon is the locus for a shuffling dance that opens communication between the physical and metaphysical worlds for the congregants.

A creolization of many West African and West Central African circle dances honoring the ancestors, the Clearing ritual that Baby Suggs coordinates is an example of what came to be known in North America as the ring shout, a dance that evolved in slave communities as a result of African tribes with shared core beliefs absorbing each others' strongest traditions. In Ibo, Yoruba, Bakongo and other African burial rituals, participants dancing at the edges of a cleared space in a counterclockwise direction – the east-to-west movement of the sun – shuffled slowly to insure that their feet did not lose contact with the ground and to imprint the earth as they circled.[97] The circular counterclockwise pattern of the dance imitated the geometric form of the Kongo cosmogram. Singing and chanting with drum and rattle accompaniments, the ring shouters communicated with the living-dead. The emotional spectacle in the Cincinnati Clearing is more akin to the shout, shouting, or holy dance witnessed in modern African-American holiness worship services. A group of shouters or a sole shouter, using feet and hands as percussives, hollers, cries, laughs, and dances "in the spirit" – an altered spiritual state akin to Voudoun possession – during the singing of a spiritual or gospel song which may have drum, guitar, piano, or tambourine accompaniment.[98]

Commencing when she puts down a mayombo-styled stick that Voudoun priests and priestesses carry, the Call, the invocation Baby Suggs issues in the Clearing modeled on a Voudoun peristyle, expresses the doctrinal ideology embedded in the shuffling-step pattern to which those gathered move. "'Here,' Baby Suggs calls, "in this here place, we flesh; flesh that weeps, laughs; flesh that dances on bare feet in grass. Love it. Love it hard. Yonder they do not love your flesh. They despise it . . . This is flesh I'm talking about here. Flesh that needs to be loved.'"[99] Rooted in call and response, an oral exchange originating in West African ancestral practice and surviving in modern sacred and secular African-American discursive forms such as the sermon and the step-show chants of fraternities and sororities, the Call that Baby Suggs, holy, issues is not a Christian sermon, nor is her method of delivery preaching. Seated on a flat rock in a clearing, Baby Suggs calls into an open space children, men, and women from the surrounding trees to laugh, dance, and cry in a synchronized order that dissolves into a chaotic emotional release. Her Call "did not tell them to clean up their lives or to go and sin no more. She did not tell them they were the blessed of the earth, its inheriting meek or its glorybound pure. She told them the only grace they could have was the grace they could imagine. That if they could not see it, they would not have it."[100] She admonishes them to love their hands, mouth, neck and most of all, their hearts. The Call, exhorting the Clearing celebrants' self-love of their flesh, which their enslavers despise, is the refusal to subordinate flesh to spirit, the exegesis of the inseparability of spirit and flesh found in Voudoun. Deren supplies insight into the unity of the two in the Haitian religion:

In Voudoun the cosmic drama of man consists not of a dualism, a conflict of the irreconcilable down-pull of flesh and the up-pull of spirit; it is, rather, an almost organic dynamic, a process by which all that which characterizes divinity – intelligence, power, energy, authority, and wisdom – evolves out of flesh itself. Instead of being eternally separated, the substance and the spirit of man are eternally and mutually committed: the flesh to the divinity within it and the divinity to the flesh of its origin.[101]

A disavowal of Christianity's warning against love of the flesh and self as spiritually corrupting, Baby Suggs's theology of the flesh rejects European Americans' physical persecution and spiritual rupture of the African other, as well as the spiritual persecution of their material selves.

The concept of the zombie best illustrates the West's disjunction of flesh and spirit, especially as the concept of the zombie grew out of the Haitian-evolved Petro rites as a metaphor for the slave, a person whose soul/psyche has been stolen. The severance of the spirit from the flesh wherein the flesh is inconsequential and void of gros-bon-ange, the psyche, but still vitalized results in an amoral mass of organic matter, purposeless humanity, the living dead. Baby Suggs's unification of the two disjointed spheres of her self occurs when Mr. Garner, the master of Sweet Home, takes her from south to north, traversing the Ohio River Kalunga to freedom and life. At that moment her body quickens, and she senses for the first time the hands and heartbeat of an autonomous, unenslaved self.

The spiritual guidance regarding the flesh that Baby Suggs bequeaths to those who survive her lives on in her granddaughter, Denver, whose maternal grandmother, Ma'am, also retained the geometric signage of the Kongo cross and circle cosmogram, as a cicatrix under her breast. Denver holds firm in her memory Baby Suggs's counsel that she should always listen to and love her body. Her refuge within walking distance of 124 Bluestone Road, a bower of "five boxwood bushes, planted in a ring ... [that] had started stretching toward each other four feet off the ground to form a round, empty room seven feet high, its walls fifty inches of murmuring leaves"[102] adumbrates that she has been passed (un)consciously the most profound Black Atlantic survival, the cross within a circle, to insure her survival in the New World. Because Baby Suggs is an African-born unchurched preacher who directly officiates at a ring shout, she is the least diluted West African traditional priest in Morrison's canon to date.

CONSOLATA SOSA – MÃE DE SANTO AND WATER
PRIESTESS YEMANJÁ

Rescued from the streets of Brazil by American nun Mary Magna and taken to the United States via Panama, Puerto Limón, and New Orleans to a convent seventeen miles outside of Ruby, Oklahoma, Consolata Sosa, the West African traditional priestess figure of *Paradise*, culturally bears African, European, and Amerindian religious beliefs and practices. Transculturally, she embodies the syncretism or "juxtapositioning" of African-Brazilian Candomblé with Catholicism and indigenous beliefs to which she was exposed until the age of nine. Over the next four decades, instruction in Catholicism from the American nuns who rear her and the Voodooisms embedded in the Black folk Protestantism that Ruby acquaintance and lay priestess Lone DuPres passes on to her when Consolata is half a century old complete her traditional religious training. Lone DuPres's blend of African-American folk Protestantism with Caribbean Dahomean, Yoruban, and Kongo-Angolan Voudoun beliefs that Fairy DuPres passed on to her from her New Orleans exposure reawakens Consolata's early memories of Candomblé in the Brazilian port town where Mary Magna kidnapped her. Her early memories of Brazil where Vodun survives undiluted shape her unconscious ascendancy to the socio-religious role of mãe de santo, a Candomblé priestess.

The Portuguese who arrived on the coast of West Africa in 1471 initiated a slave trade that supplied their South American colony founded in 1500 with untold numbers of West Africans. Many of these enslaved peoples continued their religious customs beyond the experiences of the Middle Passage, just as they had carried them out in their West African homelands. In the northeastern coastal cities of Salvador da Bahia, the most African of the Brazilian cities, and Rio de Janeiro, pães de santo and mães de santo resisted the adulteration of Candomblé, the worship and rites of the Yoruba orishas.[103] European Catholicism never subverted the Yoruba orishas, the Dahomean pantheon of gods, or Kongo-Angolan beliefs and practices. In Consolata's American setting, a Baptist church, a Methodist church, and a Pentecostal church within one mile of each other in the distant Ruby are institutional Christian foils to the uninstitutional African traditional beliefs that passed through the Caribbean to the North and South American continents.

During a trip to Brazil in the 1980s, Morrison heard an account of an attack on a convent of African-Brazilian nuns who rescued abandoned children from the streets and who were practitioners of Candomblé.

A group of local men, the account maintained, considered the nuns an outrage and executed them posse-style. The story recounted to Morrison resembles an account concerning a terreiro, a house of Candomblé, which operated in 1785. Authorities raided the terreiro located on the outskirts of Cachoeira, a town northwest of the coastal city of Salvador, after receiving reports that those who lived within its walls conducted magical ceremonies in the temple. "The nature of the materials confiscated and the ethnicity of the occupants suggest that the house was dedicated to the vodun, a religious pantheon with its origins in ancient Dahomey (currently Benin). The spiritual leader of the house, a freedman named Sebastião, appears to have established a reputation as a <u>curandeiro</u> (healer) and magician."[104] Morrison later learned that the incident she heard about involving the nuns never in fact happened, but for her "it was irrelevant ...[,] since it said much about institutional religion and uninstitutional religion, and how close they are."[105] The fabricated account served as the impetus for the plot of *Paradise*. Nine men of Ruby, an all-Black Oklahoma town, massacre Consolata Sosa and four other women living in a former convent. The men mount the assault convinced that the women are a coven, a cult "more like witches" than bitches,[106] and the root of all the misfortune and evil now visited upon their once morally unblemished town. To the men who hunt down the Convent women, what they judge as witchcraft are remnants of a legitimate world religion.

Consolata officiates as a Candomblé mãe de santo at a cross and circle gathering in the cellar of the Convent, which easily figures as a terreiro, a sanctuary headed by a mãe de santo and devoted to a single orixá. A Candomblé terreiro typically includes a barracão, a central room used for major ceremonies; roncós, separate rooms where novices or devotees spend much of their time in seclusion; the living quarters of the priest(ess); and a garden of natural and cultivated vegetation that provides the priest(ess) with sacred plants.[107] The Convent ostensibly proliferates with Catholic icons, yet covertly it is a terreiro excised of a Christ but replete with a garden containing circularly grown plants and a rare strain of specially cultivated dark purple hot peppers that will not thrive elsewhere. There is no Jesus iconography in the Convent, signifying that a Christian ethos should not be imposed upon Consolata's priesthood within its perimeter. At the back of the altar as "[c]lean as new paint is the space where there used to be a Jesus" on a huge cross. As the nine men search the Convent, the sun, as it rises in the window behind the cross without a Jesus, symbolizes the necessary circular accompanying geometric icon for a cross in a Candomblé terreiro.[108] The name of the order of nuns who formerly occupied the Convent, the Sisters of the

Sacred Cross, equally applies to Consolata and her four devotees. The subterranean terreiro setting of the Vodun-informed cross and circle ritual that the women perform when Consolata accedes to the priesthood reflects the historical reality that the religious beliefs, practices, and icons of the African diaspora have been driven figuratively underground in the African-American consciousness. Christian hegemony subverts African survivals.

The placement of the Kongo cosmogram in the sanctuary's cellar also augments the construction of Consolata as the Candomblé water priestess Yemanjá, the complement of the African-descended Rada loa of Voudoun, La Sirène, (an aspect of the loa Erzulie) who resides under the sea. She is depicted as a mermaid with ample breasts, the symbol of her maternal, nurturing nature, and her oceanic colors are blue, white, and green. In the Convent made of sandstone "[t]he bathtub rests on the backs of four mermaids – their tails split wide for the tub's security, their breast arched for stability."[109] The first exchange that Consolata has with the newly arrived Mavis Albright, who announces that she is on her way to California, concerns her desire to see the sea again. Furthermore, the colors of the sea and Yemanjá recur in imagery connected with the Convent and its associates. A faded white sign with blue letters that once advertised the Convent's school for Native girls directs visitors to its grounds from the access road. Consolata buys "blue-tissued roles of surgical cotton" intended "for the girls menstrual periods" on her first foray into Ruby.[110] Soane Morgan, Consolata's closest Ruby associate, wears a "summer-weight crepe [dress], pale blue with a white collar" when she is first introduced in the narrative.[111] And Sweetie Fleetwood wanders to the Convent in white loafers and a pale blue dress. Often clad in a sailcloth apron, Consolata heads a religious house surrounded by "acres of bluestem."[112] And blue and white are the colors Consolata is wearing at her death; she quickly slips "on a dress, blue with a white collar" when she hears intruders in the Convent.[113] The Virgin Mary is Yemanjá's and therefore Consolata's Christian parallel. Thus the blue-eyed Mary Magna who rears her is the direct complement to the green-eyed Consolata.

A Candomblé manifestation of the Madonna and a complement to Yemanjá, Piedade, or rather her memory, pervades Consolata's consciousness. The cerulean Piedade is the guardian Virgin of the sea who gives safe harbor to those at risk of perishing beneath its flood. Off the coast of Salvador on Itaparica, the largest island in the All Saints Bay, stands Capela de Nosso Senhora da Piedade (Our Lady of Piety Chapel) erected in 1622 in honor of the Virgin.[114] However, Morrison's conflation of Piedade, "a woman black as firewood,"[115] with the most important Virgin of Brazil, Our Lady Aparecida, centers the representation of Consolata squarely within Brazilian religious iconography and the trope of Yemanjá. The Catholic church's patron saint of Brazil, Our Lady Aparecida is black, "at least in terms of the physical icon."[116] In 1717 a group of fisherman on the Paraíba River caught in their net a black wooden statue of the Virgin Mary that they named Aparecida after the Brazilian city Aparecida do Norte, where the rescued Madonna was later enshrined in a Basilica built for her. Frei Agostino de Jesus, a carioca monk from São Paulo, sculpted the statue which is less than three feet tall, around 1605. How it came to be underwater or how long it had been there is not known – but it must have been there for years. The face and hands of Our Lady Aparecida, the only parts of the statue's body visible as flesh, are dark brown and she balances herself on a crescent moon. In the African-Brazilian tradition, the Black Madonna Aparecida is connected with the orixá Oxum (Oshun), the Mother of Africa and the patroness of pregnancy, children, rivers, seas, beauty, seduction, shrewdness, and wisdom. Oxum rules the sweet waters – rivers, brooks, and streams – and is closely related to Yemanjá. Consolata's celebration of Piedade underscores her affiliation "with the Candomblé *orixá* Yemanjá who is associated with the Virgin Mary and is a symbol of motherhood."[117]

Yemanjá's marine nature underwrites Consolata's personality, for Yemanjá, the Candomblé orixá, is the divinity of the ocean and the moon that governs its ebb and flow.[118] African Brazilians transformed Yemanjá, the Yoruba orisha of the Niger River in Nigeria, into the goddess of the sea in Bahia. Her elemental linkage with nature is typical since the orixás govern provinces of the natural world:

The orixás are nature gods. They are associated with distinct provinces of the natural world – water, air, forest, and earth – and it is from these primary sources that they gather and impart their axé, or vital energy. Each physical domain, in turn, corresponds to an array of perceived personality traits. The orixás are archetypes for the range of behaviors exhibited by their mortal followers. They embody the strength and foresight of their adherents as well as their weaknesses.[119]

Yemanjá is the guardian of axé, the animating life force that is comparable to the gros-bon-ange in Voudoun, and its principal medium, blood. Consolata's possession of the sea orixá's animating life force extends Mary Magna's life and revitalizes Soane Morgan's son Scout after his truck crash. Stepping in their dying flesh, she pinpoints the receding light of their axé and expands it again. She, like Yemanjá, is the guardian of women, the womb, childbirth, fertility, and witchcraft. As Mary Magna weakens, a wave of female visitors enters the Convent's walls because maternal issues lead them to its door. Mavis irresponsibly leaves infant twins in a hot Cadillac to die of heat stroke. She flees her husband and surviving children, ending up at the Convent. Pregnant and feigning the need for an abortion, Soane comes to the Convent to meet the woman who has had an affair with her husband, Deacon. Believing that her lying about wanting an abortion caused her miscarriage, Soane laments the sinful lie she told that led to the loss of her third child, a daughter. An unmarried but pregnant Arnette Fleetwood, daughter of one of the nine men who later invade the Convent, arrives at its doors after unsuccessfully attempting to abort the fetus she carries. The baby arrives prematurely and survives only a few days. Sweetie, her sister-in-law, overstressed from taking care of four children whose life forces have never connected with their flesh, walks aimlessly for seventeen miles and is taken in at the Convent overnight. And Pallas, the last and youngest of Consolata's devotees, denies her pregnancy by either Carlos, an unfaithful boyfriend, or a rapist. When the Ruby men invade the Convent, Consolata, sleeping next to Pallas's baby, rises. Her last words express concern for the sleeping infant she leaves unattended.

Changes in Consolata's womb induce her mãe de santo initiation. Ten years after her affair with Deacon Morgan that awakens her "stone-cold womb,"[120] Consolata changes her life at forty-nine with the start of the "change of life," menopause. Lone DuPres, Ruby's midwife and lay priest-ess, comes to the Convent at the moment when Consolata, hot and perspiring profusely, faints from dizziness connected with the cessation of her menses and the loss of salt. Lone's prescription, a hot salt drink, restores the elemental imbalance of the sea-traited Consolata as well as quickens a woman who has grown increasingly enamored with death and the cemetery. In Voudoun salt is believed to rejuvenate the zombie, the living dead. The womb's role in regeneration, forging spirit and flesh, and the impeding surcease of its unifying potential heightens Consolata's awareness of the importance of their inseparability. Her affair with Deacon Morgan ends in an epiphany for Consolata who, biting his lip and tasting his blood, realizes that she has been closed off for too long from her own flesh. In a flash of contempt, Deacon is repulsed by her vampirism, but she is energized by the animating life force of his blood.

Consolata's sun-seared vision, wearing of sunglasses, and preoccupation with the cemetery come after her affair ends with Deacon whose person-ality, as well as his twin brother Steward's, mimics an orixá. His tempera-ment follows the representation of Oxóssi, the masculine orixá of the hunt and the forest who is never satisfied materially or romantically. Oxóssi's brother Ogoun, the divinity of iron and war, is the orixá whose character "heads" the personality of Steward Morgan.[121] Twins, soldiers, and the grandsons of Zechariah Morgan who was ironmonger and forger of the Oven's message-bearing lip, Deacon and Steward were the gentle packers of the Oven's iron plate for its final transfer to Ruby. Now the twin brothers carry deadly iron. Deacon advances from the early morning hunting of quails to the early morning hunting of women; Steward, in Ogoun fashion as the consummate warrior, fends off evil and vanquishes enemies: he shoots Consolata.

An orixá of maturity and placid temperament, Yemanjá selects devotees to instruct spiritually in her secluded sea haven. Once a part of the sacred, cloistered house, they perform domestic chores, shave their heads, and receive new names. Each takes up residence for as little as a few months or as long as seven or more years. They may disappear from their home for many years then return with tales of their exploits in her undersea haven. Rituals involving dancing are performed to induce trances that allow the spirits of their head, the Voudoun maît-tête equivalents, to possess them.

Varying lengths of residence, shorn heads, ritualized dancing, and spirit possession are all parts of the Convent experience under Consolata's direction. Mavis, Consolata's first devotee, arrives at the Convent in 1968 and is present at the massacre on the morning of July 4, 1976, the 200th anniversary of America's independence. She moves back and forth between the Convent and the outer world, and after the massacre all the devotees return a final time to their homes with shaven heads. All four women dance in the rain at Consolata's behest on the night preceding the celebration of the nation's bicentennial, releasing pent-up experiences from their pasts that have keep them emotionally bound. Consolata "fully housed by the god who sought her out in the garden, was the most furious dancer" of the group.[122] The "housing" of Consolata by the man with the African-Caribbean cadence, cascading tea-colored hair, and apple-green eyes like her own unifies her metaphysical self with her physical self. He is the spiritual filling of her flesh. Earlier in the day, Consolata prepares the proper propitiation, a sacred meal featuring the sacrificial food of Yemanjá, two hens, for the initiation service. Cleaning them twice, Consolata cooks them with small quartered potatoes cut with the cross-roads symbol and apples with their cores, vertical axes, removed then filled with raisins swollen in wine-spirits. Each of her initiates' lives is reviewed while she prepares the offering to consecrate her priesthood. At the dinner she calls the Convent women to divine service. They are not obligated to serve, but if they choose to, they are notified, "Someone could want to meet them."[123] The fulfillment of their participation is god summoning; a spirit will in all probability mount them, filling or housing their flesh as well.

Consolata takes "charge like a new and revised Reverend mother,"[124] an ialorixá, a mãe de santo, guided by the sea orixá. In a Yemanjá ceremony an altar takes the form of a circle, the symbol of the renewal of life. The women scrub the cellar floor until its stones are like rocks on a shore, before ringing it with candles. Within the circle Consolata sketches templates, tracings of the Convent women's nude body silhouettes in various poses drawn in chalk and white paint. With the exception of Pallas, the youngest of the group, who "lay on her side, knees drawn" up in fetal position, the women replicate crosses with their body positions. "Gigi flung her legs and arms apart," figuring an X; Mavis struck a floater's pose, "arms angled" out horizontal to her vertical torso with knees pointing inward. Seneca lay on her back with her "hands clasping her shoulders."[125] Later, they add a ground-painting of a green cross, a sign attached to birthing from Mavis's past, to prepare for other personal vevers that will radiate from the cross and circle center.[126] The personal symbols the women add–a heart, a pierced phallus, serpent fangs–are common vever symbols associated with the loa and orixás.

In Voudoun priests and priestesses draw vevers at the base of trees and crosses with flour or ashes to honor and consecrate the ground for a divinity during a ceremony. Deren notes that the vever is not derived from Africa but has been interpolated from Indian belief into the Voudoun Rada African rites:

The cabbala-like character and function of the drawings does not suggest any African tradition, but is similar to the intricate drawings of the Aztec and Indians . . . In the Codex Ferjervary-Mayer, the first sheet is devoted to the figure of a cross-pattee combined with a St. Andrew's cross, which is supposed to represent basic principles of Aztec belief; the five regions of the world, the nine lords of the night, the four trees supporting the four quarters of heaven.[127]

Robert Farris Thompson contradicts Deren's position, citing an African precedent for the devotional drawings:

[Vevers] take their name from an archaic Fon term for palm oil used in the making of simplified squares or rectangles on the ground for certain Dahomean deities. Essentially they take the structure from a reinforcing merger of Fon and Kongo tradition of ritual ground designs, with the cruciform cosmograms of Kongo and neighboring territory the dominating influence . . . The Kongo and Angola cruciforms invoked God and the collective dead, but the Haitian ground-painting invoked a host of deities and emblems inherited from many lands.[128]

Thompson asserts that the Bakongo believed in "drawing a point" or "tracing in appropriate media" to bring about "contact between the worlds" that "result[ed] in the descent of God's power upon that very point."[129] In Brazil complex chalked forms of Kongo and Angola origins have been melded with Yoruba, Dahomean, Catholic, and Amerindian practice in Macumba, another African-derived religion prominent in Rio de Janeiro. "Macumba priests, in the beginning, invoked spirits through simple chalked designs drawn on the ground and called 'marked points' (*pontos riscados*),"[130] circular blazons symmetrically rendered and disposed.

Situating the Convent seventeen miles due north of the all-Black Ruby, whose geography and demographics echo the Yowa cross and circle formation, reiterates such circular blazons, calling forth the African traditional view and belief system by which the Convent and Ruby should be gauged. A vertical axis, Central Street, "a road straight as a die,"[131] runs through the center of Ruby from the "flawlessly designed" Oven that is "[r]ound as a head" to Sargeant's Feed and Seed store at the town's northernmost perimeter. To celebrate the street's completion and naming, a celebratory horse race along the town's central north-south axis, Central Street, took place. Dividing the north and south sides of Ruby and within hearing distance of the Oven is a stream, the Kalunga diameter of the town. A roofed shelter common to a peristyle stands near by. It is here, at the radius of Central Street, that strangers in cars circled three or four girls, and twenty-five Ruby men with guns circled the strangers in the cars, forming a concentric pattern. Deacon Morgan circles the Oven routinely before heading north up Central Street to the bank he owns and manages.

In the northern hemisphere of Ruby, descending from Sargeant's Feed and Seed store to the Oven, are five streets that horizontally cross the vertical Central Street. To the east of Central and in descending order are St. Peter Street, St. Matthew Street, St. Mark Street, St. Luke Street, and St. John Street. Each continues across Central on its western side with corresponding secondary names: Cross Peter, Cross Matthew, and so forth. In the southern hemisphere of Ruby, and the realm of the dead with respect to the cruciform cosmogram, the south country beyond the Oven and streambed is an area that is uninhabited by the residents of Ruby, a town where reputedly no ones dies.[132] The African-American Ruby community, like the Bottom of Medallion in *Sula*, resides in the top or northern hemisphere of the town named in remembrance of its first resident to be buried but not die within its limits. Naming the town after Ruby insures permanent name-calling of its first living-dead.

Reviewing the novel, John Leonard states that "Although Morrison doesn't say so, the ancients believed that rubies were an antidote to poison, warded off plague, banished grief and diverted the mind from evil thoughts. A 'perfect ruby' was the philosophers' stone of the alchemists."[133] But the red brilliance of the ruby, cut round as is the case with most gemstones, also carries the lore of being the Lord Sun or sun gem illustrated as a total solar eclipse that generates four points of illumination around its darkened corona, imaging once again the circle and the four moments of the sun.[134] Ruby's population, 360, is the exact number of degrees in a circle, and no other town is accessible for "ninety miles around" or 180 miles, the degrees of a semi-circle.

The four women who take up residence at the Convent evince varying degrees of openness to an African traditional consciousness and cosmology. For example, Gigi, the second Convent devotee to arrive and perhaps the most cynical of the lot, is duped twice because she innately embraces animism. First, Mikey Rood – her jailed boyfriend whose surname conspicuously invokes the crucifix – convinces her that on the outskirts of his hometown, Wish, Arizona, there is an animistic rock formation of desert lovers, a black "man and woman fucking forever. When the light changes every four hours they do something new."[135] And she believes Dice – a man she meets on the Santa Fe rail line – who concocts a tale about the matchless ecstasy a human can feel if s/he squeezes between two Ruby, trees that have grown in each other's arms.[136] The pre-Convent experiences of Mavis Albright, however, the first and longest devotee under Consolata's guidance, foreshadows covertly the West African traditional ancestral geometric worship that Consolata will implement in her priesthood.

To find safe emotional and physical harbor at the Convent overseen by the maternal Yemanjá sea divinity who is also the guardian of childbirth and axé, is therapeutic to Mavis who has given birth to five children but negligently left the last two, newborn twins, in a hot car to die of heatstroke while she purchased wieners in the local Higgledy Piggledy supermarket. Taking a raincoat and her daughter's yellow galoshes, the apparel of the mariner, in her flight from her husband and surviving children, Mavis encounters a waitress dining on crab cakes on her way to Paterson, New Jersey, where Birdie Goodroe, her mother whose surname has a fish-egg suffix, lives. Mavis precedes her induction into Consolata's terreiro with a metaphoric highway navigation of the Yowa. Upon her arrival in Paterson, Mavis, driving along a hall of trees, "managed to coast across the intersection [a crossroads], and incline" her husband's Cadillac against the curb.[137] Leaving Paterson, she heads west on Route 70 (Interstate 70) for California in the colors of Yemanjá, a "light blue pantsuit, drip dry, and a white cotton turtleneck."[138] Mavis's journey across country horizontally bisects the mid-region of the

United States. Spanning the nation, and in descending order, Interstate highways 94, 90, and 80 run parallel to and north of Interstate 70. To the south of Interstate 70 and in descending, parallel order are Interstate highways 40, 20, and 10. As she drives the country's diameter, a memory involving a circular "journey" she took as a child that brought her intense pleasure returns to illuminate Mavis's movements in the present moment:

As more and more of the East was behind her, the happier she became. Only once had she felt this kind of happiness. On the Rocket ride she took as a kid. When the rocket zoomed on the downward swing, the rush made her giddy with pleasure, when it slowed just before turning upside down through the higher arc of its circle, the thrill was intense but calm. She squealed with the other passengers, but inside was the subtle excitement of facing danger while safely stopped in strong metal. . . . Now in flight to California, the memory of the Rocket ride and its rush were with her at will.

According to the map the way was straight, all she had to do was find 70, stay on it until Utah, make a left on down to Los Angeles. Later she remembered traveling like that – straight.[139]

After Topeka, Kansas, at a point that vertically bisects the country in the heart of the central time zone (and a parallel to Ruby's Central Street), Mavis panics, and turning left off Interstate 70 she descends the vertical axis. Driving in a circle, she arrives, a lost traveler, at the Convent, seventeen miles from Ruby.

Consolata's message on the nonmaterial animation of flesh reaffirms the core doctrine that the Vodun priest brought to the Americas. In Candomblé

the cosmos is characterized by a simple opposition between the realm of the spirits, orun, and the realm of the material, aiê . . . Hell, heaven, and purgatory are alien concepts to the Candomblé way. Rather than chain the body and soul to an unknowable European paradise, Candomblé resonates with the power to improve the lives of people during their brief passage through aiê [the mortal realm].[140]

The symbol of the crossroads is predicated upon the intersection of the spiritual and physical planes. Separating one from the other results in imbalance. The tangible earth is just as essential as intangible air. The two are a unity. Lone DuPres warns Consolata not to separate God's elements, not to divide his spirit from his creations. The Reverend Pulliam and Reverend Misner, at the wedding of K. D. (Kentucky Derby, aka Coffee) Smith and Arnette Fleetwood, a sacrament of the Church whereby male and female are united in spirit and flesh, debate the intersection of the two. Reverend Pulliam positions God, the metaphysical entity, as distant and disinterested in the mortal self, that is, "God is not interested in you."

Conversely, Reverend Misner, with a wooden cross in his folded arms in silent protest, urges, "He [God] is you," flesh and spirit are one.[141] The dispute between the junior and senior members of Ruby over the Oven's message turns on the same tension. The older anti-African generation doggedly asserts that the writing on the Oven's lip, "The Furrow of His Brow," was once and should remain "Beware the Furrow of His Brow."[142] God and man are an irreconcilable dualism. They view God as discrete from themselves, a force to be feared and revered. The town's youths, however, incorporate themselves within an African-centered divinity that allows them to "Be the Furrow of His Brow,"[143] be one as flesh and spirit.

Apart from the sexual molestation she experienced on the Brazilian streets, Consolata, like the Virgin Piedade, has lived the greater part of her life alienated from her flesh and the principal doctrine of an African-Brazilian belief system because as the ward of a Catholic nun her spirit has been privileged over her flesh. Permitting Catholicism to dominate, she has chained her soul to an unknowable European paradise that cannot be accessed in the here and now, only in the hereafter. Her biting of Deacon Morgan's lip and licking the blood drawn punctuate her hunger for her own flesh and the axé found in the life-giving fluid. The vevers of the Convent women's bodies that she traces in the cellar circle are not of the established orixás but formed in each of the women's fleshed images. And the vevers summon their fleshed selves to them "like magnets. They had to be reminded of the moving bodies [flesh] they wore, so seductive were the alive ones [spirit] below."[144]

Consolata's priestly text is an analogue to Baby Suggs's exhortation of flesh love in the Clearing ring shout scene in *Beloved*. Both messages are rooted in the Voudoun belief that "the cosmic drama of man consists not of a dualism, a conflict of the irreconcilable down-pull of flesh and up-pull of spirit [as is found in Christianity]. Instead of being eternally separated, the substance and spirit of man are eternally and mutually committed: the flesh of the divinity within it and the divinity to the flesh of its origin."[145] Although her priestly role is more ambiguous than Baby Suggs's, Consolata ascends to the headship of a women-centered house of Candomblé in a self-appointed way that is in keeping with her Brazilian equivalent.

***

Morrison refines the representation of conjurers to reclaim the socio-religious reality of the banganga, religious specialists who were once the spiritual core of African and African-American communal existence. These physical and metaphysical mediators – the houngan, the mambo, the pae de santo, and the mae de santo who emerged in the Americas – directed the religious lives and physical and psychological healing of countless members of the African diaspora who sanctioned their priestly investiture. Although ostensibly absent from the socio-religious landscape of contemporary African-American society, semblances of African medicine (wo)men and priest(esse)s present themselves in contemporary life in unassuming ways. Morrison's composites of Soaphead Church, Shadrack, Pilate Dead, M'Dear, Circe, Baby Suggs, and Consolata Sosa emphasize that these social roles are by no means extinct but have only been distorted from their origins or morphed into figurations more pliable for twentieth-century survival.

Morrison's imposition of the circle and cross cosmogram onto the physical spaces where specialists reside and the projection of the physical traits and behaviors of the Voudoun loa and Candomblé orixás onto their personalities recuperate the operations of those religious personages as they function in the past and present moments. Both literary practices are designed to negate the belief in Christianity's absolute eradication of traditional survivals and to symbolize that African traditional cosmological artifacts have been merely folded, along with Indian beliefs and practices, into compatible elements from the Christian tradition. Many of those beliefs may yet retain their own integrity. Morrison's grounding of her settings and characters in a founding iconographic heritage that thrives at the very core of American life is nothing short of genius. She illustrates with profound certainty that alternative methods of spirituality, healing, and knowing require serious inspection in the canon of American literature and life.

6

Identifiable Blackness: Toni Morrison's literary canon at the Western crossroads

Of the music, myths, and forms of performance that the African brought to the Western Hemisphere, I wish to discuss one specific trickster figure that recurs with startling frequency in black mythology in Africa, the Caribbean, and South America. This figure appears in black culture with such frequency that we can think of it as a repeated theme or topos ...

This topos that recurs throughout black oral narrative traditions and contains a primal scene of instruction for the act of interpretation is that of the divine trickster figure of Yoruba mythology, Esu-Elegbara. This curious figure is called Esu-Elegbara in Nigeria and Legba among the Fon in Benin. His New World figurations include Exú in Brazil, Echu-Elegue in Cuba, Papa Legba (pronounced La-Bas) in the pantheon of the loa of Vaudou [Voudoun] of Haiti, and Papa La Bas in the loa of Hoodoo [Voodoo] in the United States ... These variations on Esu-Elegbara speak eloquently of an unbroken arc of metaphysical presupposition and a pattern of figuration shared through time and space among certain black cultures in West Africa, South America, the Caribbean, and the United States.   Henry Louis Gates, Jr. *The Signifying Monkey*[1]

In 1988, the year Henry Louis Gates, Jr. published *The Signifying Monkey*, putting forward a vernacular theory that establishes the West African divinity Esu-Elegbara's link to African-American discourse and literary tradition, Toni Morrison's *Beloved* received the Pulitzer Prize for Fiction, and *Song of Solomon*, the Morrison novel that many critics believed should have first received the award, was ten years old. Five of the eight novels that now compose her canon had been published, each containing cosmological beliefs, subscriptions of the cross and circle of the Kongo Yowa, or figurations of gods originating in traditional West Africa embedded in African-American settings. While *The Signifying Monkey* neither treats Toni Morrison's works nor references her as a writer, Gates's identification of Esu-Elegbara of the West African "mythic" world and his influence on African-American discourse by way of the Signifying Monkey, the divine trickster's manifestation in the New World, affirms Morrison's approach to writing within the cultural purview of Blackness. Legba, who stands at the crossroads of African and African-American spiritual beliefs in the Western hemisphere, is only a part of the cosmological whole with which Morrison subliminally inscribes her novels to incorporate in her fiction West and Central African traditional ways of being and knowing that presently linger in the personal and collective (un)consciousness of African Americans. *Beloved* and *Song of Solomon* contain not only subscribed New World figurations of Legba as this study has demonstrated – Sixo in the later novel and Pilate Dead in the earlier work – but also New World manifestations of divinities emanating from Yoruba, Fon, Ibo, and other traditional cultures. Published between *Beloved* and *Song of Solomon* and set in the Caribbean, *Tar Baby* (1981) alludes to the spatial relocation of these African traditions to the Western hemisphere. It is ironical and fitting that Esu-Elegbara arises as the West African keystone in Gates's scholarship and as a principal figure that ties Africa with America in Morrison's fiction. The crossroads guardian who "opens the gate," Legba is not the most powerful god of his pantheon, but he is the most important. Through him the other gods enter. And through his exhumation in the Americas, in both Gates's African-influenced African-American vernacular theory and Morrison's literary art, other identifiably Black West African figures may receive cultural identification and theoretical attention.

Twenty years after the Signifying Monkey's emergence as the functional equivalent of Esu-Elegbara and the grounding of an African-American theory of criticism inscribed within the African vernacular tradition, concrete identification of and speculation on Morrison's inscriptions of West and Central African traditional linguistic and socio-religious survivals in her fiction are only now being excavated. After what is undoubtedly a relentless conceptual effort on Morrison's part to qualify the socio-religious roles, perceptions, beliefs, and behaviors that survived the Middle Passage in African America, vernacular study of Morrison's novels issuing from the trajectory that Gates formulates seems a logical next step for interrogating her work. Given her devotion to "truth in timbre," and the aural capturing of the cadence and rhythms of Black discourse, it would be useful to explore the ways in which Morrison's treatment of the Black vernacular might be theorized alongside Gates's treatments of Zora Neale Hurston's *Their Eyes Were Watching God* (1937), Ishmael Reed's *Mumbo Jumbo* (1972), and Alice Walker's *The Color Purple* (1982).

In light of Morrison's diligence in subliminally inscribing specific West and Central African traditional social and religious beliefs and practices such as the traditional view of evil or the spatialization of time in her fiction, then how might sexual license, communal ritual, gender relationships, the function of the artist, or a number of other concepts in her fiction be read through traditional cultures from Senegambia to Kongo-Angola or from the creolizing of these cultures in the Caribbean from the seventeenth century onward? Morrison, for example, gives us recurring treatments of the thwarted female artist, a salient feature of Black women's writing,[2] but how do Morrison's portraits converge and diverge with, for example, the West African traditional notion of the artist who is part of and responsible to the community and the Western configuration of the artist who speaks from an "isolated ivory tower" through the "supreme individual."[3] Maya Deren, on her first trip to Haiti, confronted the different perception of the artist when she approached the Voudoun priest under whom she served to film his ceremonies. She writes that "He understood virtually nothing of cinema and I was uncertain of his reaction, since his own standing in the community would be jeopardized by such a permission. Beside, in his culture, the artist as a singular individual did not exist."[4] Olaudah Equiano also validates the plurality of artists throughout his native Guinea (Nigeria) in *Interesting Narrative* (1789). "We are almost a nation of dancers, musicians, and poets," Equiano boasts.[5] A wealth of Morrison scholarship waits at the crossroads of African and African-American critical explication.

Although it is generally known that Morrison copiously researches the histories that substructure her fiction, the presence in her work of West and Central Africanisms that have Middle Passage precedents came first, according to her own admission, by way of her personal recollections and insights. She credits stories and experiences from her youth with informing her literary renderings of African cultures. The stories she heard as a girl in her hometown of Lorain, Ohio, furnished the primary grist for her treatments of Black belief systems, and her childhood world contained people who talked about their dreams and visions as if they were real and who had visitations from people who had passed on and connections to material things that were not "shocking" or "empirically verifiable."[6] The people who shaped her cosmological worldview had ways of knowing generally discredited by Western culture. In a 1985 interview with Bessie W. Jones and Audrey Vinson, Morrison states that her initial writing drew from her memory; she did not trust much research when she wrote her first novels because most history books or published sources on African and African-American cosmologies were unreliable. The information that she needed in the early years of her writing was unwritten.[7] A year later, in an interview that Christina Davis arranged with Morrison to commemorate the thirtieth anniversary of the First International Conference of Black Writers and Artists that was held at the Sorbonne in 1956, Morrison reaffirmed that initially, in order to draw linkages between African and African-American cultures, she relied on her own recollections:

When I first began to write, I would do no research in that area because I distrusted the sources of research, that is, the books that were available, whether they were religion or philosophy and so on. I would rely heavily and almost totally on my own recollections and, more important, on my own insight about those recollections, and in so doing was able to imagine and to recreate cultural linkages that were identified for me by Africans who had a more familiar, an overt recognition (of them). So much of what is true about Afro-Americans is not only the African but the American – we are very much that and trying to separate those things out can be very difficult, if you *want* to separate them out.[8]

While growing up, Morrison also heard the charms and traditions of Native Americans who were married to enslaved people in her family. Her Native American maternal great-grandmother, her Alabama African-American maternal grandparents, and other members of her family "talked a great deal about Jesus – [and] selected out of Christianity all the things they felt applicable to their situation – but they all kept this other body of knowledge that we call superstitions."[9] These cultural "superstitions" passed on to her were entered into her novels. In these interviews, both given within two years of *Beloved*'s publication, Morrison speculated that she could now go to some written sources for cultural information, but certain areas of her African and Native American ancestries would still have to be gleaned from her memory or have to be exhumed from her (un)consciousness by being reminded of them.[10] With respect to her knowledge of cultural connections between African and African-American literatures at that time, she maintained that she was "only discovering those links in a large sense – that is, as a reader and as a scholar" but she was unsure which ones were genuine and which ones were not.[11]

Memories later recollected and incorporated into her fiction have become increasingly self-conscious through Morrison's insights about those recollections and through African collaboration and corroboration. Morrison's initial turning inward and relying almost totally on her own recollections for Africanisms, however, demonstrates the communality of experiences, beliefs, and practices retained by the one yet reflective of those that the many possess. The role of the Africanist artist, as stated above, is not the solitary individual set apart from the community looking on from a superior vantage point as is typical of the Western perception of the artist. She is an intrinsic member of the community, and her personal experiences reflect, validate, and critique the common experiences of the community at large.

Morrison maintains that all her novels are about love, but her relentless drawing upon African traditional religions that permeate all departments of life and her treatment of religious beliefs and practices, cultural elements that are the most resistant to temporal and spatial changes, invariably make all her novels also about religion. Her intertwining of Christianity and beliefs particularly specific to West Africa in almost undetectable ways demonstrates her keen awareness of the closeness of institutional and uninstitutional religions. Time and again, Morrison's plots return to the uninstitutional affirmation of the inseparability and unity of flesh and spirit that refocuses attention on the institutional dichotomizing of the two as irreconcilable binaries.

Classified as spirit-possession religions, Vodun, Voudoun, and Candomblé are deemed incompatible with Christianity, whose defining moment comes when a dead man reappears to converse with the living that are last with and closest to him. As continuing proof of his metaphysical transfiguration and life in the afterworld, he sends to his living circle of disciples and the earth-bound world a holy spirit that "descends" upon them and gives them the power to speak in unknown or unlearned languages in order to communicate with men from different lands and perfectly and continuously with god.[12] The twentieth-century manifestation of the Holy Spirit in institutional churches since its 1906 outpouring in a former African Methodist Episcopal Church on Azusa Street in Los Angeles points out the political relevance of Morrison's literary art drawing attention to religions and cultures that view themselves as different from one another having more in common than they realize. The events at Azusa Street touched off the twentieth-century revival of spirit manifesting itself in people of all races, classes, and religious denominations. The goal of Morrison's fiction lies not only in reclaiming African survivals but also in calling attention to religious and cultural ironies and establishing evolutionary parallels, if not continuums, between ideologies, worldviews, and cultures – one labeled sacred, the other pagan– that have been relentlessly pitted against each other.

For many Western readers, definitive identifications in this study of the various traditional socio-religious roles and perceptions in Morrison's novels will expand their insight into twentieth-century African works of fiction and demand reinspection of texts in the Black literary tradition on this side of the Atlantic. The journey that the Guinean writer Camara Laye's protagonist Clarence takes in *The Radiance of the King* (1954) that moves him backward in space and time, and the assortment of people he encounters along the way – such as a tall beggar who guides him and the timeless witch/priestess Dioki endowed with psychic powers and snake familiars – prepares us to understand Milkman's journey in *Song of Solomon* and his encounters with Pilate and Circe.[13] Nigerian novelist Ben Okri's *The Famished Road* (1991), winner of the 1991 Booker Prize for Fiction, introduces an abiku spirit-child as the protagonist in the first book of his metaphysical trilogy – completed by *Songs of Enchantment* (1993) and *Infinite Riches* (1998) – that sheds enormous light on the reincarnation of Beloved and her transcendence of time. Okri's abiku, whose mother shortens his name to Azaro because his full name Lazaro is too close to the New Testament Lazarus whom Christ raised from the dead, gathers in the fields at the crossroads with other spirits waiting to be reborn. The West African traditional world that is only faintly visible in Morrison's novels becomes sharply defined in relief to Laye's, Okri's, and other African novels.

A return to African-American fiction with the conscious design of uncovering the African palimpsest upon which non-Africanist interpretations have superimposed themselves is essential to centralizing the Blackness of American works. Even a collection of short stories such as Charles W. Chesnutt's *The Conjure Woman* (1899), with seemingly seven straightforward "conjure" plots, bears revisiting. In "Po' Sandy" Uncle Julius McAdoo recounts the story of Tenie, a traditional priestess, transforming the enslaved Sandy into an animistic tree unifying his spirit and flesh that has loa significance. Attention diverted to the humanity of Annie, the European-American woman who is sentimentally moved by Julius's story, distracts the reader's attention from the religious implications of the story's conclusion. A trickster figure that lives on the Lumberton plank-road and makes his appearance in the first of the seven stories, "The Goophered Grapevine," sitting on a pine log lying horizontally under a vertical elm, Uncle Julius, may be interpreted as a Legba figure. He wants to use the Lumberton plank-road schoolhouse built from Sandy's tree-transfigured body as a place of worship for the half of his congregation that has seceded from the ironically named Sandy Run Colored Baptist Church over the question of temperance, a term that in addition to meaning total abstinence from alcoholic liquors means the quality of exercising balance or reconciling extremes. A trickster himself, Chesnutt consciously and/or unconsciously imbues his characters and natural landscapes with the crossroads and traits of divinities derived from traditional Africa.[14] Hurston's novels and autobiography, *Dust Tracks on a Road* (1942) are rife with sun (circle), tree (vertical axis), and horizon (horizontal axis) imagery. Even her last novel *Seraph on the Suwanee* (1948), that treats characters of European ancestry, contains a tree circling scene and veiled references to the loa. Ann Petry's *The Street* (1946), published as Hurston's literary career was drawing to a close, also juxtaposes Christian and traditional beliefs, blurring the interpretation of its Cross symbolism. Other African-American works – such as Henry Dumas's *Ark of Bones and Other Stories* (1970) in which Dumas includes allusions to Voodoo and experiments with time and the African vernacular, or Octavia Butler's *Kindred* (1979), a novel that passes for science fiction but whose representations of time travel and physical connections with the ancestors reflects a West and Central African sensibility – demand revisionist, Africanist readings.

In the final pages of *The Black Atlantic* (1993), Paul Gilroy writes that along with other African-American novelists, Morrison's "work accepts that the modern world represents a break with the past, not in the sense that premodern, 'traditional' Africanisms don't survive its institution, but because the significance and meaning of these survivals get irrevocably sundered from their origins."[15] Acting responsibly as a writer, Morrison concerns herself with exigencies that the cultural contours of distinctly modern experiences place on her, as well as other artists, to reunite significance and meaning with origins to (re)figure a modern, diasporic reality. "There's a great deal of obfuscation and distortion and erasure, so that the presence and the heartbeat of black people has been systematically annihilated in many, many ways and the job of recovery is ours," Morrison states. "It's a serious responsibility and one single human can only do a very very tiny part of that, but it seems to me to be both secular and non-secular work for a writer."[16]

Notes

1 FINDING THE ELUSIVE BUT IDENTIFIABLE BLACKNESS WITHIN
THE CULTURE OUT OF WHICH TONI MORRISON WRITES

1. Toni Morrison, "Rootedness: The Ancestor as Foundation," in Mari Evans, ed., *Black Women Writers (1950–1980): A Critical Evaluation* (New York: Doubleday, 1984), p. 342.
2. Ibid., p. 341.
3. Gay Wilentz, "An African-Based Reading of *Sula*," in Nellie Y. McKay and Kathryn Earle, ed., *Approaches to Teaching the Novels of Toni Morrison* (New York: MLA, 1997), pp. 128–9.
4. Toni Morrison, "Unspeakable Things Unspoken: The Afro-American Presence in American Literature," *Michigan Quarterly Review* 28.1 (Winter 1989), pp. 7, 6.
5. The term "collective (un)conscious" in this study straddles the conscious and unconscious, personal and collective awareness of survivals that acculturation did not disrupt, that oral history continued in whole and fragmented forms, and that the unknown operations of inherited, genetic, or ancestral memory may explain. Wilder Penfield in *The Mystery of the Mind: A Critical Study of Consciousness and the Human Brain* (New Jersey: Princeton University Press, 1975) addresses memory accounted for by the latter terms as "racial memory" (p. 63). Carl Jung spoke of the "collective unconscious" as a description for the part of the psyche not obtained through personal or individual acquisition. Contents of the collective unconscious have never been in the conscious mind. They are universal, impersonal, and identical in all individuals. They are preexistent, inherited forms, always and everywhere present, that are shaped from archetypes largely found in myths. Dreams and the active imaginations are sites where these archetypes express themselves. Conversely, the "personal unconscious," content once in the consciousness but now forgotten or repressed memories, consists of complexes. Jung theorized that it is possible for a person to tap into experiences s/he has never lived and recall them as if they were her or his own. See Carl Jung, *The Archetypes and the Collective Unconscious* (Princeton: Princeton University Press, 1959).
6. Robert Farris Thompson, in *Flash of the Spirit: African and Afro-American Art and Philosophy* (New York: Vintage 1984), p. 103, states that "Spelling Kongo

with a 'K' instead of a 'C', Africanists distinguish Kongo civilization and the Bakongo people from the colonial entity called the Belgian Congo (now Zaïre) and the present-day People's Republic of Congo-Brazzaville, both of which include numerous non-Kongo peoples. Traditional Kongo civilization encompasses modern Bas-Zaïre and neighboring territories in Modern Cabinda, Congo-Brazzaville, Gabon, and northern Angola. The Punu people of Gabon, the Teke of Congo-Brazzaville, and the Suku and the Yaka of the Kwango River area of Kongo in Zaïre, and some of the ethnic groups of northern Angola share key culture and religious concepts with the Bakongo and also suffered, with them, the ordeals of the transatlantic slave trade. The slavers of the early 1500's first applied the name 'Kongo' solely to the Bakongo people. Then gradually they used the name to designate any person brought from the west coast of Central Africa to America."

7. The Marassa-Trois is a constellation of three that affirms the cosmic totality or unity in opposition to a dualism even when the whole is segmented horizontally or vertically into seemingly liberated parts. Bruler-zin is a Voudoun fire ritual that revivifies or recharges the life spirit.

8. Wade W. Nobles, "African Philosophy: Foundations for Black Psychology," in Reginald L. Jones, ed., *Black Psychology* (New York: Harper and Row, 1980), pp. 32, 30.

9. Ibid., p. 32. Nobles identifies African Americans' learning to read as a primary disruptor of the oral traditions that "gave tremendous importance to the mind or memory" and recitation to preserve the cultural past. The prohibition of teaching the enslaved to read unknowingly fostered the continuation of oral cultural transmissions and retentions in the United States. Because Blacks were segregated geographically and socially from the dominant culture, the process of acculturation for them did not escalate significantly until the mid twentieth century. "Not until the television 'explosion' of the early 1950s did the African orientation come fully into contact with Western (Euro-American) styles of behavior and the American way of life" (p. 32).

10. Edward M. Pavlić, "'Papa Legba, Ouvrier Barriere Pour Moi Passer': Esu in *Their Eyes* and Zora Neale Hurston's Diasporic Modernism." *African American Review* 38.1 (Spring 2004), 61–85.

11. John S. Mbiti, *African Religions and Philosophy* (New York: Doubleday, 1970), pp. 2, 1.

12. Nobles, "African Philosophy," p. 24.

13. Bettye Jean Parker, "Complexity: Toni Morrison's Women," in Danille Taylor-Guthrie, ed., *Conversations with Toni Morrison* (Jackson: University Press of Mississippi, 1994), p. 62.

14. "Conversation with Alice Childress and Toni Morrison," *Black Creation Annual* 6 (1974–5), p. 92.

15. Sylvia R. Frey and Betty Wood, *Come Shouting to Zion: African American Protestantism in the American South and the British Caribbean to 1830* (Chapel Hill: University of North Carolina Press, 1998), pp. 58, 21. In, "The Production of Witchcraft/Witchcraft as Production: Memory, Modernity,

and the Slave Trade in Sierra Leone," *American Ethnologist* 24.2 (1997), pp. 856–76, Rosalind Shaw discusses the economic benefit that powerful people in Sierra Leone's Temne area derived from witch divining that escalated during the Atlantic slave trade. Because they had no powerful patrons to protect them from sale, low-status persons were turned into witches and thus trade goods.

16. Robert Farris Thompson and Joseph Cornet, *The Four Moments of the Sun: Kongo Art in Two Worlds* (Washington, D.C.: National Gallery of Art, 1981), p. 15.

17. Ibid., p. 33, note 4.

18. See Alfred Hauenstein, "Considérations sur le motif décoratif croix ainsi que différentes coutumes accompagnées de gestes et rites cruciformes chez quelques tribus d'Angola," *Bulletin der Schweizerischen Gesellschaft für Anthropologie und Ethnologie* 43 (1966/7), and Newbell Niles Puckett, *Black Names in America: Origins and Usage*, ed. Murray Heller (Boston: G. K. Hall, 1975).

19. Vashti Crutcher Lewis, "African Tradition in Toni Morrison's *Sula*," in Joanne M. Braxton and Andrée Nicola McLaughlin, eds., *Wild Women in the Whirlwind: Afra-American Culture and the Contemporary Literary Renaissance* (New Brunswick: Rutgers University Press, 1990), p. 316.

20. Ibid., p. 317.

21. Holly Fils-Aimé, "The Living Dead Learn to Fly: Themes of Spiritual Death, Initiation and Empowerment in *A Praisesong for the Widow* and *Song of Solomon*," *Mid-Atlantic Writers Association Review* 10.1 (June 1995), p. 9.

22. Wilentz, "An African-Based Reading of *Sula*," p. 127.

23. Therese E. Higgins, *Religiosity, Cosmology, and Folklore: The African Influence in the Novels of Toni Morrison* (New York: Routledge, 2001), p. x.

24. Morrison, "Rootedness," p. 342.

25. Three examples of critical scholarship that investigate Voudoun elements in Zora Neale Hurston's *Their Eyes Were Watching God* are Derek Collins, "The Myth and Ritual of Ezili Freda in Hurston's *Their Eyes Were Watching God*," *Western Folklore* 55.2 (Spring 1996), pp. 137–54; Daphne Lamothe, "Vodou Imagery, African-American Tradition and Cultural Transformation in Zora Neale Hurston's *Their Eyes Were Watching God*," *Callaloo* 22.1 (Winter 1999), pp. 157–75; and Edward M. Pavlić, "'Papa Legba, Ouvrier Barriere Pour Moi Passer': Esu in *Their Eyes* and Zora Neale Hurston's Diasporic Modernism," *African American Review* 38.1 (Spring 2004), pp. 61–85.

2 DAHOMEY'S VODUN AND KONGO'S YOWA: THE SURVIVAL OF WEST AND CENTRAL AFRICAN TRADITIONAL COSMOLOGIES IN AFRICAN AMERICA

1. Sterling Stuckey, *Slave Culture: Nationalist Theory and the Foundation of Black America* (New York: Oxford University Press, 1987), p. 12.

2. Other historiographers and histories that have documented African transatlantic religious retentions include Eugene Genovese, *Roll, Jordan, Roll: The*

World the Slaves Made (1974); Elsa Goveia, *Slave Society in the British Leeward Islands at the End of the Eighteenth Century* (1965); Lawrence W. Levine, *Black Culture and Black Consciousness: Afro-American Folk Thought from Slavery to Freedom* (1977); Walter Rodney, "Upper Guinea and the Significance of the Origins of Africans Enslaved in the New World" (1969); and Peter H. Wood, *Black Majority: Negroes in Colonial South Carolina from 1670 through the Stono Rebellion* (1975).

3. The African Diaspora Map outlining the scope of the dispersion to 1873, based on research by Joseph E. Harris. October 5, 2003 www.howard.edu/library/ diaspora/diasp800:gif >.

4. Sylvia R. Frey and Betty Wood, *Come Shouting to Zion: African American Protestantism in the American South and the British Caribbean to 1830* (Chapel Hill: University of North Carolina Press, 1998), p. xi.

5. Ibid., p. 9.

6. Albert J. Raboteau, *Slave Religion, The "Invisible Institution" in the Antebellum South* (New York: Oxford University Press, 1978), pp. 5–7.

7. Shipping records show that slavers also brought Africans to the American South as far away as Mozambique and Madagascar. See Walter Minchinton, Celia King, and Peter Waite, eds., *Virginia Slave-trade Statistics 1698–1775* (Richmond: Virginia State Library, 1984). In addition to "'coasting' – primarily taking captives who lived close to the ocean ports, trade along the Gambia and Senegal rivers in Upper Guinea allowed interior penetration of extraordinary distances. The same was true of the Kongo-Angola region where long-distance trade from Central Africa and beyond was important to the coastal exchange. See David Birmingham, *Trade and Conflict in Angola: The Mbundu and Their Neighbours Under the Influence of the Portuguese 1483–1790* (Oxford: Clarendon, 1966), pp. 133–61; Philip D. Curtin and Jan Vansina, "Sources of the Nineteenth-Century Atlantic Slave Trade," *Journal of African History* 5.2 (1964), 185–208; Walter Rodney, "Upper Guinea and the Significance of the Origins of Africans Enslaved in the New World," *Journal of Negro History* 54.4 (October 1969), 327–45; and Jan Vansina, "Long-Distance Trade Routes in Central Africa," *Journal of History* 3.3 (1962), 376–90.

8. Discounting an independent conception of a Supreme Being, Sir A. B. Ellis, the acclaimed nineteenth-century anthropologist who studied the Tshi, Ewe, Gã, and Yoruba-speaking peoples, prematurely reported in his early research among the West African Tshi that the superior God was a loan god, "the Christian God, borrowed [from missionaries] and thinly disguised." He later admitted that he had erred. See A. B. Ellis, *The Ewe-Speaking Peoples of the Slave Coast of West Africa: Their Religion, Manners, Customs, Laws, Languages, Etc.*, (1890) (Chicago: Benin, 1965), p. 36.

9. Frey and Wood, *Come Shouting to Zion*, p. 11, and Robin Law, *The Slave Coast of West Africa, 1550–1750: The Impact of the Atlantic Slave Trade on an African Society* (New York: Oxford University Press, 1991), p. 11.

10. Frey and Wood, *Come Shouting to Zion*, p. 11.

11. Maya Deren, *Divine Horsemen: Voodoo Gods of Haiti* (New York: Dell, 1970). In my study the spelling of Voudoun and other terminology related to the African religion follows Maya Deren's English rendering of them phonetically as close as possible to the Haitian French Creole pronunciation. The Candomblé terms follow the principal Portuguese spellings.

12. Ibid., p. 59.

13. Stuckey, *Slave Culture*, p. 11.

14. Alfred Hauenstein, "Considérations sur le motif décoratif croix ainsi que différentes coutumes accompagnées de gestes et rites cruciformes chez quelques tribus d'Angola," *Bulletin der Schweizerischen Gesellschaft für Anthropologie und Ethnologie* 43 (1966/67), 34. See also Robert Farris Thompson and Joseph Cornet, *The Four Moments of the Sun: Kongo Art in Two Worlds* (Washington, D.C.: National Gallery of Art, 1981), p. 44.

15. Ibid., p. 28.

16. Robert Farris Thompson, *Flash of the Spirit: African and Afro-American Art and Philosophy* (New York: Vintage, 1984), p. 108.

17. Ibid.

18. Thompson and Cornet, *Four Moments of the Sun*, p. 33, note 17 quoting Philip Curtin at a lecture given at Calhoun College, Yale University, spring 1977. The Kongo law gesture of blocking evil and securing futures, a gesture with left hand on hip, right hand forward, is common in both art and life. The gesture is invoked "when one advocate veers from substance or ethical expectation in such a way that miscarriage of justice suddenly is threatened" (p. 122). These gestures are interlaced in American popular culture to the point that it is impossible to watch American television during prime time on any given night without witnessing an example. The gesture of blocking evil may appear as randomly as a "Talk to the hand" joke on the situation comedy *8 Simple Rules* starring John Ritter, or as an Arby's fast food commercial slogan, "Talk to the mitt."

19. The cross (tree) and circle configuration also appears in cluster images that are abstract in nature. In *Song of Solomon* (New York: Plume, 1977), the Waterford crystal bowl that has left a cloudy gray watermark on the Deads' mahogany table holds twigs of pussy willow and Scotch pine. The watermark, even when the crystal bowl is not there, calls attention to remembrances that have been sublimated to the unconscious, what is psychologically or spiritually present even when it is materially absent (pp. 11–12). During a discussion in *Beloved* (New York: Plume, 1987) between Paul D and Stamp Paid outside what used to be a church, a horseback rider approaches looking for a slaughter-house, a house of death, on Plank Road, a road that signifies a straight axis. The mounted rider chides Paul D for drinking at a building with a cross atop it even if it is no longer a church. As the rider departs, Stamp Paid traces circles in the palm of his left hand with two fingers (p. 231). During his third search for his mother Wild, whose physicality is associated with a white oak whose roots grow backward, Joe Trace in *Jazz* (New York: Plume 1992) crawls the underground vertical and horizontal axes. Emerging head first from the vertical axis's south end, Joe faces a river. He enters a side crevice and slides

through it "on his behind," an action that is "like falling into the sun" (pp. 176, 183). And in *Paradise* (New York: Knopf, 1998), a rising sun frames a cross without a Jesus in the altar room of the Convent as the Ruby gunmen storm the building looking for its female inhabitants (p. 12).

3 BANDOKI: WITCHES, AMBIVALENT POWER, AND
THE FUSION OF GOOD AND EVIL

1. Toni Morrison, *Sula* (New York: Plume, 1973), p. 118.
2. "Conversation with Alice Childress and Toni Morrison," *Black Creation Annual* 6 (1974–5), p. 92.
3. Gay Wilentz, "Civilizations Underneath: African Heritage as Cultural Discourse in Toni Morrison's *Song of Solomon*," in David L. Middleton, ed., *Toni Morrison's Fiction: Contemporary Criticism* (New York: Garland, 1997), pp. 128–9.
4. Toni Morrison, *Beloved* (New York: Plume, 1987), p. 164.
5. Toni Morrison, *Paradise* (New York: Knopf, 1998), pp. 18, 276.
6. Allen Alexander, "The Fourth Face: The Image of God in Toni Morrison's *The Bluest Eye*," *African American Review* 32.2 (1998), p. 293.
7. Ibid.
8. Although resistance to representing absolute good and evil grounds Morrison's narrative within an Africanist worldview, a monistic perspective is not exclusive to Africa. The Indians of Mexico consider a wholly evil spiritual force as illogical since good and evil are essential to the same spiritual force. Eastern cultures, those of India and Persia for example, have divinized fusions of good and evil. The Hindu pantheon of gods and spirits in Madras, and India's mother-goddess, Mahadevi, who combines in her person the totality of existence, are ascribed both good and evil. Buddhism, which lacks a belief in God but "argue[s] that what a man *does* causes him to become what he *is*, and so defines him as 'naturally' embodying both good and evil acts and states," fits within the monistic parameter. See David Parkin, *The Anthropology of Evil* (Oxford: Blackwell, 1985), p. 9. Both Manicheism and Confucianism, each made up of two coeternal cosmic principles of good and evil that are separate and opposed to one another, are examples of dualistic theodicies.
9. "Evil," *Anchor Bible Dictionary*, ed. David Noel Freedman (New York: Doubleday, 1992).
10. Ibid.
11. Carl Jung, "The Problem of the Fourth," in Jung, *Jung on Evil*, ed. Murray Stein (Princeton: Princeton University Press, 1995), p. 58. The mid-first-century Neopythagoreans, following Pythagoreanism of 600 years before, believed that the world was composed of opposites and in the idea that the cosmos and all things, even abstractions, resembled numbers and have numerical values. Symbols, triangles, and spheres played an important part in their ideology.

12. Carl Jung, "The Spirit of Mercurius," in *Jung on Evil* p. 42.

13. Imagining the world as flat and square, the Ewe divided the horizon into four quarters. The universe was envisioned as a rectangular box with an arched top. The arched top was the sky and its bottom the earth. The four points represented the north, south, east, and west of the compass. See A. B. Ellis, *The Ewe-Speaking Peoples of the Slave Coast of West Africa: Their Religion, Manners, Customs, Laws, Languages, Etc. 1890* (Chicago: Benin, 1965), p. 31.

14. Herodotus, *The History of Herodotus*, trans. George Rawlinson (New York: Tudor, 1928), p. 99, and Herodotus, *The Histories*, trans. Robin Waterfield (New York: Oxford University Press, 1998). "Similar signs are said to be in use in Egypt, (as far back as 3,000 B.C.), in Tripoli, Senegal, Futa, the Hausa States and other places in Africa," states D. Olarimwa Epega in *The Basis of Yoruba Religion* (Nigeria: Ijamido, 1971), p. 17; Nigerian scholars maintain that either the Yoruba people emigrated from Egypt or, inversely, they emigrated from Nigeria's Ile-Ife to Egypt. See Martin Bernal, *Black Athena: The Afroasiatic Roots of Classical Civilization* (New Brunswick: Rutgers University Press, 1987); Cheikh Anta Diop, *Precolonial Black Africa: A Comparative Study of the Political and Social Systems of European and Black Africa, from Antiquity to the Formation of Modern States*, trans. Harold Salemson (New York: Lawrence Hill, 1987), pp. 31–3; and Ulysses Duke Jenkins, *Ancient African Religion and the African-American Church* (Jackson, N.C.: Flame International, 1978), p. 73.

15. Carl Jung, "Answer to Job," in *Jung on Evil*, p. 150.

16. R. H. Charles, Introduction, "The Book of Enoch," in Charles, *The Apocrypha and Pseudepigrapha of the Old Testament in English, with Introductions and Critical and Explanatory Notes to the Several Books* (Oxford: Clarendon, 1913), pp. 163–87.

17. Morrison, *Sula*, pp. 97–8.

18. Ibid., p. 114. Gay Wilentz discusses the communal mythologies that Sula's birthmark engenders with respect to its indicator of an ancestral figure and predictor of future events in "An African-Based Reading of *Sula*," in Nellie Y. McKay and Kathryn Earle, eds., *Approaches to Teaching the Novels of Toni Morrison* (New York: MLA, 1997), pp. 130–1.

19. Shadrach in the Old Testament Book of Daniel 3:24–5 completes a trinity with Meshach and Abednego. The crucial climax of his story comes with the appearance of a metaphysical fourth in the fiery furnace after he and his companions have resisted bowing to the golden statue of Nebuchadnezzar.

20. Morrison, *Sula*, p. 39.

21. Ibid., pp. 49, 57, 58.

22. Ibid., p. 105.

23. From the beginning of the text whose first section date is "1919" but contains events set in 1917 to Sula's death in 1940, there are twenty-three years. From Sula's death to the novel's end, twenty-five years pass.

24. Morrison, *Sula*, pp. 58, 59.

25. Ibid., pp. 60–1.

26. Robert W. Pelton, *Voodoo Secrets from A to Z* (New York: A. S. Barnes, 1973), p. 20, and Maya Deren, *Divine Horsemen: Voodoo Gods of Haiti* (New York: Dell, 1970), p. 337.

27. The reader should note that the tree that Sula climbs with Chicken Little is a double beech tree and the cemetery that Nel passes at the end of the novel is Beechnut Park. Morrison repeats the tree association with death. In *Song of Solomon* Ruth makes arrangements for Linden Chapel Funeral Home to prepare Hagar's body and her granddaughter's burial service is held at Linden Baptist Church (p. 320).

28. Morrison, *Sula*, p. 173.

29. Vashti Crutcher Lewis, "African Tradition in Toni Morrison's *Sula*," in Joanne M. Braxton and Andrée Nicola McLaughlin, eds., *Wild Women in the Whirlwind: Afra-American Culture and the Contemporary Literary Renaissance* (New Brunswick: Rutgers University Press, 1990), pp. 316–25.

30. Morrison, *Sula*, p. 174

31. Ibid., p. 171.

32. Robert Farris Thompson and Joseph Cornet, *The Four Moments of the Sun: Kongo Art in Two Worlds* (Washington, D.C.: National Gallery of Art, 1981), p. 27.

33. Morrison, *Sula*, p. 174.

34. Thompson and Cornet, *Four Moments of the Sun*, p. 44.

35. Parkin, *Anthropology of Evil*, p. 12.

36. John Kekes, *Facing Evil* (Princeton: Princeton University Press, 1990), p. 45.

37. Parkin, *Anthropology of Evil*, pp. 10–11.

38. Kekes, *Facing Evil*, p. 45.

39. Herein lies a conundrum or an expression of evil that has yet to be qualified and categorized. If the African traditional witch practices involuntarily and unconsciously, then her evil is unchosen and, therefore by Western definition, not immoral because moral evil requires the operation of the human will.

40. Sylvia R. Frey and Betty Wood, *Come Shouting to Zion: African American Protestantism in the American South and British Caribbean to 1890* (Chapel Hill: University of North Carolina Press, 1998), p. 15.

41. Ibid., pp. 15–16.

42. Thomas E. Lawson, *Religions of Africa, Traditions in Transformation* (New York: HarperCollins, 1985), p. 23.

43. Frey and Wood, *Come Shouting to Zion*, p. 12, and Geoffrey Parrinder, *African Traditional Religion* (New York: Hutchinson's University Library, 1957), p. 101.

44. Edward E. Evans-Pritchard, *Witchcraft, Oracles, and Magic among the Azande* (Oxford: Clarendon, 1958), p. 21.

45. Ibid.

46. Ibid., pp. 124–5.

47. The failure of witchcraft to affect strangers parallels the failure of conjuration to affect European Americans during slavery.

48. In *Slave Counterpoint: Black Culture in the Eighteenth-Century Chesapeake and Lowcountry* (Chapel Hill: University of North Carolina Press, 1998), p. 622, Philip D. Morgan writes that "a number of African words associated with magic, particularly magic aimed at causing harm, were in use well into the twentieth century. The Hausa word *huduba*, meaning 'to arouse resentment,' was simplified to *hudu*, meaning 'to cause bad luck'; the Mende word *ndzoso*, meaning 'spirit or magic,' was simplified to *joso*, meaning 'charm, witchcraft.' Other words with essentially similar meaning were also employed, such as *juju* for 'evil spirit,' *kafa* for 'charm,' *moco* for 'witchcraft or magic,' *wanga* for 'charm, witchcraft,' and most famous of all, *wudu* for 'sorcery.'"

49. Morrison, *Sula*, p. 144,

50. Ibid., p. 57.

51. Geoffrey Parrinder, *Witchcraft: European and African* (New York: Barnes and Noble, 1963), p. 129.

52. Andrew Sanders, *A Deed Without a Name: The Witch in Society and History* (Oxford: Berg, 1995), p. 131; Evans-Pritchard writes of contemporary and earlier traditional practice that "Witches are very seldom slain, for it was only when a man committed a second or third murder, or murdered an important person, that a prince permitted his execution" (*Witchcraft, Oracles and Magic*, p 5). Parrinder, states that "The Tiv believe that there are anti-social folk who go about spreading death and trouble. At times resentment against them comes to a head, when there are too many deaths, and uprisings occur to suppress them" (*Witchcraft*, p. 137).

53. Lawson, *Religions of Africa*, pp. 60–1.

54. Epega, *Basis of Yoruba Religion*, p. 26.

55. Simon Bockie, *Death and the Invisible Powers: The World of Kongo Belief* (Bloomington: Indiana University Press, 1993), p. 46.

56. Ibid.

57. Ibid., pp. 46–7.

58. Buakasa Tulu Kia Mpansu, "Le Discours de la Kindoki ou Sorcellerie," *Cahiers des Religions Africaines* 4.11 (1972), p. 29. Because West and West Central African groups use many words to designate the art of exercising unusual power, I have chosen the Kikongo words "kindoki" to designate the ambivalent art and "ndoki" (the singular of "bandoki") to designate its practitioner. The Kikongo terms serve as a reminder not to obfuscate their meanings with Western definitions that make no distinction between the use and the users of psychic power and the casting and the casters of spells with medicines and charms.

59. Bockie, *Death and the Invisible Powers*, pp. 43, 47

60. Evans-Pritchard, *Witchcraft, Oracles and Magic*, p. 41.

61. Morrison, *Sula*, p. 115. Pilate's physical markers in Morrison's *Song of Solomon* (New York: Plume, 1977) parallels Sula's and indicate to groups of Blacks that she encounters on her way to and in Virginia that she is not a normal person. Pilate has "smooth smooth skin," is hairless, scarless, and wrinkleless. The absence of an obligatory "birthmark," a navel, incontrovertibly corroborates

her unnaturalness, for "people who were born natural" have one (p. 144). Had they known that Pilate was born of a dead mother, her post-mortem delivery would have cinched her potential for invisible harm. The discoloration over Sula's eye substantiates an identical communal deduction.

62. Lawson, *Religions of Africa*, p. 24; Parrinder, *Witchcraft*, p. 134.
63. Morrison, *Sula*, p. 54.
64. Ibid., pp. 54–5.
65. Lewis, "African Tradition in Toni Morrison's *Sula*," p. 319, and P. Amaury Talbot, *Tribes of the Niger Delta: Their Religions and Customs* (London: Cass, 1967), p. 45.
66. Morrison, *Sula*, p. 57.
67. John S. Mbiti, *African Religions and Philosophy* (New York: Doubleday, 1970), p. 209.
68. Morrison, *Sula*, p. 61.
69. Ibid.
70. Trudier Harris, *Fiction and Folklore: The Novels of Toni Morrison* (Knoxville: University of Tennessee Press, 1991), p. 82.
71. Claudia Tate, "Toni Morrison," in Danille Taylor-Guthrie, ed., *Conversations with Toni Morrison* (Jackson: University Press of Mississippi, 1994) p. 164, and Wade W. Nobles, "African Philosophy: Foundations for Black Psychology," in Reginald L. Jones, ed., *Black Psychology* (New York: Harper and Row, 1980), p. 30.
72. Cauldrons commonly carried the engraved image of Cernunnos, the stag-god and nature divinity. Around AD 200 Christians perverted his horns into the devil and pagans, mostly women, were burned at the stake as witches.
73. Morrison, *Sula*, p. 75.
74. Ibid., p. 78.
75. Newbell Niles Puckett, *Black Names in America: Origins and Usage*, ed. Murray Heller (Boston: G. K . Hall, 1975), pp. 449–50. In Ngala Sula means "betray," which Sula also does with respect to Nel. In Kikongo it means "Electric fish" (eel) which suggests her connection to Shadrack. A variation of the title character's name, Sola, in Kikongo means "to make a clearing in the woods."
76. Geoffrey Parrinder, *West African Psychology: A Comparative Study of Psychological and Religious Thought* (New York: AMS, 1976), p. 165.
77. Alan Gauld and A. D. Cornell, *Poltergeists* (Boston: Routledge and Paul, 1979), p. 16.
78. Morrison, *Sula*, p. 74.
79. A. R. G. Owen, *Can We Explain the Poltergeist?* (New York: Garrett, 1964), p. 179.
80. Bockie, *Death and the Invisible Powers*, p. 40.
81. Ibid.
82. Morrison, *Sula*, pp. 147–8; (emphasis mine), and Morrison, *Beloved*, p. 133. For different reasons, Beloved dreams of exploding and being swallowed.
83. Bockie, *Death and the Invisible Powers*, p. 42.

84. Morrison, *Sula* p. 89.
85. Ibid., pp. 89–90.
86. Ibid., p. 118.
87. Parrinder, *Witchcraft*, pp. 136–7.
88. Morrison, *Sula*, p. 113.
89. Morrison posits appeasement and flight as optional maneuvers for avoiding the ire of the suspected ndoki in *Song of Solomon*. The root worker who examines Pilate's smooth stomach and the women of a migrant camp insist that she leave "with more than her share of earnings, because they fear she might hurt them in some way if they anger her. They also feel pity along with terror at having been in the company of something God never made" (p. 144). A second group of migrants "simply left her one day, moved out while she was in the town buying thread" (p. 145). From then on, when her lack of a navel was discovered, "[m]en frowned, [and] women whispered and shoved their children behind them" (p. 149).
90. Morrison, *Sula*, pp. 117–18.
91. Mbiti, *African Religions and Philosophy*, p. 278.
92. Evans-Pritchard, *Witchcraft, Oracles and Magic*, pp. 19–20.
93. Masamba Ma Mpolo, "Kindoki as Diagnosis and Therapy," *Social Science & Medicine: An International Journal* 15B.3 (July 1981), p. 406.
94. Mbiti, *African Religions and Philosophy*, pp. 203–4.
95. Ibid., p. 277.
96. Morrison, *Sula*, p. 100.
97. Ibid., p. 92.
98. Mbiti, *African Religions and Philosophy*, p. 278.
99. Harris, *Fiction and Folklore*, pp. 75–6.
100. Morrison, *Sula*, p. 112.
101. Ibid., p. 142.
102. Thompson and Cornet, *Four Moments of the Sun*, p. 107.
103. Bockie, *Death and the Invisible Powers*, p. 39.
104. Morrison, *Sula*, p. 118.
105. Ibid., pp. 117–18,
106. Mbiti, *African Religions and Philosophy*, pp. 272–3.
107. Ibid.
108. In graduate school I had a Ghanaian friend who had eighteen mothers, or rather his father had eighteen wives. His mother had been the first wife, but shortly after my friend's birth his parents divorced. His father soon remarried. The second wife met the divorced first wife in the marketplace, befriended her, and after some time requested that the husband remarry her. He did.
109. Wilentz, "An African-Based Reading of *Sula*," p. 132.
110. Ibid.
111. Morrison, *Sula*, p. 146.
112. Ibid., pp. 144–5.
113. Wilentz, "An African-Based Reading of *Sula*," p. 131.

114. Morrison, *Sula*, pp. 51–2.
115. Deren, *Divine Horsemen*, pp. 40–1.
116. Ibid., p. 41
117. Morrison, *Sula*, pp. 168–9.
118. Ibid., p. 170.
119. Murray Stein, Introduction, *Jung on Evil*, p. 9.
120. Bockie, *Death and the Invisible Powers*, p. 47.
121. Morrison, *Sula*, p. 172.
122. Ibid., p. 77.
123. Mpolo, "Kindoki as Diagnosis and Therapy," p. 405.
124. Morrison, *Sula*, p. 150.
125. Mbiti, *African Religions and Philosophy*, p. 202.
126. Bockie, *Death and the Invisible Powers*, p. 53.
127. Parrinder, *Witchcraft*, p. 141. Parrinder also states that witchcraft may be "caught," "bought," or gained "as a heritage from a dying relative," p. 142.
128. Bockie, *Death and the Invisible Powers*, p. 43.
129. Morrison, *Sula*, p. 41.
130. Sir James George Frazer, *The Golden Bough: A Study in Magic and Religion* (New York: Macmillan, 1963), pp. 793–4.
131. Elaine Breslaw, "Non-Christian Beliefs," in Breslaw, ed., *Witches of the Atlantic World* (New York: New York University Press, 2000), p. 98. Indigenous belief in sympathetic magic was not different from the philosophical school of Neoplatonism revived in the seventeenth century that asserted that there was no disconnect between the material and spiritual worlds. In *Beloved* Sethe tosses hair from her comb into the fire (p. 61).
132. Mbiti, *African Religions and Philosophy*, p. 202.
133. Morrison, *Sula*, p. 67.
134. Ibid., p. 30.
135. Ibid., p. 38.
136. An earlier Morrison usage of the name Dewey appears in *The Bluest Eye* (New York: Washington Square, 1970). Miss Marie, one of three prostitutes, has a "fabled" love for Dewey Prince. She tells Pecola Breedlove, the novel's adolescent blues protagonist, that she and Dewey Prince "ran away and lived together like married for three years"(p. 47). Mary Magdalene, the scandalized "Marie" of the Bible whose identity some New Testament scholars argue has been textually and historically compromised because of scriptural proximity with a repentant prostitute that Jesus cured of evil spirits, had a legendary love for the Son of the Trinity, the King of kings and Prince of Peace and in fact, some argue, may have been the wife of Jesus. The publication of Dan Brown's *The Da Vinci Code* (New York: Doubleday, 2003) has opened scholastic debate on the true relationship between Jesus and Mary Magdalene.
137. Toni Morrison provides an introduction for Camara Laye's *The Radiance of the King* (New York: New York Review Books, 2001), pp. xi–xxiv. See also Bessie W. Jones and Audrey Vinson, "An Interview with Toni Morrison," in

Taylor-Guthrie, ed., *Conversations with Toni Morrison* p. 179, and Christina Davis, "An Interview with Toni Morrison," in ibid., p. 228.

138. Deren, *Divine Horsemen*, pp. 38–9.
139. Ibid., p. 39.
140. Ibid.
141. Ibid., p. 40.
142. Ibid., p. 41.
143. Ibid., p. 56.
144. John 3:4.
145. Harris, *Fiction and Folklore*, pp. 74, 71, 73 (emphasis mine).
146. Ibid., pp. 74, 75.
147. Deren, *Divine Horsemen*, p. 150.
148. Morrison, *Sula*, p. 93. See also Exodus 20:12.
149. Deren, *Divine Horsemen*, p. 222.
150. Ayoade Joy Asekun, "Binary Fusions: Examining the Concepts of Good and Evil in Toni Morrison's *Sula* and *Beloved*," seminar paper, University of Tennessee (1997), p. 3.
151. Ayoade Joy Asekun, "Making the Connection: African Cosmology in Toni Morrison's *Beloved* and Paule Marshall's *Praisesong for the Widow*," unpublished MA thesis, University of Tennessee (1998), pp. 22, 23.
152. There is something in Sethe's psychological complexity that affirms her right to kill her children. As human dispenser of harming and protecting kindoki, Sethe is Beloved's figurative ndoki predecessor. Her surviving children play "die witch" (p. 205) just in case they will need to keep her harming kindoki at bay. Morrison's imbuing Sethe with cannibalistic fear, the fear of eating herself and being eaten by others, and inscribing by way of scarification a chokecherry tree on her back, a variation of the cross in the circle cicatrix under Ma'am's breast, encourage the reading of Sethe's social role from a West African traditional perspective.
153. Morrison, *Sula*, p. 78.
154. Bluestone is frequently encountered as an ingredient in mojo hands that African-American Voodooists made for protection from evil. It is sometimes mentioned in old recipes for floorwash that spiritualists used to purify the home in the interest of keeping out evil spirits. Also known as blue vitriol, Salzburg vitriol, Roman vitriol, and blue copperas, bluestone is actually copper sulphate, a naturally occurring odorless crystalline substance that is electric blue in color and highly toxic. In *Sula* Hannah's lovers "protect her from any vitriol that newcomers or their wives might spill" (p. 45).
155. Morrison, *Beloved*, pp. 8, 13.
156. In addition to designating a carnival performer, a "Two-Headed Man" is also a name for a Voodoo priest.
157. The brand under Ma'am's breast, the "boxwood bushes, planted in a ring" where Denver plays (p. 28), the chokecherry tree cicatrix on Sethe's back, and the Clearing where Baby Suggs calls to the black community gathered for worship are other cross and circle signages.

158. Morrison, *Beloved*, p. 200.
159. Ibid., p. 164.
160. Parrinder, *African Traditional Religion*, p. 60.
161. Morrison, *Beloved*, p. 5.
162. Morrison, *Beloved*, pp. 8, 13, 37.
163. Parrinder, *West African Psychology*, p. 116. Belief in reincarnation underlies Hinduism and Jainism. Buddhism does not teach the existence of a soul but does speak of a stream of existences. The Jews did not teach successive existences but did posit that the soul preexists its mortal life.
164. Mbiti, *African Religions and Philosophy*, p. 110.
165. Morrison, *Beloved*, p. 255.
166. Deren, *Divine Horsemen*, p. 138.
167. Chikwenye Okonjo Ogunyemi, *African Wo/man Palava: The Nigerian Novel by Women* (Chicago: University of Chicago Press, 1995), p. 62.
168. Asekun, "Making the Connection," pp. 32–3.
169. Morrison, *Beloved*, p. 164.
170. Deren, *Divine Horsemen*, p. 143.
171. Morrison, *Beloved*, p. 242.
172. Zora Neale Hurston, *Tell My Horse* (Philadelphia: Lippincott, 1938), p. 144.
173. Ibid., p. 145.
174. Deren, *Divine Horsemen*, p. 266. In Appendix A, Deren narrates a marriage ceremony to Erzulie in which a golden ring set with a blue stone is passed through smoke and presented to the groom.
175. Ibid., p. 141.
176. Pamela E. Barnett, "Figurations of Rape and the Supernatural in *Beloved*," *PMLA* 112 (1997), p. 418.
177. Ibid., p. 426, note 4.
178. The belief in cannibalizing witches has centuries-old roots in Africa, yet the word cannibal originated in the Caribbean to describe New World Carib Indians. Other tropes of cannibalism in *Beloved* figuratively articulate the power of fleshed as well as unfleshed evil to consume the human body, soul, and psyche. Morrison depicts the events, memories, and emotional scars of slavery as physical, human consumption. Metaphorical cannibalism that tears away at the psychic wholeness appears again in the fellatio abuse in Alfred, Georgia, that Paul D witnesses. Eating and its control symbolize traumatizing, hegemonic power that over time annihilates the body and soul/psyche of the victim. An instrument of torture, the iron bit looms large as the unparalleled oral weapon of domination that the dominant culture's commissioners of moral evil wield with the optimal objective of killing the inner life force of the enslaved. Offending the tongue, disallowing expectoration, the iron bit deprives its wearer of the power of life-sustaining consumption and self-affirming speech. Invariably its effects shoot to the eyes, vanquishing the psyche and humanity of its wearer.
179. Bockie, *Death and the Invisible Powers*, pp. 47–9.
180. Parrinder, *Witchcraft*, p. 133.

181. Deren, *Divine Horsemen*, p. 18.
182. Morrison, *Beloved*, p. 58.
183. Ibid., p. 250.
184. In Paul Gilroy's "Living memory: a meeting with Toni Morrison," in his *Small Acts: Thoughts on the politics of black cultures* (London: Serpent's Tail, 1993), Toni Morrison, commenting on Sethe's real-life counterpart, states that "Margaret Garner didn't do what Medea did and kill her children because of some guy. It was for me this classic example of a person determined to be responsible" (p. 177). Gilroy adds that "The Garner story illustrates more than the indomitable power of slaves to assert their humanity in restricted circumstances. It encapsulates the confrontation between two opposed philosophical and ideological systems and their attendant conceptions of reason, history, property, and kinship. One is the product of Africa, the other is an expression of Western modernity" (pp. 177–8).
185. Morrison, *Beloved*, pp. 256, 258–9.
186. Parrinder, *West African Psychology*, p. 167.
187. Morrison, *Beloved*, p. 239.
188. Ibid., p. 261.
189. Barnett, "Figurations of Rape," p. 421.
190. Morrison, *Beloved*, p. 257,
191. Quoted in Bockie, *Death and the Invisible Powers*, p. 51. Wesley H. Brown, "Marriage Payment: A Problem in Christian Social Ethics among Kongo Protestants," unpublished PhD dissertation, University of Southern California (1971), p. 37.
192. Nobles, "African Philosophy, p. 30.
193. Dinitia Smith, "Mixing Tragedy and Folklore," *New York Times* (January 8, 1998), pp. B1–B2.
194. Bernard Rosenthal, "Dark Eve," in Elizabeth Reis, ed., *Spellbound: Women and Witchcraft in America* (Wilmington, Del.: Scholarly Resources, 1998), pp. 78–9.
195. George Brown Tindall, *America: A Narrative History* (New York: Norton, 1984), pp. 57–8.
196. Morrison, *Paradise*, p. 18.
197. Ibid., p. 8.
198. The other two principal patriarchs of the exodus from Fairly to Haven are Juvenal DuPres, also from French Louisiana, and Drum Blackhorse from Mississippi, another textual precedent for African and Indian cooperation and amalgamation. "In Oklahoma Negroes, Indian and God mixed, all else was fodder' (Morrison, *Paradise*, p. 56). Also, while tracking the walking man with the satchel, Zechariah experiences his sound after he completely dissolves in front of him as a cross: "footsteps again, pounding . . . in back, to the left, now to the right. Or was it overhead?" (Ibid., p. 98).
199. Compare the geographic ordering of Accra, the capital city of Ghana. The city has a semicircular "Ring Road" at its action center that is divided into Ring Road East, Ring Road Central, and Ring Road West. Four major circles

named for famous African leaders link Ring Road interchanges from east to west: Danquah Circle, Sankara Circle, Nkrumah Circle, and Lamptey Circle.

200. Morrison, *Paradise*, p. 11.
201. Ibid., pp. 18, 4.
202. A foundling like Consolata, Lone is of dubious origin. Her given name, selected because the exodusters who founded Haven discovered her alone in front of a sod house that presumably contained her dead mother, proves to be the course of her life. Her French surname, DuPres, traces Fairy DuPres – the exoduster woman who reared her – back to the Louisiana French and an African Middle Passage ancestry that passed through the French Caribbean and perhaps Haiti. Lone never marries, is childless, and at eighty-six years old, despite thirty-two successful deliveries as Ruby's midwife, is rumored to have caused the misfortune of the four damaged Fleetwood children.
203. The four Fleetwood children suffer from a condition that renders them lifeless lumps of flesh; therefore they need round the clock attention to insure they do not die. One of the four, Save-Marie, dies. Lone calls her gift of pulling the dying back to life "stepping in"; Consolata calls it "seeing in" (Morrison, *Paradise*, p. 247.)
204. Morrison, *Paradise*, p. 245.
205. Ibid.
206. Ibid., p. 244.
207. Ibid., p. 263.
208. Ibid.
209. Ibid., p. 265.
210. Ibid., p. 264 (emphasis mine).
211. Melville J. Herskovits, *The Myth of the Negro Past* (New York: Harper, 1941), pp. 207–13.
212. Morrison, *Paradise*, pp. 142, 145–6.
213. Ibid., p. 17.
214. Ibid., p. 8.
215. Ibid., p. 276.
216. Because of Vodun and Candomblé acceptance of sexual fusion and balance, many hounfors and houses of Candomblé are headed by and draw initiates who are homosexual or lesbian.
217. Ibid.
218. An alternate reading of Consolata's vampirism appears in chapter 5 on banganga in this study.
219. While I discuss the "hunger" of the women in physical/material terms, there is a spiritual reading that is equally valid.
220. Morrison, *Paradise*, p. 171.
221. Ibid., p. 261.
222. Jones and Vinson, "Interview with Toni Morrison," p. 178.
223. Claudia Tate, " Toni Morrison," in Taylor-Guthrie, ed., *Conversations with Toni Morrison* p. 168.

4 KANDA: LIVING ELDERS, THE ANCESTRAL PRESENCE, AND
THE ANCESTOR AS FOUNDATION

1. T. Cullen Young, "The Idea of God in Northern Nyasaland (Malawi)," in Edwin W. Smith, ed., *African Ideas of God* (London: Edinburgh House, 1966), p. 38.
2. Toni Morrison, "Rootedness: The Ancestor as Foundation," in Mari Evans, ed., *Black Women Writers (1950–1980): A Critical Evaluation* (New York: Doubleday, 1984), p. 343.
3. Ibid., p. 343.
4. Christina Davis, "An Interview with Toni Morrison," in Danille Taylor-Guthrie, ed., *Conversations with Toni Morrison* (Jackson: University Press of Mississippi, 1994), p. 227.
5. "Conversations with Alice Childress and Toni Morrison," *Black Creation Annual* 6 (1974–5), p. 92.
6. Barbara Christian, "Fixing Methodologies, *Beloved*," in Elizabeth Abel, Barbara Christian, and Helene Moglen, eds., *Female Subjects in Black and White: Race, Psychoanalysis, Feminism* (Berkeley: University of California Press, 1997), p. 367.
7. Ibid., p. 365.
8. Ibid., pp. 368, 364.
9. Robert Farris Thompson and Joseph Cornet, *The Four Moments of the Sun: Kongo Art in Two Worlds* (Washington, D.C.: National Gallery of Art, 1981), p. 28.
10. Sandra Pouchet Paquet, in "The Ancestor as Foundation in *Their Eyes Were Watching God* and *Tar Baby*," *Callaloo* 13 (1990), pp. 499–515, identifies Thérèse as the "dominant ancestral figure," but also states that "Son as [Jadine's] lover assumes the role of ancestor, instructive and protective." Joanne M. Braxton, in "Ancestral Presence: The Outraged Mother Figure in Contemporary Afra-American Writing," in her *Wild Women in the Whirlwind: Afra-American Culture and the Contemporary Literary Renaissance* (New Brunswick: Rutgers University Press, 1990), pp. 299–315, maintains that Pilate "represents the ancestral past" but does not account for the role her father performs as her living-dead guide.
11. Sylvia R. Frey and Betty Wood, *Come Shouting to Zion: African American Protestantism in the American South and the British Caribbean to 1830* (Chapel Hill: University of North Carolina Press, 1998), p. 12.
12. See chapter 5 on banganga in this study.
13. Morrison, "Rootedness," p. 342.
14. John S. Mbiti, *African Religions and Philosophy* (New York: Doubleday, 1970), p. 97.
15. Ibid., pp. 32–3.
16. Edwin W. Smith, "The Whole Subject in Perspective: An Introductory Survey," in Smith, ed., *African Ideas of God* (London: Edinburgh House, 1966), p. 24.

17. Geoffrey Parrinder, *African Traditional Religion* (New York: Hutchinson's University Library, 1957), p. 60.
18. Mbiti, *African Religions and Philosophy*, p. 109
19. Ibid.
20. E. Thomas Lawson, *Religions of Africa, Traditions in Transformation* (New York: HarperCollins, 1985), p. 62.
21. Mbiti, *African Religions and Philosophy*, p. 110.
22. Toni Morrison, *Sula* (New York: Plume, 1973), p. 149.
23. Toni Morrison, Interview, *In Black and White: Conversations with African American Writers*, San Francisco Newsreel, 1992.
24. Mbiti, *African Religions and Philosophy*, pp. 21, 23.
25. Ibid.
26. Mbiti, Ibid., asserts that "Numerical calendars, with one or two possible exceptions, do not exist in African traditional societies as far as I know. If such calendars exist, they are likely to be of a short duration, stretching back perhaps a few decades, but certainly not into the realm of centuries" (p. 25).
27. The lunar month displaces the numerical month. Cyclical events, rain season, planting, harvesting, dry season, displace the set numerical year.
28. Mbiti, *African Religions and Philosophy*, pp. 24–5.
29. Richard Wright, *Black Power* (New York: Harper, 1954), p. 175.
30. Morrison, *Beloved* (New York: Plume, 1987), p. 60.
31. Ibid., p. 36.
32. Ibid., p. 183.
33. Ibid., p. 257.
34. Especially important because it is used as a lingua franca – a medium of communication between peoples of different languages – in large parts of Africa, Swahili is one of the most widely known Bantu "people" languages in Africa (ntu means "person" and ba pluralizes "person," thus Bantu translates as "people"). Bantu languages extend in a semi-circle from Nigeria in the west, along eastern Kenya and Tanzania, to Kongo-Angola and Namibia. With Arabic roots and used by the Portuguese and other slave traders as a lingua franca, Swahili has been criticized as a bastard African language. After I spoke with speakers of and experts in Kikongo, Lingala, and other Bantu languages who agreed with Mbiti's exposition of time in the traditional sense, I selected his well-articulated explication of African temporality.
35. In Akan culture the counterclockwise spiral with an arrow indicating an unspecified continuation into the past is called Abode Santen (also Abode Santan). A symbol of eternity, it is a pattern that is not as commonly printed on Adinkra cloth as some of the other symbols.
36. Mbiti, *African Religions and Philosophy*, pp. 28–9.
37. Ibid., p. 32.
38. Morrison, *Beloved*, p. 274.
39. Mbiti, *African Religions and Philosophy*, p. 34.
40. Ibid., p. 33.
41. Ibid., pp. 33–4.

42. Christian, "Fixing Methodologies," pp. 366–7.
43. Morrison, *Beloved*, p. 210.
44. Ibid.
45. Ibid.
46. Jerome S. Handler, "Survivors of the Middle Passage: Life Histories of Enslaved Africans in British America," *Slavery and Abolition* 23.1 (2002), pp. 38, 43. Slave captains and others of European descent wrote first-hand accounts of the transatlantic trafficking of Africans as chattel. But extant accounts from the perspective of the cargo, the collected memories of Africans who survived and wrote autobiographically or reported biographically of their transportation between Africa and the Caribbean or American shores, like Royall's, are few. Archibald John (or Aneaso) Monteith, an Ibo from Nigeria; James Albert Ukawsaw Gronniosaw from northeastern Nigeria; and Venture Smith (born *c.*1729) from the Gold Coast give minimal information about the Middle Passage. Gronniosaw's and Smith's narratives appear in Vincent Carretta's *Unchained Voices: An Anthology of Black Authors in the English-Speaking World of the Eighteenth Century* (Lexington: University of Kentucky Press, 1996), pp. 32–58, 369–87.
47. Handler, "Survivors of the Middle Passage," pp. 27, 38, 39. Handler, who identifies fifteen autobiographical accounts by Africans who survived the Middle Passage (twelve by males and three by females, of which Royall's is one), states that nine give no details of the voyage, five give minimal details, and one, Equiano's, gives maximum details.
48. Olaudah Equiano, *The Interesting Narrative of the Life of Olaudah Equiano, or Gustavus Vassa, The African. Written by Himself* (New York: St. Martin's Press, 1995), pp. 55–6.
49. Handler, "Survivors of the Middle Passage," p. 39. Basing his argument on textual analysis, S. E. Ogude questions details and the location of Equiano's birth and upbringing but not his African nativity. Vincent Carretta, basing his claims on archival research, argues that Equiano, a true native of South Carolina, fabricated his Nigerian birth from oral history and reading for rhetorical and financial ends. See S. E. Ogude, "Facts into Fiction: Equiano's Narrative Reconsidered," *Research in African Literatures* 13 (Spring 1982), pp. 31–43, and Vincent Carretta, "Olaudah Equiano or Gustavus Vassa? New Light on an Eighteenth-Century Question of Identity," *Slavery and Abolition* 20.3 (December 1999), pp. 96–105.
50. The text of *Beloved* does not provide details of Baby Suggs's birthplace. A *Newsweek* article, however, quotes Morrison as affirming that "Baby Suggs came here out of one of those ships." See Walter Clemons, "The Ghosts of 'Sixty Million and More,'" *Newsweek* (September 28, 1987), p. 75.
51. Before cotton was king in the lowlands of colonial South Carolina, the principal naturalized staple and export was rice. Indigo, also produced after 1740, made up one-third of South Carolina's total exports.
52. American English dictionaries define nana as a grandmother, nurse, or nurse-maid, and cite it as being "of baby-talk origin." The Oxford English

Dictionary lists no origin. Nanã, the Yoruba orisha, is best known in African-Brazilian Candomblé.

53. Morrison, *Beloved*, p. 62.
54. Ibid.
55. Ibid., p. 30.
56. Peter H. Wood, *Black Majority: Negroes in Colonial South Carolina from 1670 through the Stono Rebellion* (New York: Knopf, 1974), p. 59.
57. Robert Farris Thompson, *Faces of the Gods: Art and Altars of Africa and the African Americas* (New York: Museum of African Art, 1993), p. 56.
58. Maya Deren, *Divine Horsemen: Voodoo Gods of Haiti* (New York: Dell, 1970), p. 59.
59. Thompson and Cornet, *Four Moments of the Sun*, p. 28.
60. Sterling Stuckey, *Slave Culture: Nationalist Theory and the Foundations of Black America* (New York: Oxford University Press, 1987), pp. 11–12.
61. Deren, *Divine Horsemen*, p. 153.
62. Wood, *Black Majority*, p. 59.
63. A significant number of Middle Passage survivors who arrived in Louisiana were from Mali. Modern incarnations of Mali culture survive in the costumes of animal designs paraded during the annual celebration of Mardi Gras in New Orleans. With its 1803 purchase from Napoleon Bonaparte, Louisiana suspended laws prohibiting slave gatherings, thereby permitting special occasions and Sunday recreation on plantations and at legally sanctioned public sites like New Orleans's Congo Square.
64. Morrison, *Beloved*, p. 30.
65. Ibid., p. 208.
66. Ibid., p. 25.
67. Ibid., p. 21.
68. Ibid., p. 21. The flame-red tongue and indigo face are also features of the Voudoun priest.
69. Maximilien Larouche, *L'image comme écho* (Montreal: Editions Nouvelle Optique, 1978), pp. 173, 199.
70. Morrison, *Beloved*, p. 160.
71. Ibid., p. 219.
72. Wona, *A Selection of Anancy Stories* (Kingston, Jamaica: Aston W. Gardner, 1899). "Do-Mek-A-See," "Put You Down a Me Wife Pot," "Tocooma A Me Fadder Ole Ridin' Harse," "Anancy and Bredda Firefly," "Anancy and the Sheep," "Anancy and Bredda Tiger," "Dry Head," "Tumbletud," "Anancy's Deserts," "Groun' Hab Yie," "Anancy and Bredda Dog," and "Anancy Meets Bredda Death" all contain trickster deceptions involving food. Also compare Son's logic concerning stealing food versus the eating of that food in Morrison's *Tar Baby* (New York: Plume, 1981), p. 118.
73. Robert Farris Thompson, *Flash of the Spirit: African and Afro-American Art and Philosophy* (New York: Vintage, 1984), p. 108.
74. Morrison, *Beloved*, p. 22.
75. Ibid., p. 267.

76. Ibid., p. 24.
77. Mbiti, *African Religions and Philosophy*, p. 33.
78. Mbiti, Ibid., reports that personal recognition of individuals who have passed on "may continue up to four or five generations" (p. 32).
79. Ibid., pp. 33, 174.
80. Morrison, *Beloved*, pp. 4, 200.
81. Ibid., p. 45.
82. Ibid., p. 87.
83. See chapter 5 on banganga in this study.
84. P. C. Bassett, "A Visit to the Slave Mother Who Killed Her Child," *National Anti-slavery Standard*, March 15, 1856, rpt. in Angelita Reyes, "Using History as Artifact to Situate Beloved's Unknown Woman: Margaret Garner," in Nellie Y. McKay and Kathryn Earle, eds., *Approaches to Teaching the Novels of Toni Morrison* (New York: MLA 1997), pp. 82–4. Bassett recorded that Mary Garner, the mother-in-law of Margaret Garner, "witnessed the killing of the child, but said that she neither encouraged nor discouraged her daughter-in-law – for under similar circumstances she should probably have done the same. The old woman is from sixty to seventy years of age; has been a professor of religion about twenty years, and speaks with much feeling of the time when she shall be delivered from the power of the oppressor" (p. 83).
85. Morrison, *Beloved*, p. 180.
86. Clemons, "The Ghost of 'Sixty Million and More,'" p. 75.
87. Morrison, *Beloved*, p. 244.
88. Ibid., p. 104.
89. Ibid., p. 244.
90. Toni Morrison, *Song of Solomon* (New York: Plume, 1977), p. 17.
91. Ibid., pp. 184, 253. Holly Fils-Aimé, in "The Living Dead Learn to Fly: Themes of Spiritual Death, Initiation and Empowerment in *A Praisesong for the Widow* and *Song of Solomon*," *Middle-Atlantic Writers Review* 10.1 (June 1995), p. 4, gives a full discussion of the zombie figuring in *Song of Solomon*. According to Fils-Aimé, the "tell-tale signs" that Morrison equates Milkman with the zombie, a figure that is not a part of Voudoun but is found in Carib Indian folklore and superstitions that have sprung up around the religion, are an integral part of the narrative. First, as is the inability of the Deads, zombies cannot remember their names. Next, living dead zombies walk with a shuffling, uneven gate. One of Milkman's legs is shorter than the other and the limp his imbalance produces disappears when he undergoes the Voudoun initiation involving the abandonment of the illusion of the ego. At the vertical and horizontal axes of the base of a sweet gum tree that cradles him during the Shalimar bobcat hunt like a grandfather's maternal hands, he relinquishes his arrogant possession of his life. Last, zombies are forbidden salt because of its quickening power. Milkman twice has the taste of salt in his mouth: once when he draws closer to resurrecting the life of his grandfather and thus his own, and again when he draws closer to resurrecting his own life from the dead. In the first instance Guitar admonishes Milkman to live his life and

purloin the gold from Pilate that will turn out to be his grandfather's human remains. In the second instance Milkman forges the liminal Kalunga line of the Danville, Pennsylvania, creek on his way to the cave that will lead to his trip to the southern town of Shalimar and the recovery of his ancestors' names and personal immortality.

92. Toni Morrison, "The Site of Memory," in William Zinsser, ed., *Inventing the Truth: The Art and Craft of Memoir* (Boston: Houghton Mifflin, 1987), p. 124.

93. Morrison, *Song of Solomon*, p. 35.

94. Morrison, "Rootedness," p. 344.

95. Morrison, *Song of Solomon*, pp. 38, 36.

96. Modeled on the loa Ayizan, Eva Peace has four sickle-pear trees in her yard (Morrison, *Sula*, p. 30).

97. Morrison, *Song of Solomon*, p. 55.

98. Compelled by graveyard love (excessive love that causes her to lose touch with her own needs and identity), Ruth Foster Dead makes 3.30 a.m. visits to Fairfield Cemetery to commune with her father who was buried there forty years earlier.

99. Morrison, *Song of Solomon*, p. 38.

100. Ibid., p. 141.

101. Ibid., p. 239.

102. Ibid., p. 169.

103. Ibid., p. 209.

104. Ibid., p. 54.

105. Ibid., p. 224. Guitar Baines draws a distinction between the living life and the dead life.

106. Morrison, *Song of Solomon*, p. 238.

107. Mbiti, *African Religions and Philosophy*, p. 35.

108. George Thomas Basden, *Among the Ibos of Nigeria: An Account of the Curious and Interesting Habits, Customs and Beliefs of a Little Known African People by One Who Has for Many Years Lived Amongst Them On Close and Intimate Terms* (Philadelphia: Lippincott, 1931), pp. 115–16.

109. William Bosman, *A New and Accurate Description of the Coast of Guinea; Divided into the Gold, the Slave, and the Ivory Coasts* (London: Printed for J. Wren, 1754), pp. 223–4.

110. C. K. Meek, *Law and Authority in a Nigerian Tribe, A Study of Indirect Rule* (New York: Barnes and Noble, 1970), p. 309.

111. Richard Francis Burton, *A Mission to Gelele, King of Dahome II* (London: Tinsley, 1864), p. 165.

112. Pilate's Darling Street residence and the activities she conducts there exemplify the simplicity of African traditional living. On the urban outskirts of a Michigan Southside near Lake Superior, her house with an unpaved perimeter sans address number, telephone, electricity, gas, and running water lacks the trappings of modernity. Organized like a home in an African village, the Darling Street residence relies on candles, kerosene, wood, and coal to supply

light and warmth. Mattresses stuffed with pine needles sparsely furnish the interior along with several five-bushel baskets filled with blackberry brambles, the evidence of Pilate's winemaking vocation. In an African setting 6,000 miles away, Pilate's analogous vocation, in addition to village specialist, would be proprietor of a palm wine house. Time is Africanist to the Darling Street matrilineage. Pilate, her daughter Reba, and her granddaughter Hagar are "not clock people," thus Milkman surmises that Pilate is ignorant of telling time "except by the sun" (p. 183). In addition to consulting the solar moment, Pilate measures time by monitoring other naturally occurring events. She bases the time it takes to prepare the perfect soft-boiled egg on the size of the bubbles rising in the boiling water plus the time it takes to perform "one small obligation" (p. 39).

113. The fishermen who discover Jake's floated-up body deposit it in Hunters Cave located on the face of a wooded hill not far from a creek. The cave's hillside location is not unlike Shalimar's Solomon's Leap, the higher of two outcroppings of rock overlooking a deep valley where Jake's bones will ultimately be transferred for burial.

114. Kavuna Simon, "Northern Kongo Ancestor Figures," trans. Wyatt MacGaffey, *African Arts* 28.2 (Spring 1995), pp. 49, 50.

115. Morrison, *Song of Solomon*, p. 334.

116. Simon, "Northern Kongo Ancestor Figures," p. 51.

117. The sweet smell of ginger (a spice so closely identified with Africa that sources credit it as both native to the continent and a naturalization the Portuguese introduced from southeast Asia), a chill, sighs, and a male specter define the animating nkuyu spirit of Jake's kimbi. Breathing the "heavy spice-sweet smell . . . that could have come straight from a marketplace in Accra" (pp. 185–6) but presently wafts mysteriously across the Kalunga-figured Lake Superior, Milkman and Guitar hear two deep airy sighs as they, on a warm autumn night with a "piercing chill," burgle the green sack containing Jake's bones suspended from the ceiling in Pilate's Southside bedroom. Guitar dismisses his sighting of a male specter standing behind Milkman as they exit with the sack through the window.

Throughout *Song of Solomon*, allusions recur that associate spicy sweetness with death and the passed-on living-dead. Pilate substitutes "Sugarman" for the name of her grandfather Solomon in her blues complaint sung at the suicidal leap of Robert Smith that opens the novel. Guitar associates his father's sawmill death with oversweet "candy. Divinity. A big *sack* of divinity" that the sawmill employer presents to the deceased's children after the accident (p. 61). And Milkman, on the night of the Shalimar bobcat hunt, abandons his prior egocentric illusions after teetering between life and death under a sweet gum tree that cradles him with the "maternal hands of a grandfather" (p. 279). The experience transforms a selfish, phallocentric Milkman who has peed on women into a dually gendered and female-respecting man. He provides mutual maternal comfort and support for Sweet, a Shalimar woman.

118. Morrison, *Song of Solomon*, p. 339.
119. Simon, "Northern Kongo Ancestor Figures," p. 53. Henry Dumas's "Ark of Bones" in *Ark of Bones and Other Stories* (Carbondale: Southern Illinois University Press, 1970) provides another possible precedent for Morrison's modern American literary adaptation of a kimbi, a big sack of divinity, in her commitment to representing Blackness as an artistic imperative. In "Ark of Bones," the title story of Dumas's collected short fiction, allusions to Ezekiel's reincarnation story in the Valley of Dry Bones and Noah's Ark, which saves humanity from destruction, dissolve into an ark on the Mississippi River filled with moaning and the bones of a multitude of Africans. Headeye, a seer and guide carrying a mojo bone with which his friend Fish-hound accuses him of working "voodoo," enters at Deadman's Landin, a "soulboat" ark, "the house of generations. Every African who lives in America has a part of his soul in this ark." Each step leading into the ark moves through time and Black men who pull the bones from the river lay out "big bones and little bones, parts of bones, chips, tid-bits, skulls, fingers and everything" (pp. 5, 10, 13, 12). One of the men pulling the bones for the river moans:

> Aba aba, al ham dilaba
> Aba aba, mtu brotha
> Aba aba, al ham dilaba
> Abab aba, bretha brotha
> Aba aba, djuka brotha
> Aba aba, all ham dilaba (p. 12)

The apparitional sighting of the vessel on the Mississippi coincides with the murder of an African American in their town. On the night when Headeye and Fish-hound encounter the ark of bones, interracial violence severs another limb from the African-descended family tree: "white folks had lynched a nigger and threw him in the river" (p. 14). Morrison credits Dumas with strongly influencing her writing, and in their images of arks of bones as well as their depictions in modern American settings of untranslatable and untranslated African languages from an earlier time and place, traditional ancestral markers survive.
120. *Drums and Shadows: Survival Studies among the Georgia Coastal Negroes* (Athens: University of Georgia Press, 1940), p. 79, records more than two dozen variations of flying African stories.
121. Ibid., p. 54.
122. Caesar Grant, "All God's Chillen Had Wings," in John Bennett, ed., *The Doctor to the Dead, Grotesque Legends and Folk Tales of Old Charleston* (New York: Rinehart, 1943), pp. 141–2.
123. Thomas LeClair, "The Language Must Not Sweat: A Conversation with Toni Morrison," in Danille Taylor-Guthrie, ed., *Conversations with Toni Morrison* (Jackson: University Press of Mississippi, 1994), p. 122.
124. Kay Bonnetti, Interview with Toni Morrison (New York: American Audio Prose Library, 1983). Transcribed by Ousseynou Traore in "Creative African Memory: Some Oral Sources of Toni Morrison's *Song of Solomon*," in Femi

Ojo-Ade, ed., *Of Dreams Deferred, Dead or Alive: African Perspectives on African-American Writers* (Westport, Conn.: Greenwood, 1996), p. 130.

125. Morrison, *Song of Solomon*, p. 266.
126. Bessie W. Jones and Audrey Vinson, "An Interview with Toni Morrison," in Danille Taylor-Guthrie ed., *Conversations with Toni Morrison* (Jackson: University Press of Mississippi, 1994), p. 173.
127. The introductory structure of the song of Solomon that the children sing reflects the three-and-one quaternary pattern. See chapter 3 on bandoki in this study.
128. Morrison, *Song of Solomon*, p. 307.
129. Ibid.
130. *Drums and Shadows*, p 154.
131. Morrison, *Song of Solomon*, pp. 306–7.
132. Ibid., p. 307.
133. "The Bilali Document," in Harold Courlander, ed., *A Treasury of Afro-American Folklore: The Oral Literature, Traditions, Recollections, Legends, Tales, Songs, Religious Beliefs, Customs, Sayings, and Humor of Peoples of African Descent in the Americas* (New York: Crown, 1976), pp. 289–90.
134. *Drums and Shadows*, pp. 161, 167.
135. Ibid., p. 182.
136. Ibid., p. 163.
137. Ibid., p. 185. Paule Marshall's *Praisesong for the Widow* (New York: Plume, 1983) features the Ibo Landing story. Marquetta L. Goodwine, ed., *The Legacy of Ibo Landing: Gullah Roots of African Culture* (Atlanta: Clarity, 1998), p. 6, records that the incident took place in May 1803 along the shores of Dunbar Creek in Georgia.
138. *Drums and Shadows*, p. 145
139. Ibid., pp. 177–8.
140. The name Queen of France, the main city in the fictional Dominique, echoes the name of Haiti's capital, Port-au-Prince.
141. The divine horsemen of the Voudoun pantheon are also timeless ancestral spirits that have been detached from the human family and undergone divinization. A discussion devoted to the blind horsemen appears below.
142. Toni Morrison, *Tar Baby*, pp. 152–3.
143. Ibid., p. 106. The avocados are a veiled food offering to a loa.
144. Jones and Vinson, "Interview with Toni Morrison," p. 186.
145. Charles Ruas, "Toni Morrison," in *Conversations with Toni Morrison*, p. 106.
146. Ibid., p. 107.
147. Ibid.
148. Morrison, *Tar Baby*, p. 305.
149. These definitions appear in the *World Almanac Encyclopedia* and the *Oxford English Dictionary*.
150. Morrison, *Tar Baby*, pp. 150–1.
151. Ibid., p. 143.
152. Ibid., p. 154.

153. Ibid., p. 10.
154. Ibid., p. 258.
155. Geoffrey Parrinder, *African Mythology* (New York: Bedrick, 1987), p. 129.
156. Ruas, "Toni Morrison," p. 102.
157. LeClair, "The Language Must Not Sweat," p. 122.
158. Morrison, *Tar Baby*, p. 183.
159. Ibid., p. 184.
160. Davis, "Interview with Toni Morrison," pp. 225–6, 27.
161. Ruas, "Toni Morrison," p. 110.
162. Davis, "Interview with Toni Morrison," p. 226.
163. Bettye Jean Parker, "Complexity: Toni Morrison's Women," in *Conversations with Toni Morrison*, p. 61.
164. Mbiti, *African Religions and Philosophy*, pp. 97–107.
165. Maya Deren, *Divine Horsemen*, p. 86.
166. Ibid. Deren notes, that "The loa did not create the cosmos; that was the function of the initial creator divinity" (p. 86).
167. Morrison, *Tar Baby*, pp. 9, 10, 127.
168. Deren, *Divine Horsemen*, p. 29.
169. Deren Ibid., pp. 27, 32–3.
170. Jean Jacques Dessalines, Haiti's first President, renamed the island in 1804. Haiti is the Carib/Arawak word meaning "the high mountains." In 1697 the Treaty of Ryswick formally ceded a portion of Hispaniola, Saint-Domingue, to France. The remaining Spanish section was called Santo Domingo, presently the Dominican Republic. Isle de la Gonave (whale), a mytical island near Haiti, parallels Morrison's fictional Isle des Chevaliers (horses) that is close to Dominique.
171. Deren, *Divine Horsemen*, p. 64.
172. Ibid., pp. 29–30.
173. Zora Neale Hurston, *Tell My Horse* (New York: Lippincott, 1938), p. 234.
174. In Morrison's *Jazz* (New York: Plume 1992), p. 144, Violet sleeps under a walnut tree "a little way from her sisters, but not too far. Not too far to crawl back to them swiftly if the trees turn out to be full of spirits idling the night away." Joe Trace falls from the walnut tree and she claims him (p. 103). Golden Gray compares Wild, who is associated with a white oak tree and the vertical center-post, to his horse pulling his phaeton, a carriage whose name – an African god's appropriated by Greece – is rife with sun and earth symbolism. He is afraid that something from her "might touch or penetrate" him (p. 144).
175. Maya Deren, dir., *Divine Horsemen: The Living Gods of Haiti*, (Mystic Fire, 1985). In some sources "vèvè" is given as a spelling for the sacred design that Deren spells as "vever." Deren bases her spellings on English phonetics since Voudoun terminologies make use of original African words blended with Creole, a mixture of French, Spanish, and the language of the Indians. I selected the spelling "Voudoun" from her text.
176. Morrison, *Tar Baby*, p. 182.
177. Deren, *Divine Horsemen*, pp. 178, 181.

178. Ibid., p. 86.
179. Morrison, *Tar Baby*, p. 183.
180. Deren, *Divine Horsemen*, p. 259.
181. Ibid., pp. 37, 47.
182. The vever for Erzulie features eight stars with a cross and X overlay.
183. Deren, *Divine Horsemen*, p. 47.
184. Morrison, *Tar Baby*, p. 179.
185. Ibid., p. 271.
186. Before 1919, the company's name was North Carolina Mutual and Provident Association. John Merrick, C. C. Spaulding, and Dr. A. M. Moore were the company's founders.
187. Toni Morrison, "Unspeakable Things Unspoken: The Afro-American Presence in American Literature," *Michigan Quarterly Review* 28.1 (Winter 1989), p. 27.
188. Morrison, *Song of Solomon*, pp. 155–6.
189. Ibid., p. 8.
190. Ibid., p. 155.
191. Elsie B. Washington, "Talk with Toni Morrison," in *Conversations with Toni Morrison*, p. 238.
192. Morrison, "Rootedness," p. 344.

5 BANGANGA: THE SPECIALISTS – MEDICINE (WO)MEN AND PRIEST(ESSE)S

1. W. E. B. Du Bois, *The Souls of Black Folk* (New York: Signet, 1969), p. 216.
2. John M. Janzen and Wyatt MacGaffey, *An Anthology of Kongo Religion: Primary Texts from Lower Zaire* (Lawrence: University of Kansas Press, 1974), p. 34.
3. Robert Farris Thompson, *Flash of the Spirit: African and Afro-American Art and Philosophy* (New York: Vintage, 1984), p. 107.
4. Charles C. Jones, *The Religious Instruction of the Negroes in the United States* (Savannah, Ga.: Thomas Purse, 1842), pp. 127–8.
5. Tulu Kia Mpansu Buakasa, *L'Impense du discours: "Kindoki" et "nkisi" en pays kongo du Zaïre* (Kinshasa: Presse Universitaire, 1973).
6. Peter H. Wood, *Black Majority: Negroes in Colonial South Carolina from 1670 through the Stono Rebellion* (New York: Knopf, 1974), pp. 289–92.
7. Albert J. Raboteau, *Slave Religion: The "Invisible Institution" in the Antebellum South* (New York: Oxford University Press, 1978), p. 75.
8. Ibid., p. 87.
9. Toni Morrison, *The Bluest Eye* (New York: Washington Square, 1970), p. 165.
10. Toni Morrison, *Paradise* (New York: Knopf, 1998), p. 244.
11. John S. Mbiti, *African Religions and Philosophy* (New York: Doubleday, 1970), p. 220.
12. Ibid., p. 219.
13. Ibid., p. 221.
14. Ibid., p. 222.

15. Ibid., p. 230.
16. Ibid., pp. 226, 229, 231.
17. Ibid., p. 245.
18. Maya Deren, *Divine Horsemen: Voodoo Gods of Haiti* (New York: Dell, 1970), p. 159.
19. Ibid., p. 164.
20. Robert A. Voeks, *Sacred Leaves of Candomblé: African Magic, Medicine, and Religion in Brazil* (Austin: University of Texas Press, 1997), pp. 54–5.
21. Mbiti, *African Religions and Philosophy*, p. 252.
22. Ibid.
23. Morrison, *The Bluest Eye*, p. 167.
24. Europeans brought Chinese indentured laborers to work in the Caribbean sugar industry as early as 1806. See Walton Look Lai's *The Chinese in the West Indies, 1806–1995: A Documentary History* (Kingston, Jamaica: The Press University of the West Indies, 1998).
25. Morrison, *The Bluest Eye*, p. 167.
26. Ibid., p. 164.
27. Ibid., p. 166.
28. Ibid., p. 180.
29. Ibid., p. 165.
30. Deren, *Divine Horsemen*, p. 86.
31. The green sack containing the remains of Solomon that hangs in the bedroom of Pilate Dead and the shoe box that holds the hair clippings of Hagar are examples of minkisi in *Song of Solomon*.
32. Morrison, *The Bluest Eye*, p. 165–6.
33. Ibid., p. 181–2.
34. Ibid., p. 165.
35. Wade W. Nobles, "African Philosophy: Foundations for Black Psychology," in Reginald L. Jones, ed., *Black Psychology* (New York: Harper and Row, 1980), p. 30.
36. Morrison, *The Bluest Eye*, p. 169.
37. Vashti Crutcher Lewis, "African Tradition in Toni Morrison's *Sula*," in Joanne M. Braxton and Andrée Nicola McLaughlin, eds., *Wild Women in the Whirlwind: Afra-American Culture and the Contemporary Literary Renaissance* (New Brunswick: Rutgers University Press, 1990), p. 317.
38. Ibid., p. 318.
39. Deren, *Divine Horsemen*, p. 134.
40. Ibid., p. 130.
41. Ibid., p. 59.
42. Ibid., p. 132.
43. Ibid., pp. 132–3.
44. Ibid., p. 31.
45. Lewis, "African Tradition in Toni Morrison's *Sula*," p. 317.
46. Morrison, *Sula* (New York: Plume, 1973), pp. 14–15.
47. Ibid., p. 8.

48. Ibid., p. 158.
49. Ibid., p. 8.
50. Ibid., p. 12.
51. Ibid., p. 11.
52. Ibid., p. 15.
53. Ibid.
54. Ibid., p. 14, and Deren, *Divine Horsemen*, p. 82.
55. Morrison, *Sula*, pp. 13, 158.
56. Ibid., p. 14.
57. Deren, *Divine Horsemen*, p. 31.
58. Toni Morrison, *Song of Solomon* (New York: Plume, 1977), pp. 30, 36.
59. Ibid., p. 18.
60. Ibid., p. 148.
61. Morrison returns to the interplay of African and Indian cultures in *Paradise*.
62. Deren, *Divine Horsemen*, p. 67.
63. Ibid., pp. 61, 67.
64. Additional information on the treatment of the Kongo kimbi and nkuyu in *Song of Solomon* appears in chapter 4 on kanda in this study.
65. Deren, *Divine Horsemen*, p. 285.
66. A "confiance" assists the mambo.
67. Morrison, *Song of Solomon*, pp. 240, 252, 256.
68. Deren, *Divine Horsemen*, p. 35.
69. Ibid., pp. 103, 104.
70. Ibid., pp. 37–8.
71. Morrison, *Song of Solomon*, p. 10.
72. Deren, *Divine Horsemen*, p. 282.
73. Morrison, *Song of Solomon*, pp. 62, 63.
74. Deren, *Divine Horsemen*, p. 282.
75. Morrison, *Song of Solomon*, p. 62.
76. Ibid., p. 28.
77. George Eaton Simpson, "The Belief System of Haitian Vodun," *American Anthropologist* 47.1 (January–March 1945), p. 51.
78. Morrison, *Song of Solomon*, p. 217.
79. Ibid., p. 215.
80. Ibid., pp. 127, 119.
81. Ibid., p. 186.
82. Deren, *Divine Horsemen*, p. 96.
83. Morrison, *The Bluest Eye*, p. 136.
84. Ibid., p. 139.
85. The mayombo legend interfaces with the Bible's Old Testament story of Moses's staff devouring the priest's staff before Pharoah. Zora Neale Hurston's works make the connection between Moses and his parallel with the West African traditional priest. While Shadrack does not carry a walking stick, Morrison emphasizes the graceful curve of his hand around the wooden door jamb of his shack.

86. Morrison, *Song of Solomon*, p. 248.

87. Because Eva Peace in *Sula* demonstrates the traits of the loa Ayizan and the African traditional priestess, she is also a possible candidate for inclusion in a discussion of sacred specialists. However, Morrison's main objective in *Sula* is to explore the African-American conception of evil, and Eva commits a questionably "evil" act, when she sets her only son, Plum, on fire. The discussion of her persona fits more appropriately within in the discussion of evil and morality. See chapter 3 on bandoki in this study.

88. Morrison, *The Bluest Eye*, p. 139.

89. Morrison, *Song of Solomon*, p. 242.

90. Herodotus, *The History of Herodotus*, trans. George Rawlinson (New York: Tudor, 1928), p. 99, and Herodotus, *The Histories*, trans. Robin Waterfield (New York: Oxford University Press, 1998).

91. The existence of a direct link between West Africa and Egypt may explain why some Nigerians believe that Esu and the Egyptian god Shu are one and the same and why there are similarities between the Yoruba Ifa System of Divination and Egyptian hieroglyphics. See Martin Bernal, *Black Athena: The Afroasiatic Roots of Classical Civilization* (New Brunswick: Rutgers University Press, 1987); Cheikh Anta Diop, *Precolonial Black Africa: A Comparative Study of the Political and Social Systems of European and Black Africa, from Antiquity to the Formation of Modern States*, trans. Harold Salemson (New York: Lawrence Hill, 1987), pp. 31–3; D. Olarimwa Epega, *The Basis of Yoruba Religion* (Nigeria: Ijamido, 1971), p. 17; and Ulysses Duke Jenkins, *Ancient African Religion and the African-American Church* (Jackson, N.C.: Flame International, 1978), p. 24.

92. Morrison, *Song of Solomon*, p. 234.

93. Frank M. Snowden, Jr., *Blacks in Antiquity: Ethiopians in the Greco-Roman Experience* (Cambridge, Mass.: Harvard University Press, 1970), pp. 161, 64. Judith Yarnall, in *Transformations of Circe: The History of an Enchantress* (Chicago: University of Illinois Press, 1994), pp. 182–3, references Morrison's inclusion of the character named Circe in *Song of Solomon* but dismisses the depiction as "unambiguously a creature of the novelist's own imagination." Yarnall's book includes ten artists' representations of Circe but makes no note of nor addresses the historical possibilities of these fourth-century BC skyphoi depicting an African Circe.

94. Mary Hamilton Swindler, *Ancient Painting, From the Earliest Times to the Period of Christian Art* (New Haven: Yale University Press, 1929), p. 298. Swindler continues by stating that "The negroid characteristics in the profiles and the exaggerated details are a far cry from ordinary Greek work and bring before our eyes some of the strangest phenomena known in the art of Greece" (p. 298).

95. Morrison, *Beloved* (New York: Plume, 1987), p. 87.

96. Ibid.

97. Sterling Stuckey, *Slave Culture: Nationalist Theory and the Foundations of Black America* (New York: Oxford University Press, 1987), p. 12.

98. The modern-day Christian shout also revisits Voudoun ritual. An individual possessed by the Holy Spirit may rear or hop on one leg while bracing the small of his or her back with one hand.
99. Morrison, *Beloved*, p. 88.
100. Ibid.
101. Deren, *Divine Horsemen*, p. 27.
102. Morrison, *Beloved*, p. 28.
103. Thompson, *Flash of the Spirit*, p. 113. In a second African-derived religion in Brazil called Macumba, which is more prominent in Rio de Janeiro, Kongo and Angola medicines and spirits dominate but have been fused with Yoruba elements of the caboclo inland Amerindian spirits and the Catholic saints.
104. Voeks, *Sacred Leaves of Candomblé*, pp. 51–2.
105. Dinitia Smith, "Mixing Tragedy and Folklore," *New York Times* (January 8, 1998), pp. B1–B2.
106. Morrison, *Paradise*, p. 276.
107. The oldest operating terreiro in Bahia is Casa Branca, established in the 1820s.
108. Morrison, *Paradise*, p. 12.
109. Ibid., p. 9.
110. Ibid., pp. 225–6.
111. Ibid., p. 43.
112. Ibid., p. 4.
113. Ibid., p. 289.
114. Capela de Nosso Senhora da Piedade (Our Lady of Piety Chapel) shares the island with Matriz de Vera Cruz (True Cross Church), built *c*.1560.
115. Morrison, *Paradise*, p. 318.
116. David J. Hess, *Samba in the Night: Spiritism in Brazil* (New York: Columbia University Press, 1994), p. 145.
117. J. Brooks Bouson, *Quiet as It's Kept: Shame, Trauma, and Race in the Novel of Toni Morrison* (New York: State University of New York Press, 2000), p. 241.
118. Other alternate spellings of Yemanjá are Iemanja, Yemoja, Jemanja, Imanja, and Ymoja.
119. Voeks, *Sacred Leaves of Candomblé*, p. 56.
120. Morrison, *Paradise*, p. 229.
121. The hunter Oxóssi shoulders an iron bow that in Deacon's case has been upgraded to the modern iron weapon, the gun. Acquisition of property and Deacon's affair with Consolata may be explained by his Oxóssi nature that is "characterized by keen intelligence and curiosity. An itinerant seeker, discoverer, and traveler, Oxóssi is never satisfied – materially, romantically, or geographically" (Voeks, *Sacred Leaves of Candomblé*, p. 56). In orixá mythology Oxóssi "mata o passaro das feiticeiras" ("Oxóssi kills a group of witches") who were angry for not having been invited to a ceremony. See Reginaldo Prandi, *Mitologia Dos Orixás* (São Paulo: Companhia das Letras, 2001), p. 113. Ossie, a trope on the name Oxóssi, is the name of the Ruby citizen responsible for organizing the horse race to celebrate the completion and naming of

Central Street. At its celebration Consolata and Deacon see each other for the first time.

Associated with the palm, Ogoun is a night wanderer. He is also associated with dandá, a plant whose rhizomes both West Africans and African Brazilians chew. Because he is juxtaposed with the Catholic Saint Anthony whom illustrators depict "as a conquering military hero sitting astride his horse while slaying a dragon," Ogoun is typically imagined as mounted on horseback (see Voeks, *Sacred Leaves of Candomblé*, pp. 125–6, 60–1). These associations compare with Steward Morgan's 4 a.m. horseback ride on Night and his habit of chewing tobacco, which has deadened his sense of taste. Moreover, Steward's need for spicy foods, hot peppers and barbecue accords with the bellicose, hot, reactive nature of Ogoun. Troping on "Red Man," a chewing tobacco brand that has the head profile of a Native American as its trademark, Morrison names Steward's brand of chewing tobacco "Blue Boy." Red and blue are the sacred colors of Ogoun, and the plot of *Paradise* follows his activities. In orixá mythology Yemanjá (Iemanja) goes into the forest to have sex with Ogoun, which, if myth were aligned with Morrison's fictional plot, would place Steward as Consolata's lover and not Deacon (see Prandi, *Mitologia Dos Orixás*, p. 105). According to the mythology of the orixás, Ogoun "violenta e maltrata as mulheres" ("violates and mistreats women") and "conquista para os homens o poder das mulheres" ("conquers for the men the power of the women"). As the myth goes, Ogoun plans an attack on women who have powers and secrets and are members of a secret society. When he arrives, dressed in powerful armor and armed to the teeth, the women scatter. Iansã was the first to flee, terrified. One of the women ran so much with fear that she disappeared from the face of the earth forever. The men expelled the women from the secret society (Ibid., pp. 105–7). Both Oxóssi and Ogoun are associated with hemp, thus the men who storm the Convent carry rope as necessary "paraphernalia" (see Morrison, *Paradise*, p. 3).

122. Morrison, *Paradise*, p. 283.
123. Ibid., p. 262.
124. Ibid., p. 265.
125. Ibid., p. 263.
126. Ibid., pp. 263, 265.
127. Deren, *Divine Horsemen*, p. 276.
128. Thompson, *Flash of the Spirit*, pp. 188, 191.
129. Ibid., p. 110.
130. Ibid., p. 113.
131. Morrison, *Paradise*, p. 110.
132. The final words of the novel, "down here in Paradise" (p. 318), suggest the lower hemisphere of Ruby, the space of the afterworld. In the *New York Times* interview with Dinitia Smith ("Mixing Tragedy and Folklore"), Morrison states that the "last word in the book should have a small 'p,' not capital P. The whole point is to get paradise off its pedestal, as a place for anyone, to open it for passengers and crew. I want all the readers to put a lowercase mark on that 'p.'"

133. John Leonard, "Shooting Women," *The Nation* 266.3 (January 26, 1998), p. 26.
134. Before Christ, the cross was an ancient symbol associated with the sun. At the corona or circumference of the eclipse, points of light at the top, bottom, left, and right – points corresponding with the four moments of the sun – stood out brilliantly.
135. Morrison, *Paradise*, p. 63.
136. Dice are used in some African cultures to "roll the bones" for divination purposes. Translated from the Spanish, Sante Fe means "holy faith."
137. Morrison, *Paradise*, p. 30.
138. Ibid., p. 32.
139. Ibid., p. 33.
140. Voeks, *Sacred Leaves of Candomblé*, pp. 63, 68.
141. Morrison, *Paradise*, pp. 142, 147.
142. Ibid., p. 143.
143. Ibid., p. 87.
144. Ibid., pp. 264, 265.
145. Deren, *Divine Horsemen*, p. 27.

6 IDENTIFIABLE BLACKNESS: TONI MORRISON'S LITERARY CANON AT THE WESTERN CROSSROADS

1. Henry Louis Gates, Jr., *The Signifying Monkey: A Theory of Afro-American Literary Criticism* (New York: Oxford University Press, 1988), pp. 4, 5–6.
2. Deborah E. McDowell, "New Directions for Black Feminist Criticism," in Angelyn Mitchell, ed., *Within the Circle: An Anthology of African American Literary Criticism from the Harlem Renaissance to the Present* (Durham: Duke University Press, 1994), p. 436.
3. Toni Morrison, "Rootedness: The Ancestor as Foundation," in Mari Evans, ed., *Black Women Writers (1950–1980): A Critical Evaluation* (New York: Doubleday, 1984), p. 343.
4. Maya Deren, *Divine Horsemen:Voodoo Gods of Haiti* (New York: Dell, 1970), p. 14.
5. Olaudah Equiano, *The Interesting Narrative of the Life of Olaudah Equiano, or Gustavus Vassa, The African, Written by Himself* (New York: St Martin, 1995), p. 36.
6. Christina Davis, "An Interview with Toni Morrison," in Danille Taylor-Guthrie, ed., *Conversations with Toni Morrison* (Jackson: University Press of Mississippi, 1994), p. 226.
7. Bessie W. Jones and Audrey Vinson, "An Interview with Toni Morrison," in *Conversations with Toni Morrison*, p. 176.
8. Davis, "Interview with Toni Morrison," p. 225.
9. Charles Ruas, "Toni Morrison," in *Conversations with Toni Morrison*, p. 115.
10. Jones and Vinson, "Interview with Toni Morrison," p. 176.
11. Davis, "Interview with Toni Morrison," p. 225.
12. Acts 2.

13. An African precedent for Morrison's third novel may be Francophone Upper Guinea novelist Camara Laye's *The Radiance of the King* (1954). Laye's protagonist, Clarence, a European who has come to Africa to find his metaphorical "pot of gold," ultimately reveres Africa as he moves back in time by traveling south into Africa's rural and far past. Morrison credits Laye with having "an enormous effect" on her writing (Jones and Vinson, "Interview with Toni Morrison," p. 179). For Morrison, reading *The Radiance of the King* "was an important thing . . . a very narcotic kind of experience, a journey . . . that was overwhelming" as she watched the errant Clarence, the anglicized prototype prefiguring the questing Milkman, "stripped as it were, going farther and farther and farther and farther back [into an African rootedness and consciousness] and the complex array of [African] people that he met" (Davis, "Interview with Toni Morrison," p. 228).

A reckless adventurer, Clarence, in his single-minded concentration on becoming rich on the African continent, reluctantly submits to Afrocentric thought, which leads to an unanticipated spiritual conversion. He discovers, like Milkman, an African identity that Western colonialism and imperialism have overwritten. A tall beggar, the Pilate Dead equivalent, shepherds the naïve European's journey from the capital city Andramé in the north of an undisclosed African country to its rural south, a spatial and directional movement that parallels his psychic immersion in and surrender to an African traditional worldview. That immersion frees him to transcend his Western arrogance and ignorance. The progressive stripping of Western clothing from his body – recalling Milkman's divestment of his beige three-piece suit, blue shirt, black tie, Longines watch, and Florsheim shoes – opens the way for Clarence's descent into African ways of knowing. Dioki, a timeless African witch-figure endowed with psychic powers and whose familiars are snakes, summons up direct parallels with the immortal Circe and her pack of Weimaraners that Milkman encounters on his southern journey of heightened ancestral awareness. The figurative ancestor, the gold-clad king who grants favors not based on rights but on an African system of social and religious reciprocity, meets Clarence face to face in the south and embraces him at the nadir of the European's figurative and literal nakedness as a wayward son. See La Vinia Delois Jennings, "Camara Laye's *The Radiance of the King* (1954) as Foundation for Toni Morrison's *Song of Solomon* (1977)," unpublished article (2004).

14. In "The Goophered Grapevine," in his *The Conjure Woman* (Ann Arbor: University of Michigan Press, 1969), Charles W. Chesnutt describes the trip that Annie and her husband John make to the old McAdoo plantation in great detail. Along the way they pass an area wrapped in the cloistral solitude of pines, and they stop at the crossroads to wait for a human being to consult about directions. "At length a little negro girl appeared, walking straight as an arrow, with a piggin full of water on her head" (p. 7).

15. Paul Gilroy, *The Black Atlantic: Modernity and Double Consciousness* (Cambridge, Mass.: Harvard University Press, 1993), pp. 222–3.

16. Davis, "Interview with Toni Morrison," pp. 224–5.

Works cited

Alexander, Allen, "The Fourth: The Image of God in Toni Morrison's *The Bluest Eye*." *African American Review* 32.2 (1998), 293–303.

Asekun, Ayoade Joy, "Binary Fusions: Examining the Concepts of Good and Evil in Toni Morrison's *Sula* and *Beloved*." Seminar paper, University of Tennessee, 1997.

"Making the Connection: African Cosmology in Toni Morrison's *Beloved* and Paule Marshall's *Praisesong for the Widow*." Unpublished MA thesis, University of Tennessee, 1998.

Barnett, Pamela E., "Figurations of Rape and the Supernatural in *Beloved*." *PMLA* 112 (1997), 418–27.

Basden, George Thomas, *Among the Ibos of Nigeria: An Account of the Curious and Interesting Habits, Customs and Beliefs of a Little Known African People by One Who Has for Many Years Lived Amongst Them on Close and Intimate Terms*. Philadelphia: Lippincott, 1931.

Bassett, P. C., "A Visit to a Slave Mother Who Killed Her Child," *National Anti-slavery Standard*, March 15, 1856. Rpt. in Angelita Reyes, "Using History as Artifact to Situate *Beloved*'s Unknown Woman: Margaret Garner", in Nellie McKay and Kathryn Earle, eds., *Approaches to Teaching the Novels of Toni Morrison*. New York: MLA, 1997, 77–85.

Bernal, Martin, *Black Athena: The Afroasiatic Roots of Classical Civilization*. New Brunswick: Rutgers University Press, 1987.

"The Bilali Document," in Harold Courlander, ed., *A Treasury of Afro-American Folklore: The Oral Literature, Traditions, Recollections, Legends, Tales, Songs, Religions, Beliefs, Customs, Sayings, and Humor of Peoples of African Descent in the Americas*. New York: Crown, 1976, 289–90.

Birmingham, David, *Trade and Conflict in Angola: The Mbundu and Their Neighbours Under the Influence of the Portuguese, 1483–1790*. Oxford: Clarendon, 1966.

Bockie, Simon, *Death and the Invisible Powers: The World of Kongo Belief*. Bloomington: Indiana University Press, 1993.

Bonnetti, Kay, *Interview with Toni Morrison*. New York: American Audio Prose Library, 1983. Transcribed by Ousseynou Traore, "Creative African Memory: Some Oral Sources of Toni Morrison's *Song of Solomon*," *Of Dreams Deferred, Dead or Alive: African Perspectives on African-American Writers*, Ed. Femi Ojo-Ade, Westport, Conn.: Greenwood, 1996, 129–41.

Bosman, William, *A New and Accurate Description of the Coast of Guinea; Divided into the Gold, the Slave, and Ivory Coasts*. London: Printed for J. Wren, 1754.

Bouson, J. Brooks, *Quiet as It's Kept: Shame, Trauma, and Race in the Novels of Toni Morrison*. New York: State University of New York Press, 2000.

Braxton, Joanne M., "Ancestral Presence: The Outraged Mother Figure in Contemporary Afra-American Writing," in Braxton, *Wild Women in the Whirlwind: Afra- American Culture and the Contemporary Literary Renaissance*. New Brunswick: Rutgers University Press, 1990, 299–315.

Breslaw, Elaine, "Non-Christian Beliefs," in Breslaw, ed., *Witches of the Atlantic World*. New York: New York University Press, 2000, 97–103.

Brown, Dan, *The Da Vinci Code* (New York: Doubleday, 2003).

Brown, Wesley H., "Marriage Payment: A Problem in Christian Social Ethics among Kongo Protestants," unpublished PhD dissertation, University of Southern California (1971).

Burton, Richard Francis, *A Mission to Gelele, King of Dahome II*. London: Tinsley, 1864.

Carretta, Vincent, "Olaudah Equiano or Gustavus Vassa? New Light on an Eighteenth-Century Question of Identity." *Slavery and Abolition* 20.3 (December 1999), 96–105.

  Unchained Voices: An Anthology of Black Authors in the English-Speaking World of the Eighteenth Century. Lexington: University of Kentucky Press, 1996.

Charles, R. H., Introduction, "The Book of Enoch," in Charles, *The Apocrypha and Pseudepigrapha of The Old Testament in English, with Introductions and Critical and Explanatory Notes to the Several Books*. Oxford: Clarendon, 1913, 163–87.

Chesnutt, Charles W., *The Conjure Woman*. Ann Arbor: University of Michigan Press, 1969.

Christian, Barbara, "Fixing Methodologies, *Beloved*," in Elizabeth Abel, Barbara Christian, and Helene Moglen, eds., *Female Subjects in Black and White: Race, Psychoanalysis, Feminism*. Berkeley: University of California Press, 1997, 363–70.

Clemons, Walter, "The Ghost of 'Sixty Million and More.'" *Newsweek*, September 28, 1987, 75.

Collins, Derek, "The Myth and Ritual of Ezili Freda in Hurston's *Their Eyes Were Watching God*." *Western Folklore* 55.2 (Spring 1996), 137–54.

"Conversation with Alice Childress and Toni Morrison." *Black Creation Annual* 6 (1974–5), 90–2.

Curtin, Philip D., and Jan Vansina, "Sources of the Nineteenth Century Atlantic Slave Trade." *Journal of African History* 5.2 (1964), 185–208.

Davis, Christina, "An Interview with Toni Morrison," in Danille Taylor-Guthrie, ed., *Conversations with Toni Morrison*. Jackson: University Press of Mississippi, 1994, 223–33.

Deren, Maya, dir., *Divine Horsemen: The Living Gods of Haiti*. Mystic Fire, 1985. *Divine Horsemen: Voodoo Gods of Haiti*. New York: Dell, 1970.

Diop, Cheikh Anta, *Precolonial Black Africa: A Comparative Study of the Political and Social Systems of European and Black Africa, from Antiquity to the Formation of Modern States*, trans. Harold Salemson. New York: Lawrence Hill, 1987.

Drums and Shadows: Survival Studies among the Georgia Coastal Negroes. Athens: University of Georgia Press, 1940.

Du Bois, W. E. B., *The Souls of Black Folk*. New York: Signet, 1969.

Dumas, Henry, *Ark of Bones and Other Stories*. Carbondale: Southern Illinois University Press, 1970.

Ellis, Sir A. B., *The Ewe-Speaking Peoples of the Slave Coast of West Africa: Their Religion, Manners, Customs, Laws, Languages, Etc.*, (1890). Chicago: Benin, 1965.

Epega, D. Olarimwa, *The Basis of Yoruba Religion*. Nigeria: Ijamido, 1971.

Equiano, Olaudah, *The Interesting Narrative of the Life of Olaudah Equiano, or Gustavus Vassa, The African, Written by Himself*. New York: St Martin's Press, 1995.

Evans-Pritchard, Edward E., *Witchcraft, Oracles, and Magic among the Azande*. Oxford: Clarendon, 1958.

"Evil," Anchor Bible Dictionary. Ed. David Noel Freedman, 6 vols., New York: Doubleday, 1992.

Fils-Aimé, Holly, "The Living Dead Learn to Fly: Themes of Spiritual Death, Initiation and Empowerment in *A Praisesong for the Widow* and *Song of Solomon*." *Mid-Atlantic Writers Association Review* 10.1 (June 1995), 3–12.

Frazer, Sir James George, *The Golden Bough, A Study in Magic and Religion*. New York: Macmillan, 1963.

Frey, Sylvia R., and Betty Wood, *Come Shouting to Zion: African American Protestantism in the American South and British Caribbean to 1830*. Chapel Hill: University of North Carolina Press, 1998.

Gates, Jr., Henry Louis, *The Signifying Monkey: A Theory of Afro-American Literary Criticism*. New York: Oxford University Press, 1988.

Gauld, Alan, and A. D. Cornell, *Poltergeists*. Boston: Routledge and Paul, 1979.

Genovese, Eugene, *Roll, Jordan, Roll: The World the Slaves Made*. New York: Pantheon, 1974.

Gilroy, Paul, *The Black Atlantic: Modernity and Double Consciousness*. Cambridge, Mass.: Harvard University Press, 1993.

"Living memory: a meeting with Toni Morrison," in Gilroy, *Small Acts: Thoughts on the politics of black cultures*. London: Serpent's Tail, 1993, 175–82.

Goodwine, Marquetta L. ed., *The Legacy of the Ibo Landing: Gullah Roots of African Culture*. Atlanta: Clarity, 1998.

Goveia, Elsa V., *Slave Society in the British Leeward Islands at the End of the Eighteenth Century*. New Haven, Conn: Yale University Press, 1965.

Grant, Caesar, "All God's Chillen Had Wings." in John Bennett, ed., *The Doctor to the Dead, Grotesque Legends and Folk Tales of Old Charleston*. New York: Rinehart, 1943.

Handler, Jerome S., "Survivors of the Middle Passage: Life Histories of Enslaved Africans in British America." *Slavery and Abolition* 23.1 (2002), 25–56.

Harris, Joseph E., The African Diaspora Map – 1. October 5, 2003, www.howard, edu/library/diaspora/diasp800:gif.

Harris, Trudier, *Fiction and Folklore: The Novels of Toni Morrison*. Knoxville: University of Tennessee Press, 1991.

Hauenstein, Alfred, "Considérations sur le motif décoratif croix ainsi que differ-éntes coutumes accompagnées de gestes et rites cruciformes chez quelques tribus d'Angola." *Bulletin der Schweizerischen Gesellschaft für Anthropologie und Ethnologie* 43 (1966–7), 34.

Herodotus, *The Histories*, trans. Robin Waterfield. New York: Oxford University Press, 1998.

The History of Herodotus. trans. George Rawlinson. New York: Tudor, 1928.

Herskovits, Melville J., *The Myth of the Negro Past*. New York: Harper, 1941.

Hess, David J., *Samba in the Night: Spiritism in Brazil*. New York: Columbia University Press, 1994.

Higgins, Therese E., *Religiosity, Cosmology, and Folklore: The African Influence in the Novels of Toni Morrison*. New York: Routledge, 2001.

Hurston, Zora Neale, *Tell My Horse*. Philadelphia: Lippincott, 1938.

Janzen, John M., and Wyatt MacGaffey, *An Anthology of Kongo Religion: Primary Texts from Lower Zaire*. Lawrence: University of Kansas Press, 1974.

Jenkins, Ulysses Duke, *Ancient African Religion and the African-American Church*. Jackson, N.C. Flame International, 1978.

Jennings, La Vinia Delois, "Camara Laye's *The Radiance of the King* (1954) as Foundation for Toni Morrison's *Song of Solomon* (1977)." Unpublished article, 2004.

Jones, Bessie W., and Audrey Vinson, "An Interview with Toni Morrison," in Danille Taylor-Guthrie, ed., *Conversations with Toni Morrison*. Jackson: University Press of Mississippi, 1994, 171–87.

Jones, Charles C., *The Religious Instruction of the Negroes in the United States*. Savannah, Ga.: Thomas Purse, 1842.

Jung, Carl, *The Archetypes and the Collective Unconscious*, ed. Sir Herbert Read et al. Princeton: Princeton University Press, 1959.

Jung on Evil, ed. Murray Stein. Princeton: Princeton University Press, 1995.

Kekes, John, *Facing Evil*. Princeton: Princeton University Press, 1990.

Lai, Walton Look, *The Chinese in the West Indies, 1806–1995: A Documentary History*. Kingston, Jamaica: The Press University of the West Indies, 1998.

Lamothe, Daphne, "Vodou Imagery, African-American Tradition and Cultural Transformation in Zora Neale Hurston's *Their Eyes Were Watching God*," *Callaloo* 22.1 (Winter 1999), 157–75.

Larouche, Maximilien, *L'image comme echo*. Montreal: Editions Novelle Optique, 1978.

Law, Robin, *The Slave Coast of West Africa, 1550–1750: The Impact of the Atlantic Slave Trade on an African Society*. New York: Oxford University Press, 1991.

Lawson, Thomas E., *Religions of Africa, Traditions in Transformation*. New York: HarperCollins, 1985.

Laye, Camara, *The Radiance of the King*. New York: New York Review of Books, 2001.

LeClair, Thomas, "The Language Must Not Sweat: A Conversation with Toni Morrison," *New Republic* 184 (March 21, 1981), 22–9. Rpt. in Danille Taylor-Guthrie, ed. *Conversations with Toni Morrison*. Jackson: University Press of Mississippi, 1994, 119–28.

Leonard, John, "Shooting Women." *The Nation* 266.3 (January 26, 1998), 25–6, 28–9.

Levine, Lawrence W., *Black Culture and Black Consciousness: Afro-American Folk Thought from Slavery to Freedom*. New York: Oxford University Press, 1977.

Lewis, Vashti Crutcher, "African Tradition in Toni Morrison's *Sula*," *Phylon: A Review of Race and Culture* 48.1 (March 1987), 91–7. Rpt. in Joanne M. Braxton and Andrée Nicola McLaughlin, eds., *Wild Women in the Whirlwind: Afra-American Culture and the Contemporary Literary Renaissance*. New Brunswick: Rutgers University Press, 1990, 316–25.

Marshall, Paule, *Praisesong for the Widow*. New York: Plume, 1983.

Mays, Benjamin Elijah, and Joseph William Nicholson, *The Negro's Church*. New York: Russell and Russell, 1969.

Mbiti, John S., *African Religions and Philosophy*. New York: Doubleday, 1970.

McDowell, Deborah E., "New Directions for Black Feminist Criticism," in Angelyn Mitchell, ed., *Within the Circle: An Anthology of African American Literary Criticism from the Harlem Renaissance to the Present*. Durham: Duke University Press, 1994, 428–41.

Meek, C. K., *Law and Authority in a Nigerian Tribe, A Study of Indirect Rule*. New York: Barnes and Noble, 1970.

Métraux, Alfred, *Voodoo in Haiti*, trans. Hugo Charteris. New York: Schocken Books, 1972.

Minchinton, Walter, Celia King, and Peter Waite, eds., *Virginia Slave-Trade Statistics 1698–1775*. Richmond: Virginia State Library, 1984.

Morgan, Philip D., *Slave Counterpoint: Black Culture in the Eighteenth-Century Chesapeake and Lowcountry*. Chapel Hill: University of North Carolina Press, 1998.

Morrison, Toni, *Beloved*. New York: Plume, 1987.

The Bluest Eye. New York: Washington Square, 1970.

Interview, in *In Black and White: Conversations with African American Writers*, San Francisco Newreel, 1992.

Jazz. New York: Plume, 1992.

Paradise. New York: Knopf, 1998.

"Rootedness: The Ancestor as Foundation," in Mari Evans, ed., *Black Women Writers (1950–1980): A Critical Evaluation*. New York: Doubleday, 1984, 339–45.

"The Site of Memory," in William Zinsser, ed., *Inventing the Truth: The Art and Craft of Memoir*. Boston: Houghton Mifflin, 1987, 101–24.

Song of Solomon. New York: Plume, 1977.

Sula. New York: Plume, 1973.

Tar Baby. New York: Plume, 1981.

"Unspeakable Things Unspoken: The Afro-American Presence in American Literature." *Michigan Quarterly Review* 28.1 (Winter 1989), 1–34.

Mpansu, Buakasa Tulu Kia, "Le Discours de Kindoki ou Sorcellerie." *Cahiers des Religious Africaines* 4.11 (1972), 5–67.

L'Impense du discours: "Kindoki" et "Nkisi" en pays Kongo du Zaïre. Kinshasa: Presse Universitaire, 1973.

Mpolo, Masamba Ma, "Kindoki as Diagnosis and Therapy." *Social Science & Medicine: An International Journal* 15B.3 (July 1981), 405–13.

Nobles, Wade W., "African Philosophy: Foundations for Black Psychology," in Reginald L. Jones, ed., *Black Psychology.* New York: Harper and Row, 1980, 23–36.

Ogude, S. E., "Facts into Fiction: Equiano's Narrative Reconsidered." *Research in African Literatures* 13 (Spring 1982), 31–43.

Ogunyemi, Chikwenya Okonjo, *African Wo/man Palava: The Nigerian Novel by Women.* Chicago: University of Chicago Press, 1995.

Okri, Ben, *The Famished Road.* London: Jonathan Cape, 1993.

Opoku, Kofi Asare, "African Traditional Religion: An Enduring Heritage," in Jacob K. Olupona and Sulayman S. Nyang, eds., *Religious Plurality in Africa: Essays in Honour of John S. Mbiti.* New York: Mouton de Gruyter, 1993, 67–82.

Owen, A. R. G., *Can We Explain the Poltergeist?* New York: Garrett, 1964.

Paquet, Sandra Pouchet, "The Ancestor as Foundation in *Their Eyes Were Watching God* and *Tar Baby*," *Callaloo* 13 (1990), 499–515.

Parker, Bettye Jean, "Complexity: Toni Morrison's Women," in Danille Taylor-Guthrie, ed., *Conversations with Toni Morrison.* Jackson: University Press of Mississippi, 1994, 60–6.

Parkin, David, *The Anthropology of Evil.* Oxford: Blackwell, 1985.

Parrinder, Geoffrey, *African Mythology.* New York: Bedrick, 1987.

African Traditional Religion. New York: Hutchinson's University Library, 1957.

West African Psychology: A Comparative Study of Psychological and Religious Thought. New York: AMS, 1976.

Witchcraft: European and African. New York: Barnes and Noble, 1963.

Pavlić, Edward M., "'Papa Legba, Ouvrier Barriere Pour Moi Passer': Esu in *Their Eyes* and Zora Neale Hurston's Diasporic Modernism." *African American Review* (Spring 2004), 61–85.

Pelton, Robert W., *Voodoo Secrets from A to Z.* New York: A. S. Barnes, 1973.

Penfield, Wilder, *The Mystery of the Mind: A Critical Study of Consciousness and the Human Brain.* Princeton: Princeton University Press, 1975.

Prandi, Reginaldo, *Mitologia Dos Orixás.* São Paulo: Companhia das Letras, 2001.

Puckett, Newbell Niles, *Black Names in America: Origins and Usage*, ed. Murray Heller. Boston: G. K. Hall, 1975.

Raboteau, Albert J., *Slave Religion: The "Invisible Institution" in the Antebellum South*. New York: Oxford University Press, 1978.

Rodney, Walter, "Upper Guinea and the Significance of the Origins of Africans Enslaved in the New World." *Journal of Negro History* 54.4 (October 1969), 327–45.

Rosenthal, Bernard, "Dark Eve," in Elizabeth Reis, ed., *Spellbound: Women and Witchcraft in America*. Wilmington, Del.: Scholarly Resources, 1998, 75–98.

Ruas, Charles, "Toni Morrison," in Danille Taylor-Guthrie, ed., *Conversations with Toni Morrison*. Jackson: University Press of Mississippi, 1994, 93–118.

Sanders, Andrew, *A Deed Without a Name: The Witch in Society and History*. Oxford: Berg, 1995.

Shaw, Rosalind, "The Production of Witchcraft/Witchcraft as Production: Memory, Modernity, and the Slave Trade in Sierra Leone." *American Ethnologist* 24.2 (1997), 856–76.

Simon, Kavuna, "Northern Kongo Ancestor Figures," trans. Wyatt MacGaffey. *African Arts* 28.2 (Spring 1995), 49–53, 91.

Simpson, George Eaton, "The Belief System of Haitian Vodun." *American Anthropologist* 47.1 (January–March 1945), 35–59.

Smith, Dinitia, "Mixing Tragedy and Folklore." *New York Times* (January 8, 1998), B1–B2.

Smith, Edwin W., "The Whole Subject in Perspective: An Introductory Survey," in Smith, ed., *African Ideas of God*. London: Edinburgh House, 1966, 1–35.

Snowden, Jr., Frank M., *Blacks in Antiquity: Ethiopians in the Greco-Roman Experience*. Cambridge, Mass.: Harvard University Press, 1970.

Stein, Murray, Introduction, in Carl Jung, *Jung on Evil*, ed. Murray. Princeton: Princeton University Press, 1995, 1–24.

Stuckey, Sterling, *Slave Culture: Nationalist Theory and the Foundations of Black America*. New York: Oxford University Press, 1987.

Swindler, Mary Hamilton, *Ancient Painting, From the Earliest Times to the Period of Christian Art*. New Haven: Yale University Press, 1929.

Talbot, P. Amaury, *Tribes of the Niger Delta: Their Religions and Customs*. London: Cass, 1967.

Tate, Claudia, "Toni Morrison," in Danille Taylor-Guthrie, ed., *Conversations with Toni Morrison*. Jackson: University Press of Mississippi, 1994, 156–70.

Thompson, Robert Farris, *Faces of the Gods: Art and Altars of Africa and the African Americas*. New York: Museum of African Art, 1993.

  Flash of the Spirit: African and Afro-American Art and Philosophy. New York: Vintage, 1984.

  and Joseph Cornet, *The Four Moments of the Sun: Kongo Art in Two Worlds*. Washington, D.C.: National Gallery of Art, 1981.

Tindall, George Brown, *America: A Narrative History*. New York: Norton, 1984.

Traore, Ousseynou, "Creative African Memory: Some Oral Sources of Toni Morrison's *Song of Solomon*," in Femi Ojo-Ade, ed., *Of Dreams Deferred, Dead or Alive: African Perspectives on African American Writers*. Westport, Conn.: Greenwood, 1996, 129–41.

Vansina, Jan, "Long-Distance Trade Routes in Central Africa." *Journal of African History* 3.3 (1962), 375–90.

Voeks, Robert A., *Sacred Leaves of Candomblé: African Magic, Medicine, and Religion in Brazil*. Austin: University of Texas Press, 1997.

Washington, Elsie B., "Talk with Toni Morrison," in Danille Taylor-Guthrie, ed., *Conversations with Toni Morrison*. Jackson: University Press of Mississippi, 1994, 234–8.

Wilentz, Gay, "An African-Based Reading of *Sula*," in Nellie Y. McKay and Kathryn Earle, eds., *Approaches to Teaching the Novels of Toni Morrison*. New York: MLA, 1997, 127–34.

"Civilizations Underneath: African Heritage as Cultural Discourse in Toni Morrison's *Song of Solomon*," in David L. Middleton, ed., *Toni Morrison's Fiction: Contemporary Criticism*. New York: Garland, 1997.

Wona, *A Selection of Anancy Stories*. Kingston, Jamaica: Aston W. Gardner, 1899.

Wood, Peter H., *Black Majority: Negroes in Colonial South Carolina from 1670 through the Stono Rebellion*. New York: Knopf, 1974.

Wright, Richard, *Black Power*. New York: Harper, 1954.

Yarnall, Judith, *Transformations of Circe: The History of an Enchantress*. Chicago: University of Illinois Press, 1994.

Young, T. Cullen, "The Idea of God in Northern Nyasaland (Malawi)," in Edwin W. Smith, ed., *African Ideas of God*. London: Edinburgh House, 1966, 36–58.

Index

227